Cambridge Studies in Social and Cultural Anthropology
Editors: Ernest Gellner, Jack Goody, Stephen
Gudeman, Michael Herzfeld, Jonathan Parry

70
The anthropology of numbers

A list of books in the series will be found at the end of the volume

The Anthropology of Numbers

THOMAS CRUMP
University of Amsterdam

CAMBRIDGE
UNIVERSITY PRESS

Published by the Press Syndicate of the University of Cambridge
The Pitt Building, Trumpington Street, Cambridge CB2 1RP
40 West 20th Street, New York, NY 10011-4211, USA
10 Stamford Road, Oakleigh, Melbourne 3166, Australia

First published 1990
First paperback edition 1992
Reprinted 1994

Printed in Great Britain by Athenæum Press Ltd, Gateshead, Tyne & Wear

British Library cataloguing in publication data
Crump, Thomas
The anthropology of numbers. – (Cambridge studies in
social anthropology).
1. Numbers. Social aspects
I. Title
306′.45

Library of Congress cataloguing in publication data
Crump, Thomas.
The anthropology of numbers / Thomas Crump.
    p.   cm. — (Cambridge studies in social anthropology)
Bibliography.
Includes index.
ISBN 0-521-38045-6
1. Numerals – Folklore.   2. Symbolism of numbers.   3. Economic
anthropology.   I. Title.   II. Series.
GR933.C78   1990
306.4′5–dc20   89-34123 CIP

ISBN 0 521 38045 6 hardback
ISBN 0 521 43807 1 paperback

Contents

Illustrations

Preface

In anthropology, a faculty library will contain any number of books applying the methods and insights of the discipline to almost any category of human thought or behaviour. At the same time, the standard monograph, investigating in detail the daily life of the population upon which it is based, may range equally widely in the choice of the topics dealt with. To all this there is, however, one exception: the use and understanding of numbers. This subject, if not completely disregarded, is treated as no more than marginal, even in cases where numerical factors dominate the day-to-day life of the people being studied. To take the case of Japan, where I have been engaged in field-work throughout the 1980's, I am myself the author of almost every journal article about popular numeracy to have appeared in the west. In the hundreds of books and articles about Japanese culture and society which I have come across, this subject is seldom given any serious attention. It would be one thing if the Japanese found numbers uninteresting, but in fact they are obsessed with numbers. Almost since my first day in Japan, some ten years ago, people I hardly know have talked to me about the way numbers rule their lives, and in this the Japanese are by no means an exceptional case. And yet there is no recognised anthropology of numbers: the object of this book, therefore, is to establish this subject.

It is still worth asking why this has not been done before. In the context of the intellectual or scientific life of the West, the problem, as it seems to me, is that the numerical sciences are presented as esoteric, self-contained and completely autonomous: this is particularly true of the world of pure mathematics as seen in G. H. Hardy's classic *A Mathematician's Apology*, whose influence, some fifty years after publication, seems quite undiminished. The one message constantly broadcast by pure mathematicians is that their subject stands far above any possible application in daily life. If anthropologists, with their feet firmly on the ground, appear, all too readily, to have heeded the warning implicit in this message, the same is no less true of the practitioners of other related disciplines. Hurford (1987:5) identifies, with remarkable precision, the reasons for this, and what he says in relation to his own subject, linguistics, applies equally to anthropology:

numerals are clearly weird, atypical of language generally, because the things they denote, numbers, are entities unlike the kind of entities dealt with in the rest of language, say persons, places, things, actions, states and qualities. [...] To the extent that numeral systems are peripheral to the core of language because they deal with mathematical concepts (a strange " because "!), they are likely to be less peripheral to the study of number. [...] Numeral systems are in clear ways well integrated with the languages in which they are embedded.

The object of my book, simply stated, is show how and why numeral systems are well integrated with the cultures in which they are embedded. Here I am particularly grateful to the late Prof. Meyer Fortes, who was the first to encourage me to pursue this object. At first I conceived of a book along much the same lines as *Literacy in Traditional Societies*, which Jack Goody edited in 1968, but once I began to take the project seriously, it soon became clear that numeracy and literacy could be equated only marginally, so that the approach of the book I have now written is quite different to that of Goody – as any reader will see.

The problems involved in writing this book have been considerable, particularly because of the small number of published works which were any help in solving them. The difficulty – clear enough from what has been said above – is twofold: first, few professional mathematicians have any interest in the cognitive assumptions implicit in their work; second few anthropologists are numerate in the sense of being able to realise how significant the numbers that occur in the course of their field-work might be in the local culture. To give but one example, Evans-Pritchard (1951:30) noted, in his study, *Kinship and Marriage among the Nuer*, that forty was the 'ideal' number of cattle to be given in bridewealth, but he never thought to ask why forty, and not some other number. This blindness to the meaning of numbers is quite general: it even extends to works dealing with such pronounced numerical phenomena as music, so that McPhee's (1979) study of Balinese music hardly reflects at all the numerical richness of Balinese culture apparent in almost any of Geertz's later studies. The sceptical reader is invited to look at any collection of anthropological monographs, to see how far he must search to find terms relating to number and arithmetic in the index. He will then have to look even further to find any systematic treatment of the significance of numbers in a local culture.

Fortunately, however, not all anthropologists are blind to the significance of numbers, and of those who are conscious of their importance, I am most grateful for having had the opportunity to talk with Louis Dumont, Clifford Geertz, C. R. Hallpike, G. B. Milner, Andrew Strathern, T. Yoneyama, R. H. Barnes, John Gay, Jonathan Parry and Paul Spencer. But one work, more than any other, is a treasure house for anyone writing a book of this kind: it is entitled *Science and Civilisation in China*, and an evening spent as the guest of its editor, Joseph Needham FRS, FBA, greatly added to my understanding of many important points of Chinese numerology. The material gathered by Dr Needham is so rich as to tempt one to concentrate, to an excessive degree, on how the Chinese use and think about numbers.

Indeed the Far East is par excellence the home of numerate civilisations. My own time spent in Japan explains the relatively large number of Japanese examples in this book, but these are no more than a small selection from material gathered in the course of field-work. (A more detailed study is planned, with the title, *The Japanese Numbers Game*.) Once again, my research would have achieved little without the generosity of the Japan Foundation and the University of Amsterdam, which provided the necessary funds, or the help of any number of Japanese colleagues and institutions. Here I would particularly like to mention M. Akasaka, H. Araki, H. Nakamaki, T. Hatta, T. Hayashi, E. Kuroda, H. Saito, K. Sakata and H. Yamada together with the Universities of Kyoto, Nagoya, Tokyo and Toyama, the Education Universities of Kyoto and Osaka, the National Abacus Education Centre, the National Museum of Ethnology and the Little World Anthropological Museum.

In the general field of the cultural and social dimension of numbers, a number of works cover a part of the ground dealt with in this book: these are to be found in the bibliography, but Bloor (1973, chapter 4 and 1976), Hurford (1987), Ifrah (1987), Lancy (1983), Menninger (1977) and Restivo (1981, 1982 and 1983) are particularly worth mentioning. My own related works are also in the bibliography. I am also conscious of gaps in my treatment of the subject which others will no doubt point out: this book already has some 90,000 words, and an exhaustive text would be at least twice as long. It is in any case but a first step along a path which can lead to any number of new insights and discoveries, and which, I hope, many others will follow.

Finally, in the autumn of 1949, at the end of my first supervision as an undergraduate reading mathematics at Cambridge, the late Prof. A. S. Besicovitch – whom I later came to know well – asked me, 'Mr Crump, please tell me one thing: why is it you read mathematics?' I do not think he found my reply entirely convincing, but I hope now that this book answers his question. Certainly the writing of it has given me the very greatest pleasure, as well as enabling me to get to know many kind and helpful colleagues, in many different parts of the world. Needless to say my gratitude extends also to all of those whom I have not been able to mention above.

Acknowledgements

The author and publisher are grateful to the following for permission to reproduce illustrative material: Figure 13, Dover Publications, New York; Figure 14, Laurence Hill & Co., Westport, Conn.; Figure 15, Cordon Art, Baarn, Netherlands; Figures 16, 17, John Weatherhill Inc., New York and Tokyo; Figures 18, 19 (reprinted from *Viator*, 6 (1975), pp. 351–90), The Regents of the University of California; Figure 20, Griffith Observatory, after W. E. Gates.

The passage from *As Time Goes By* on page 1 is used by kind permission of Redwood Music Ltd, 14 New Burlington Street, London W1X 2LR and Warner Chappell Music Inc., 9000 Sunset Boulevard, Los Angeles CA 90069, U.S.A.

The passage on page 47 is taken from *The Lawless Roads* (published in the United States under the title *Another Mexico*) by Graham Greene. Copyright 1939, renewed © 1967 by Graham Greene. Reprinted by permission of Viking Penguin, a division of Penguin Books USA Inc., William Heinemann Ltd and the Bodley Head Ltd.

The passage on page 52 from *Suite Anglaise* by Julien Green is reprinted by permission of Editions du Seuil © Julien Green, 1988.

1

The ontology of number

The ontogenesis of number

> This day and age we're living in give cause for apprehension,
>> With speed and new invention,
>> And things like third dimension,
> Yet we get a trifle weary, with Mr. Einstein's theory,
>> So we must get down to earth,
>> At times relieve the tension.
> No matter what the progress, or what may yet be proved,
> The simple facts of life are such they cannot be removed.
>
> ...
>> The fundamental things apply,
>> As time goes by.   *Herman Hupfeld, 1930*

When it comes to mankind's use and understanding of numbers, what are the simple facts of life? Are there any fundamental things which always apply? Are numbers part of a reality which exists independently of the lives and deaths of individual human beings and the rise and fall of civilizations'? (Restivo 1983: 231). If this is so, then the characteristics of numbers are largely defined in terms of the ways in which they can combine with one another, according to the rules of what we call 'mathematics', or, in confining its application to numbers, simply 'arithmetic'. In that case, following Frege, we are confronted with 'the principal problem of arithmetic. [...] How do we apprehend logical objects, in particular numbers?' (Cited Hodes 1984). But whatever may be fundamental about numbers, one must still ask what are the simple facts of life, and much of this book is an attempt to answer this question in its relation to numbers. The foundations cannot be laid without, first, having some sort of *cognition* of numbers, and some command over numerical techniques. Both are determined in different ways by context: a compulsive gambler on cockfights in Bali will derive his cognition of numbers from the general culture of the island, but the application will make use of special skills developed so as to win as much as possible.

The cognitive base, examined in detail in chapter 2, cannot exist without some set of *signs* representing the series of *natural* numbers, 1, 2, 3...The representation is inevitably partial, since the series of natural numbers is infinite.[1] It takes the form of words 'one', 'two', 'three' and so on,

1

representing the lowest numbers in the series, up to a limit determined by the resources of the local language. These words, in whatever language it may be, are almost always distinctive (Hurford 1987: 4), and divorced from the rest of the vocabulary. The young child may first become acquainted with these words by means of a ritual *activity* (ibid.: 106) of *symbolic* counting (Lancy 1983: 142), such as is sometimes incorporated into nursery rhymes, but the symbols are *unnatural*. This may be the reason why anthropologists have been guarded in their approach to numerical symbolism. As Lévi-Strauss has pointed out in a recent work (1985), in the societies which traditionally interested anthropologists the symbolism was rooted in natural phenomena, so that – to give but one example – in parts of the world as widely separated as Australasia and North America, populations were divided into clans bearing the names of animals.[2] Such systems point towards the concrete, where unnatural systems can only point towards the abstract. Although at an elementary level the use of numbers may not be mathematical at all (and some cultures may go no further than this), sooner or later 'arithmetic is involved in the interpretation of numeral expressions, though nowhere else in language, so numerals are, prima facie, odd' (Hurford 1987: 5). And since arithmetic has to do with numbers rather than the numerals which denote numbers, one has, in some way, to transcend the symbolic base. Much of this book is taken up with this process in a variety of different contexts. But it is sufficient if 'for the time being, a number is simply something that can be named by a numerical expression' (ibid.: 8).

The logical problem is then to discover what exactly numbers are: this requires relating the *symbolic* numbers, according to the definition just given, to the series of natural numbers, 1, 2, 3,...Since, however, as chapter 3 shows, a viable society need not even have 'words' for a handful of low numbers, let alone rules of syntax for combining them to represent higher numbers, this requirement is by no means easy to satisfy. The point would seem to be reinforced by the fact that the indefinite extension of the realm of numbers to incorporate all the demands of the cognitive domain at some point requires a written notation. This provides then the earliest record of 'cognitive style', that is the primary mode of thinking about numbers (Davis and Hersh 1983: 307), in the historical development of advanced numerical systems. The evidence is unmistakable that the cognitive basis of number, at this point in history, was defined by the need to record quantities of concrete objects (Friberg 1984: 78) and not by that of facilitating the development of arithmetic in the abstract.

One would think, intuitively, that prehistoric cognitive style could not have been less concrete, but this conclusion is contradicted by research in the many pre-literate societies known to modern anthropology. Lévi-Strauss' study of the importance of groups of ten in the mythology of North-American Indians, shows how the purely arithmetical properties of the number, 10, determined both structure and interpretation (Lévi-Strauss 1971). Indeed the invention of the written recording of numbers occurred in a context calculated, if anything, to demythologize numbers.

We do not have to accept 'the dogma that the intuition of the natural number system is universal is not tenable in the light of historical, pedagogical or anthropological experience' (Davis and Hersh 1983) at the cost of being deprived of any firm foundation for continued discussion. If some anthropologists, for example Sahlins, would seem to welcome such deprivation, the purpose of this book, as that of any scientific work, is to present its subject matter to readers who have some cultural identification with its author. I accept the general application of the proposition stated by Brainerd (1973b: 247), that 'the structure of mathematics is in some sense isomorphic with the structure of reality', to all numerical praxis, traditional as well as modern. My conclusion will then be that this proposition also characterises, at least in part, most traditional cognitive styles. This view also makes it possible to define numeracy in terms of the ability to understand and work with the structure of mathematics, at such level of development as is feasible given the linguistic resources of the local culture. More particularly, where the definition is such as to include mathematical notation and calculating instruments, however rudimentary, it becomes clear that the greater these resources are, the more significant is the potential role of numeracy. It is therefore realistic to recognise that levels of numeracy not only vary greatly from one culture to another, but also that they can do so within any one culture, particularly one that is at all complex. This will often prove to be the result of a traditional pre-literate society having to come to terms with an imposed system of school education based on Western models.

There is, none the less, no inherent need for the user to be conscious of any abstract properties of numbers, even at the elementary level of realising that some are odd, while others are even. Numbers as a purely formal system are independent of external reality. Then, even if 'nobody need be aware that there is an isomorphism[3] between the two' (Hofstadter 1980: 53), in practice it is perfectly possible to project properties of the formal system on to a real situation, if the structures of the two are congruent. I provide many such instances in this book.[4] For the moment, however, the point can be made by equating the two sides of a street with the two formal categories of numbers, odd and even, and then to rule that on even days of the month cars may be parked on one side, and on odd days, on the other. If one can imagine a non-numerate society, which still had cars, there would be no great problem in establishing a rule which achieved the same result without appealing to the isomorphism. On the other hand, the problem would be of a quite different order if parking were regulated according to whether or not the number of the day of the month was prime. This would depend not only upon a fairly advanced development of the abstract properties of the formal system, but

3

also upon establishing a systematic relationship between ordinal and cardinal numbers. This, as the following section will show, cannot be taken for granted.

The general truth, however, is that where numerical techniques are known – even at the elementary level of separating numbers into odd and even – they are used as 'paradigms of identity' (Bloor 1983: 92), so that 'mathematics is normative', (ibid.: 91, citing Wittgenstein 1964, V, 41) and numeracy becomes an indispensable cultural accomplishment. The reality is that use is made of certain operations and techniques which are central to the training given to children, and are fastened upon, so as to become memorable patterns: 'it's an ethnological fact – it's something to do with the way we live' (Wittgenstein 1970: 244, 249). The truth of the proposition that a 'language-game, even in mathematics, can implicate our whole life' (Bloor 1983: 100), will be abundantly proved in the following pages,[5] for mathematics is not so much a science, but a 'language for other sciences' (Davis and Hersh 1983: 343). Further, it is 'hard to think of any branch of mathematics which does not depend on real numbers' (ibid.: 370).

The question then is: what are the characteristics of mathematics, in its application to traditional use and understanding of number? The answer is to be found partly in praxis, and partly in cognitive style. As to the former, it is useful to start with Resnick and Ford's (1981) 'partitioning of the "mathematics space" into number facts, algorithms, and problem solving' (Lancy 1983: 187). Number facts are basically what are learnt in mastering the numerical vocabulary of one's own language. Algorithms are more or less standard procedures for applying this knowledge in culturally defined contexts. The constant use of such algorithms may generate, at least among some individuals, true mathematical concepts, which can be recognised because they do not 'embody regularities of our sensory experiences of the physical environment, but regularities of these regularities, and relations between them at a high order of abstraction' (Skemp 1980: 9). This introduces, once again, the fundamental question of the relation of the power of abstraction to the use and understanding of numbers. Here, following Lancy (1983: 110), there must be 'some point in the acquisition and practice of mathematics when understanding number as an abstraction becomes necessary. It is still not clear where that point lies, nor the extent to which growing up in a nonnumerically ordered society, hinders the attainment of this level of abstraction'. On the other hand, in certain numerical contexts, such as music or games, the power of abstraction may be found, even where it is absent in the rest of the local culture.

Where the power of abstraction is insufficiently developed, traditional numeracy is constrained by the fact that '...counting and ordering are the only *experimental* techniques in arithmetic' and that these are insufficient to 'prove even the most elementary theorem, such that the number of primes is

4

unlimited' (Hofstadter 1980: 58). In the result traditional use of numbers tends to be characterised by the endless, and often extremely complex, application of algorithms – that is, of fixed procedures, which produce some new statement out of basic numerical facts. Elementary arithmetic, as taught in primary school, is of this kind, even though the algorithms now taught are hardly a hundred years old (Davis and Hersh 1983: 91). As for cognitive style, the continued use of algorithms means that mathematics is seen, essentially, as a means for generating results. This is just like the modern computer, which of its nature can only apply pre-set procedures. This is quite different from the insights generated by the dialectic of modern mathematics (Davis and Hersh 1983: 182f), which are such that 'today many, perhaps most, mathematicians have no[...]conviction of the objective existence of the objects they study' (ibid.: 252). In traditional numeracy, the whole art lies in interpretation and application, rather in the way that a modern heart specialist looks at an electrocardiogram, without needing to understand much about the actual mechanics of the instrument he is using.[6]

This leads to considerable problems, for it means that the numerical institutions of traditional societies must be functional, which leads to the question as to whether there is a sort of cultural ecology of numbers. The cases I cite in this book will make clear that in some cultures far more use is made of numbers than in others: at one extreme there are, for instance, the Balinese who seem not to be able to do anything without numbers, while at the other, there are the Bemba of Zambia, who would readily dispense with them altogether. The explanation has surprisingly often a historical basis in the process of diffusion: it is no accident that the Balinese are Hindu wet-rice cultivators, so that both their religion, and an economy based upon the meticulous control of irrigation, provide some explanation for their obsession with numbers. Even at this level, numerical institutions can be ordered in terms of their efficiency and user-friendly characteristics: in the realm of language, for instance, the place-value system of written numerals has generally superseded all competing systems. In particular, the more abstract a numerical institution – and such institutions are of their nature abstract – the greater its power of diffusion. Once again, both music and games provide many examples.

It does not follow, however, that the present book requires a categorical answer to the question I ask in the first paragraph, about the independent reality of mathematics. Is it then sufficient to accept the 'constructivist' view of the Dutch mathematician, L. E. J. Brouwer, that in mathematics nothing can be accepted as meaningful, or even be recognised as existing, unless it can be derived by a finite process whose starting point is the natural numbers, although this is hardly acceptable to most modern mathematicians (Davis and Hersh 1983: 334 and Russell 1980)? Or must we accept the logicist view, attributed to Plato, that mathematical objects are real, and their existence an objective fact, quite independent of our knowledge of them?[7] (We can also be content with a subjective variant, attributed to Kant according to which 'the truths of[...]arithmetic are forced upon us by the way our minds work; this explains why they are supposedly true and independent of experience. The intuitions of time and space[...]are objective in the sense that they are universally valid for all human minds' (ibid.: 329).) Finally there is the formalist view, according to which mathematics is a game, with rules made up of symbols and formulae (ibid.: 410), which is certainly the approach of many traditional numerical institutions. In this last case, one has an instance of the contrast (discussed in greater detail in chapter 11) between constitutive systems, where formal rules define the field of operation, and regulative systems which govern operations carried out in a field with its own separate existence.

The real issue is whether the theme of the present book can be treated holistically. The final chapter will reconsider this question in the light of all the preceding instances of the use and understanding of numbers. The question to bear in mind is whether the constructivist, logicist and formalist views are believed, each in their own contexts, because each corresponds to a certain conceptualisation – or application – of numbers: according to the first view, numbers are no more than what man makes of them; according to the second numbers are, in the words of Einstein (cited Davis and Hersh 1983: 68), 'the symbolic counterpart to the universe', an ideal, pre-existing non-temporal reality, open, at least in part, to discovery by man; according to the third, man makes the rules of the game, but the powers then given to numbers are outside his control. In a book in which the main focus is on culture and cognition, the question as to which view is correct, or in what circumstances, can be left open: in every separate case, the facts must speak for themselves. All that is needed is some workable definition of number, combined with a systematic treatment of the different instances of number which can occur in a traditional culture. The following section of this chapter provides the necessary definition, on the basis of the classification into ordinal, natural and cardinal numbers, which proves to be at least compatible with almost any cognitive domain, while in the final section I define the scope of the book, and the way in which its subject matter is organised.

Ordinal, natural and cardinal numbers

Order (according to Russell 1920: 31) is a property of the members of any set in which there is a recognised relation of precedence and succession. Once such a relationship is established between any two members of the set, it is a simple matter to prove that it imposes one single order upon all the members. Any recognisable order, however it occurs, always depends upon the application of some principle: this is a requirement with any collection of objects, however heterogeneous. The contents of a shopping basket, for example, could be ordered on the basis of weight or cost. If no such principle is available, then no order can be imposed, but this case is unimportant, for where order is desired, necessity proves to be the mother of invention when it comes to finding an acceptable principle. The opposite case is much more common: circumstances dictate the principle to be applied, so that, for instance, seniority within the family is determined according to age. Any principle depending on time has a built-in order, since with any two instants of time, one must precede the other.[8] I shall show in chapter 7 how the principle of order determines the traditional use and understanding of time.

The case of time always shows how order can be represented, according to context, by its own terminology. Therefore, we have the distinctive names for the days of the week or the months of the year, a principle which in some traditional societies has been extended to recurring periods of much longer duration.[9] It does not matter that the terms defining order constantly, and even frequently, recur, at least so long as ambiguity is avoided. Indeed the use of such terms can be extremely convenient, as can be seen by considering a sentence such as: 'In Holland grocery stores are closed on Tuesday afternoons.' Of course such a statement, judged cognitively, takes much for granted, but this causes no difficulty in any context in which it is likely to be made. The cognitive demands can be even stricter, as can be seen from the sentence, 'I have been invited to a party next Tuesday afternoon', which is only meaningful if it can be located within one definite week.[10]

The case of cyclic order, implicit in much of the terminology of time, is extremely fundamental, of common occurrence and will constantly recur in this book. It is more difficult to establish in purely logical terms (Russell 1920: 40f.), and the cases vary according to the number of points in the cycle. In the binary case, represented by the Yin–Yang principle discussed in chapter 4, the endless alternation between two points make it impossible to establish precedence. Does night follow day, or day follow night? But with three points the problem can be solved, as I illustrate in chapter 10 with the Japanese game of Janken. With four points, one has the familiar example of the compass points, and with five, the different orders of the five elements, also discussed in chapter 4. These cases of low-number cycles are significant for illustrating the isomorphisms recognised between different instances of cycles with the same number of points, so that, for instance, the Chinese used the five elements to organise space on the basis of the four cardinal points and a centre at which opposing forces cancelled each other, thereby preserving the harmony of the whole system (Needham 1980: 286). But at the same time the mathematical properties of the group constituted by the five elements were independent of this or any other particular application.

The existence of cyclic sets also demonstrates that ordered sets may contain only a finite number of members, but in practical use ordering always

7

implies a closed domain. A phrase such as 'in the two hundred and fiftieth year of his life' plainly does not refer to any ordinary mortal, though logically and grammatically there is nothing wrong with it. The important distinction to be made is between sets, which by definition have a fixed number of ordered members, such as the days of the week, and those for which no precise upper limit need be known. The first case allows for the concept introduced by Gerschel (1962: 696) of the 'nombre marginal', defined as 'un nombre qui n'existe pas, puis qu'il surpasse d'une unité le dernier nombre réel, mais qui, en vertu des lois de la fiction, gagne en extension ce qu'il perd en compréhension'. This would explain the significance of the 1001 nights: Shahrazād was saved because she succeeded in surviving one night longer than the number of nights which could be counted. In this case it is no coincidence that 1000 is the cube of 10, but it is particularly in relation to binary numbers that the *nombre marginal* becomes significant. The case of 33, which exceeds by one the fifth power of 2, is an example which I shall use a number of times in this study.

Returning to the principle of isomorphism, once this is recognised, then the next logical step is to order the isomorphic sets according to the number of members contained in each, so that the first term of the series will designate those with two members, the second those with three, and so on. (The one member set is a quite different construction, left out of the present analysis, largely for historical reasons[11].) The insight, which allows this step to be taken, is the breakthrough to the use of natural numbers, as we know them: 1, 2, 3,.... Up to this point the existence of the series of natural numbers, however implicit in the ordered sets within the cognitive domain, can still be excluded from it. What it does require, on the present analysis, is the capacity to categorise in a perfectly abstract way, so that number provides the means of putting into one and the same category completely heterogeneous collections of things, whose only common property is that they have the same number of members (Russell 1920: 14).

Applying this lesson to traditional societies, one is faced with the problem, noted by Lancy (1983: 66–7), that grouping collections together, on the basis of numerical equivalence, is not necessarily part and parcel of every culture which uses numbers. It is not even certain whether there is an intellectual basis for such a process, ripe for development in every individual, which will actually be realised if the cultural factors are favourable. What Western culture takes for granted, in its command of numbers, may be the result of a historical process, leading to the extreme division of labour, and the general use of writing and formal schooling, a process that is only now just beginning to make an impact on non-Western cultures.

The use of natural numbers (without which there is no question of numeracy) implies a system of symbols apt to designate them. In the first instance these symbols may be taken to be in the form of spoken words, although there may be no logical necessity for this. It would seem to follow that once the use of the natural numbers is admitted, these symbolic numbers, or 'numerals', can be used to 'count' the number of members of any ordered set, so as to establish an 'ordinal number' corresponding to the last member of that set. In this way the numbers *one, two, three*... up to *eleven* can be used to count the months from January to November, so as to make November the *eleventh* month. This establishes the ordinal number as the relation number of a well-ordered series. It is thus a species of serial number (Russell 1920: 93). The dilemma according to Russell, is that 'a set of terms has all the orders of which it is capable. Sometimes one order is so much more familiar and natural to our thoughts that we are inclined to regard it as the order of that set of terms;[12] but this is a mistake' (ibid.: 29f), even though 'in counting, it is necessary to take the objects counted in a certain order' (ibid.: 17). His conclusion is supported by experiments carried out in Papua-New Guinea which fail to show any relationship between an understanding of the number concept and the notion of *ordinality* – that things can be arranged in order of magnitude (Lancy 1983: 142). Lancy notes the case of Ponam, one of the countless languages of Papua New Guinea, in which there is no general system of ordinals beyond *first, middle* and *last*, even though the numerical system is otherwise relatively advanced.[13] On the other hand, the elementary cognition of a pre-literate population in Papua New-Guinea can hardly be taken as a confirmation, let alone a proof, of advanced and esoteric propositions in mathematical logic (which belong to a conceptual domain quite beyond any such cognition), nor even as sufficient to falsify the results of experimental work in development psychology, such as that done by Brainerd (1973a, 1973b).

Once the number of a set is divorced from the order of its members, the individual identity of each number is lost. This is inherent in the transformation from ordinal to cardinal numbers. An ordinal is an adjective, which is only significant if it qualifies something; a cardinal number is a substantive, which can stand alone. The cardinal number is an abstraction, and as I have already noted, any particular cardinal number is the only common property of all collections which have that number of members. How then do we know how many members there are in any collection of things before us? The commonsense answer (at least in our own culture) is to count them, but, as Russell says, 'counting cannot define numbers, because numbers are used in counting' (Russell 1920).[14] It follows, then, that if we want to use numbers for counting, they must have some definite meaning, and be something more than symbols capable of being manipulated in the processes of arithmetic. Where Russell is content to find this meaning in the logical theory of arithmetic, we are wise not to follow him, for we would then lose all possible contact with the cognitive domain of any traditional culture. It is better simply to accept that counting depends upon

9

an intellectual resource, consisting of a set of symbols, in the first instance taking the form of spoken words – in English starting with 'one, two, three' – whose actual range of application will in practice be much narrower than is theoretically possible. These words will therefore always be an imperfect, because essentially incomplete, representation of cardinal numbers as established and defined by the logical theory of arithmetic. Russell, himself, noted that 'it must have required many ages to discover that a brace of pheasants and a couple of days were both instances of the number 2: the degree of abstraction is far from easy', even though he probably did not realise that there were cultures, such as that of the Hopi of the American desert, in which cognition did not extend this far.

The linguistic resources of any cognitive domain largely determine how cardinal numbers are conceived. When these resources are sufficient, then the cardinal numbers can combine with each other in ways that we recognise as belonging to arithmetic, and in the general context of language this property is quite unique (Hurford 1975: 3). The scope of arithmetic is greatly enhanced by two factors: the first is a good, written notation, the second, the availability of efficient means of calculation. Deficiencies in the first factor can largely be made good by the second, so that the abacus made advanced calculation possible long before the place-value principle on which it was based was incorporated into the written form of numbers. Effective calculation, then, only requires a suitable set of algorithms: in Japan and China these governed the use of the abacus, the written numerals being used only for the purposes of recording numbers.[15]

The deficiencies of notation and the means for calculation has often led to pre-occupation with elementary arithmetical structures which require only the use of low numbers. An instance of this is the magic square – of which an example is given in figure 1 – invented by the Chinese more than two thousand years ago, and brought by them to a remarkable degree of perfection (Needham 1959: 55ff.). The Chinese tradition also shows the importance of alternative numerical systems, such as the binary system which is the basis of the I Ching (which I discuss in chapter 4) and which also provides the winning strategy for the game of *Nim*, described in chapter 10. Indeed, the Chinese use and understanding of binary numbers foreshadowed the principle, established by von Neumann in relation to computers – which also work with binary numbers – that the same codes represent both the numerical input and the calculations imposed upon it by the program. Once again the autonomy of cardinal numbers is established in the context of arithmetic.

To summarise, the scheme set out in this section assumes a sort of numerical ontogenesis based on the order: ordinal numbers,[16] natural numbers, cardinal numbers. This corresponds to the process of psychogenesis established by development psychology (Brainerd 1973b: 221f.) – a subject I

10

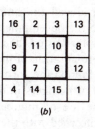

(a)

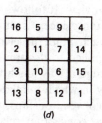

(b)

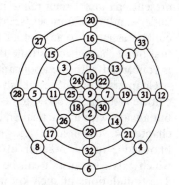

(c)

(d)

Fig. 1. Magic squares.

discuss further in chapter 2. The assumption, if intuitively attractive, is hardly susceptible to rigorous proof, and Lancy's work in Papua New Guinea would seem to contradict it. On the other hand, all the alternative logical arguments, which tend to assume a reversed order of priority, make cognitive assumptions that are unacceptable in the present context, quite apart from any internal contradictions they may contain.[17] For present purposes it is sufficient to accept the view of Brainerd (1973a: 103), that 'because there is no universally acceptable mathematical basis for choosing between ordinal and cardinal theories the choice becomes a subjective matter'. It is, however, not necessary to accept the intuitionist view that 'the series of numbers is an innate intuition, present at birth in all members of the human species', even though there is no categorical answer to Lancy's question, 'At what point does genetic evolution stop and cultural evolution take over in managing the development of cognition?' It is sufficient that the numerical systems are consistent with the demands made upon them, whether or not in the form of arithmetical calculation. The theoretical choices I make for the purposes of this book are consistent with its essential cognitive approach: such logical contradictions as they may involve are outside its frame of reference.

The typology of the uses of number

Given the classification of numbers established in the previous section, the question is, how are the different classes of number used in different cultural contexts? The different possible answers to this question provide the subject

11

matter of my book. Having introduced the ontology of numbers in the present chapter, I then relate it to the development of the individual's own understanding of number (see chapter 2), and then to place it in the linguistic context essential to any actual representation of number (see chapter 3). The first three chapters constitute the foundation for the rest of the book, which is concerned with the application of numbers in different contexts.

Chapters 4 and 5 establish the use of number in culture and society: culture is, broadly, taken to be concerned with the organisation of concepts, but always with a practical end in view. It follows that the subject matter of chapter 4, cosmology and ethnoscience, is not concerned with pure knowledge in the manner of much modern science, but with knowledge which exists because it can be applied to decision making in everyday life. The foundations of such knowledge are as much metaphysical as physical. Chapter 5 is more about the way in which numerical principles are directly applied to the regulation of human relationships, whether economic, social or political. To some extent the conceptual relationships established by chapter 4 provide the model for the social relationships dealt with in chapter 5: if, however, there is little overlap between the themes treated in these two chapters, this may be as much the result of the way I have organised this book as it is of any inherent difference between them.

In chapter 6 I consider what is often taken to be the most fundamental practical application of numerical techniques. It is often claimed that arithmetic developed in response to the need to measure, or even that in the cognition of traditional societies, mathematics and measurement were one and the same thing. Such claims are not essential to chapter 6, which simply investigates the utility of measurement, and the practical and conceptual problems involved.

In chapter 7, *Time*, I deal with the use of number to bring order and understanding to something that is part of all human experience. The natural phenomena marking the passage of time are an enormous stimulus to thinking numerically: if time is in any sense to be managed, numerical techniques are indispensable. All phenomena, viewed from the perspective of time, are subject to an order of precedence. This explains why, in chapter 7, I concentrate upon the typology of ordinal numbers. Periods of time, measured in terms of duration in fixed units, and then related to other measurable quantities, such as money, are a minor part of the traditional cognitive domain. Money, the subject of chapter 8, is in a sense the exact opposite of time. It is the numerical institution par excellence, and the endless calculations which money requires show that the role of cardinal numbers is dominant.

In chapters 9, 10 and 11 I deal with specific, but important, instances of the use of numbers. These provide the opportunity for analysing three different realms with almost unrestricted scope for numerical fantasy and creativity.

12

As an animal species, man could do without music, games or art: these all belong to what the modern world calls leisure. But what would the purpose and meaning of life be without them? The lesson will be that it is precisely in the contexts of music, games and art, that the most advanced numerical techniques, as much as the most sophisticated numerical institutions, developed.

Other instances of the application of numerical techniques, say in medicine or agriculture, are also included: medicine is one of the ethnosciences dealt with in chapter 4, and the organisation of time, the subject of chapter 7, is often directed to the needs of agriculture. The organisation of any book is, of course, largely a matter of the author's choice, but the subject matter almost invariably proves to have its own autonomy. This is particularly true of a book about numbers, for if there is one lesson I have learnt from writing this book, it is that numbers in a sense control the wills of those who make use of them. The respect and attention given to numbers in the many different cultures I have examined shows how widespread is this sense of being controlled by numbers.

Finally, in chapter 12 I reflect on the conclusions reached in the preceding eleven chapters, to see how much can be learnt from their characteristic synoptic approach. In particular, the content of these chapters will be seen to define the meaning and scope of the title of this book. If, in this first chapter, little has explicitly been said about what I mean by the *anthropology of numbers*, it is because this meaning can only unfold, gradually, as the narrative proceeds. Every chapter adds something to the complete picture, whether it be a particular perspective, or some significant detail, which illuminates the whole composition.

2
The cognitive foundations of numeracy

The mind of the individual

The simplest approach to the cognitive basis of numeracy is to assume that there is no essential differentiation between the minds of different individuals, nor between the different numerical systems which such individuals must learn to master as they grow up. The first assumption, although regarded as fundamental by psychologists, is essentially biological. Man is one species, so that, subject to certain pathological exceptions, the neurophysiology of man is completely uniform. The pathological exceptions, generally related to injuries to the brain and patent defects in the operation of the sensorimotor system of individual subjects, are important, for they dominate much of the experimental work done by psychologists interested in cognition.[1] Experiments related to the normal case rely largely on statistical surveys, designed to demonstrate a normal distribution of some measurable index[2] among the class being surveyed, which is likely to be defined according to such culturally neutral factors as age and sex. This leads, in the case of numeracy, to the second assumption made above, which is essentially logical or, perhaps better, epistemological. It has been stated in its simplest form by Stark (1958:162): 'Surely, there can only be one science of numbers, forever self-identical in its content'. For heuristic reasons, I simply assume the truth of this proposition at the present stage of the argument in order to procede further with the discussion.

To start with, therefore, I work with one biological and one epistemological paradigm. Subject to these constraints, the mind of the child is seen as developing, from earliest infancy, through a number of successive phases, to a point where its mastery of numbers will enable it to carry out any number of established numerical operations whose ends are generally practical. This is the basic theory of development psychology of Jean Piaget (1896–1980) which, according to Lancy (1983) is still 'the only one available[...][even though] it leaves whole areas of mathematics untouched (e.g. numerical operations), while giving inordinate attention to a few (e.g. probability, measurement and Euclidean geometry)'. If the experimental work in this

14

field carried out in recent years was incompatible with this theory, its deficiencies in relation to numerical operations would be critical, but this is not the case. So following Lancy, I adopt Piaget's developmental psychology as the basis of the present analysis.[3]

In the first months of life the sensorimotor system does not equip the child to differentiate between its own actions, as a subject, and the properties of the objects which those actions encounter. At the same time the child is endowed with an innate neurophysiological capacity, not only to co-ordinate its actions, but to develop its intellect in the direction of the 'progressive substantiation of the other' (Piaget 1972), which is the first step towards socialisation. The brain of the child has, at birth, certain 'neural co-ordinations', but this does not mean that '"the logic of neurons" contains in advance that of propositions at the level of thought' (Piaget, 1972, p. 61). Action comes before perception, so that, to begin with, the child's only interest in objects is in manipulating them in some way: this first phase is known as sensorimotor assimilation. It is only later that the child relates objects to each other, which is the essential basis of any conceptual scheme. This process begins to develop even in the first six months of life. This second phase, of representative assimilation, is essential to human knowledge, for the first problem of knowledge is the construction of intermediaries: these, being essentially symbolic, are defined and communicated by the culture in which the child grows up. As Pieron (1959:211) puts it, 'a child, at birth is a candidate for humanity; it cannot become human in isolation; but has to learn to become a man in contact with other men'. Therefore, 'what is achieved at the level of animals through biological inheritance, is thus achieved by man through assimilation, i.e. by a process that is one of humanising the child's psyche' (Leontiev 1981:135). The most important symbols which the child confronts, from the very beginning of its life, are to be found in speech, and the most important event in the life of the young child – generally at about the age of two – is that the 'development of thought and speech, till then separate, meet and join to initiate a new form of behaviour' (Vygotsky 1962:43). This process almost certainly represents a decisive re-structuring of the physiology of the brain, but the science of neurophysiology has not reached the point of being able to reduce this process, or its results, to any accurate description of what has actually taken place.[4] It is an important instance of the psychological phenomenon known as '*Aufhebung*', a German word which connotes not only raising something up to a higher level, but also destroying the means used to achieve this result. The process is familiar to us from St Paul (1 Cor. xiii:11): 'When I was a child, I spoke like a child, I thought like a child, I reasoned like a child; when I became a man I gave up childish ways.' The only thing is that *Aufhebung* occurs not just once, but at each successive stage of intellectual development and 'in the history of behavior these transitional systems lie between the

15

biologically given and the culturally acquired' (Vygotsky 1978:46). At whatever stage is reached, the individual becomes gradually conscious of new perceptions, which cannot be incorporated into existing patterns of thought. These must be recast in order that the individual has once again a sense of 'cognitive clarity':[5] the pieces of the puzzle fit together again.

With language, the basis of all intellectual progress after the first two years of life, the process is essentially complete by the end of the fifth year and in every case the physiology of the brain must then correspond, somehow, to the structure of the mother tongue (Fry 1979:34). There is, however, no evidence that linguistic factors can change the order in which numerical skills are acquired, although they may make the acquisition of the most advanced skills more difficult (Lancy 1983:142). At a certain advanced level, where numerical techniques depend upon visual representations, they need no longer be tied to any one language. Adopting a three-stage model proposed by Lancy, the basic cognitive processes provided by nature in Stage I, are taken over by culture and shaped to its own ends in Stage II, while the processes engendered in Stage III have the potential to supersede the culture that bred them. In the learning of arithmetic, reaching this last stage, to say the least, is made much easier by the use of written notation, but in such essentially numerical activities as may be found, for instance, in music and games, this is not necessary, however much the Western world may take it for granted. The same conclusion is true also of such activities as shopping in supermarkets, which, as Lave (1988:168) points out, 'challenges claims for the hegemony of school taught math over every day practice[...]such claims do not hold up under empirical scrutiny. But these claims are accepted as valid by [those] whose everyday practice invalidates them.'

The end-point of the development process, as it relates to numbers, is formalisation, on the one hand, and operational utility on the other. Starting from a position of innate, instinctive co-ordinations, in the transition to 'intelligence', the hereditary programming of content disappears, at least in part, to be replaced by new constructions based on abstractions, to which the child then adapts its behaviour. The first part of the process, which is logico-mathematical, is one of interiorisation, while the second part, being based on learning and experiment, is one of exteriorization. This, once more, is the process of *Aufhebung*. The question is, what form do these reconstructions take, and in what order do they occur?

According to Piaget's (1952:3–4) development psychology, the basis of thought is the functional need for conservation. That is, thought rests on the proposition that the objects confronting the child in the external world are permanent, so that they can be conceived of in terms that are constant. If it is intuitively obvious that a system of thought cannot develop on any other basis, this is no proof that the proposition is true. Life is a process of learning that things are not what they seem to be. The child needs the process of

16

Aufhebung to be able to cope: otherwise the intellectual achievements of man would have been impossible. This is why the permanent object represents 'the most primitive of all principles of conservation'. In practice the application of the principle to the conservation of quantity presents the child with considerable difficulties. A liquid, poured from one container to another, will be judged to vary in quantity, according to the size and number of containers (ibid.: 5). The same liquid in a tall glass will be seen as 'more' than in a short glass, showing that the perception of quantity, in one single dimension, is more elementary than being able to reason that the volume of the liquid cannot be changed by process of transfer. The dominant principle is thus ordination rather than conservation, that is, of selecting some quantitative criterion according to which different objects can be arranged in order systematically. In the normal case conservation is not a problem since the objects to be ordered will not have been confused by deliberate transfers between them. All that ordination requires is a set of transitive, asymmetrical relations between the relevant objects, so that between any two of them there will be a palpable criterion which ranks one higher than the other. This is far from meaning that any child, presented with a collection of such objects, knows a systematic procedure for setting them out in order according to that criterion.

Now the most common example of ordination is the counting of things (Brainerd 1973a: 103). In one way this is a very simple operation, with which children have little trouble once the spoken language used contains the numerals necessary for carrying it out (Lancy 1983: 179). In any such case, the child will also master the numerals in a number of discrete steps (Ginsburg 1977: 3), beginning with the numbers from 1 to 7, and then proceeding, at later stages, to the mastery of those from 8 to 15, from 16 to 30, until it finally has a cognitive grasp of the whole system (Piaget 1972: 42). Taking only the first step, the child will first learn these numerals as a single utterance, sometimes making mistakes. Now according to Piaget (1952: 61), 'there is no connection between the acquired ability to count and the actual operations of which the child is capable'. The problem arises when the ordered series of numerals is applied to any collection of objects, for then the child must realise that the ordering of these objects is imposed by the number words, 'one, two, three...' and not by any intrinsic property of the objects themselves. Thus given a set of Russian dolls, these do not have to be fitted inside each other – an essentially ordinal process – in order to be counted. On the other hand if this is what the child wants to do, the dolls need only be arranged in order of size, without needing to be counted at all: indeed this procedure could be carried out in a numerical culture so elementary that it did not dispose of any means for actually counting them. But where the dolls are counted, there is then the obstacle that they lack, because of the differences in size, the uniformity necessary for them to be members of a single class. It follows that unless the class to be counted is uniform, the counting process will require a process of abstraction. This reduces the case to one of a set 'formed of equal elements only distinguishable by their position', in which case 'the elements can be arranged in any order, provided that there is an order and that it permits of each element being counted once and once only. This is[...] "vicariant order", which means that either of two elements can be the first or the second, provided that there always is a first and a second. In such a case the order can be disregarded and the significance of the correspondence becomes primarily cardinal, since the equivalence between the sets can be established irrespective of order' (Piaget 1952:96) .

The paradox is that neither the ordinal nor the cardinal process requires any explicit numeration. As for the former, the game of *janken*, discussed in chapter 10, shows that between any of three basic positions – scissors, stone and paper – there is an established order, but not one that is expressed in numerical terms. In the gestures used by the players to represent these three positions, the subordination of scissors to stone, of stone to paper, and of paper to scissors, is based on metaphor, and according to the Barthes' (1967:60) semiology, must be seen as systematic. The child who plays 'scissors' wins against the one who plays 'paper', because in the cultural system to which the players belong, *scissors* cut *paper*. The game itself requires no such specific cultural props, and could be equally played in any culture possessing an isomorphic system, even if scissors and paper – or for that matter stone – were unknown to it. Any arithmetical analysis requires not metaphor, but metonomy, but the problem then is that almost any possible notation – such as calling the three positions, P, Q and R, would contain a contradictory assumption, such as R < P, when everyone knows that R comes later than P in the alphabet. Now any mathematician knows that the order in this case is not transitive, by virtue of the definition inherent in the rules of the game: he will also know that the mathematical basis is what Barthes (1967:59) calls syntagmatic and not systematic. The 'syntax' is not, and could not be based on the series of natural numbers, so it is not surprising that the Japanese children who constantly play janken are always content with the metaphorical system: they would be in very deep water if they were to try to replace it with anything more abstract. In development psychology the two representations are very widely separated.

That the cardinal process can do without numeration is more difficult to show: a number of cases, such as those of the Wedda of Ceylon or the Plateau Tonga of Southern Africa, who can deal in quantities which their language is quite unable to express, illustrate the point, even if they hardly prove it. The logical basis of cardinal number is also independent of explicit numeration. But both in this case, and that of ordinal numbers, the question arises as to what it is that relates the two to each other. This is the role of the natural numbers, or integers, that we know in the familiar form, 1, 2, 3,

4, ... and so on. In one special case, relating only to the numbers from 1 up to about 7, objects are counted by means of a mental process named 'subitization' by Miller (1956), which means that regardless of their arrangement, the number present is perceived instantaneously.[6]

Now the natural numbers, in the context of cognition, are a *symbolic* system, belonging to language, and defined by the local culture. None the less it seems that 'symbolic counting is a universal skill that develops gradually with age and is relatively unaffected by variations in the counting system employed, culture, cognitive development or schooling' (Lancy 1983:142). The symbolic numbers, as recognised by development psychology or cultural anthropology, correspond to the natural numbers defined by the mathematics or logic, but are a sub-class, since the natural numbers are an infinite series, which the symbolic numbers, by force of circumstance, can never be.

In the general case, the child, if it is to learn the natural numbers operationally, must learn that they are significant in two quite different ways. First, they have the meaning represented by the 'numerals' in the child's mother tongue. The mastery of this meaning belongs to the informal learning process, although it occurs at a relatively late stage in it. The reason is simply that children 'cannot plan strategies for dealing with things once and only once; and they find it hard to make a one-to-one correspondence between the numbers they say and the things they touch' (Ginsburg 1977:15). Second, the natural numbers have any number of properties, whether alone, or in combination, which are purely arithmetical: it is not easy for a child to see that addition is commutative, so that $2+1 = 1+2$ (ibid.: 168), or, at a more advanced level, to realise that numbers will be either odd or even, and that the sum of two odd or two even numbers will always be even, while that of an odd and an even number will always be odd. Here the cognitive process will depend more on formal learning, focussed upon the mastery of technical skills, such as a master teaches to an apprentice. The beginning of this process, say at the level of learning the multiplication tables at the age of seven or eight (Piaget 1972:43), requires the child to have grasped the principle of conservation in its application to numerical collections (ibid.: 72), but true logical insights into what is involved in the process come at a much later age. It is true for every stage 'that sign operations appear as a result of a complex and prolonged process subject to all the basic laws of psychological evolution. *This means that sign-using activity in children is neither simply invented nor passed down by adults*; rather it arises from something that is originally not a sign operation and becomes one only after a series of *qualitative* transformations[...]linked like stages of a single process, and[...] historical in nature' (Vygotsky 1978:46). Observation confirms that 'people use rather simple strategies while learning a skill such as addition and multiplication. These strategies involve a succession of small steps, such as successive incrementing by one. As the skill develops, many of the individual results are stored in memory and can be retrieved effortlessly' (Posner 1973:113). Finally, it is not every child who will complete the journey, to the point that it has mastered all the numerical skills practised within its own culture,[7] (and here it must be recognised that there may be 'several [alternative] strategies for performing arithmetic operations[...][which] may or may not be affected by the numeration system' (Reed and Lave 1979:572)). The end of the journey, at least in any advanced culture, is outside the purview of any general development psychology.[8]

The point reached in the previous paragraphs makes possible a threefold classification of cultures which will provide the background for the following section of this chapter. There will be, first, elementary cultures in which numerical skills will be conceived of in purely operational (or practical) terms, with mastery not restricted to any class of specialists: such cultures will almost always be pre-literate. Second, there are the cultures in which such skills, being arithmetically more advanced, are the recognised prerogative of specialists, who will also often be literate. These, however, will not be concerned to develop new numerical techniques, or advance the frontiers of knowledge: such cultures are in this sense pre-scientific, even though the arithmetical knowledge they dispose of may historically be the product of scientific process. Third, there are the modern cultures, which set no limits to the advance of mathematical knowledge or the development of new numerical techniques: such advances are expected, and society is organised so as to encourage them. These cultures, which include our own, are only marginally relevant to any study of traditional numeracy.

The position described above is now somewhat confused by the fact that in many pre-literate[9] societies formal education has been introduced in the form of schools built on a Western model. This circumstance has provided the context for much of the recent research into the use and understanding of numbers in traditional societies. This line of scholarship begins with Gay and Cole's (1967) study of learning among the Kpelle of Liberia, but the present focus on New Guinea, presented in detail in Lancy (1983), is perhaps more important. In any case the main interest is in the cognitive consequences of Western elementary education. The most important conclusion is that for those growing up in traditional societies contending with Western education there are two alternative ways of becoming skilled in the use of numbers: these may be called 'traditional' and 'modern'.

Apprenticeship, based on the transmission of acquired knowledge, in the context in which it will later be applied, is the basis of traditional instruction in numerical skills. School, in which such skills are not taught with a view to their direct application, if any, outside the institutional context, is the basis of modern instruction. Both institutions have in common the protracted transmission of acquired knowledge of numerical *systems* to specified age-groups, with the understanding that those who successfully complete the course will in some sense be 'qualified' (Reed and Lave 1979:569). But the use of the skills acquired, and the value of the qualifications achieved, are quite different, and determine the level of performance in either context. Apprenticeship inculcates practical thinking directed to the application of such skills to the carrying out of any task recognised as falling within the scope of the craft. The criterion for distinguishing between skilled from amateur performance is to be found both in the quality of the work, and the economy of effort in carrying it out. It is not, however, sufficient to reduce cognition, in this context, to problem solving *per se*, for this takes no account of the cognitive consequences of using arithmetic in the exercise of professional skills. There is in fact a dialectical process in which the constant interaction between the craftsman, and the tasks which he has to perform, creates a permanent corpus of arithmetical theory, which is the basis of each individual's cognition. Lave (1988:57) has shown that the same transformation takes place with *just plain folks* engaged in supermarket shopping in California, where 'success and frequency of calculation[...]bear no statistical relationship with schooling, years since schooling was completed, or age'. This argues 'against transmission and internalization as the primary mechanisms by which culture and individual come together' (ibid.: 177). This is in complete contrast with an academic setting, in which arithmetic is presented as autonomous, with practical applications being merely incidental; in pure mathematics they are not even that (Lave, Murtaugh and de la Roche 1985:94).

Two general points emerge from the above discussion. First, the superior performance of Western children in numerical skills taught in *school* is the result of the relatively high level of proficiency required for graduation, which in the local culture is established as an essential *rite de passage* to the world of economic opportunity. At the same time, what children in the mainstream of a modern culture learn at school has a good fit with the cognitive domain of their own home: put more simply, such children learn substantially what their parents learnt before them. The problem arising when such schooling is made available, or is imposed, outside its true cultural context, is that it has a bad fit with the cognitive domain of the children's home background. Many such children 'perceive themselves as members of a caste who can realistically anticipate little in the way of economic opportunity. Hence [they] have little incentive to work hard at academic studies. The problem is primarily economic and motivational, not cognitive' (Ginsburg and Allardice 1984:198) – a conclusion abundantly confirmed by Lancy's research in a quite different part of the world, Papua New Guinea.[10] If, in such a context, a breakthrough is achieved, then the price paid is that 'the educated individual joins a "world culture" and has far more in common with his or her similarly educated counterparts on the other side of the world than with uneducated kinsmen in his or her hometown or village' (Lancy 1983).

The second observation, although no more than implicit in the whole process of modernisation, is critical for the present study. The underlying assumption of the research cited is that, above all, economic factors determine the direction and level of acquisition of numerical skills. Any comprehensive research into the use of numbers in traditional societies leads to the conclusion that this is a very questionable assumption: the examples I give in the following chapters should make this abundantly clear.

Culture and cognition

Although Piaget himself never seemed to worry about it, to base a whole theory of development psychology on experiments, carried out with French-speaking children, in twentieth-century Geneva, would seem to beg any number of critical questions. After all, cognition, which is central in any such theory, is about the individual's reaction to different sorts of experience and belief. In any culture, the individual is conditioned to respond, in a characteristic way, to different collections of interrelated items of knowledge, each of which constitutes a 'cultural system'. Even if, in the majority of known cultures, numerical phenomena constitute one such system, the actual content will still vary from one culture to another. On the other hand, such numerical systems are highly 'consonant' at a popular level, simply because their usefulness depends upon their being free of internal contradictions.[11] Furthermore, these systems, more than any other, are reducible to a common paradigm, simply because of the elementary properties of numbers which I introduced in Chapter 1. Operational mastery will also depend on skills, as well as the means of transmitting them, which are culture-specific. For example, there are still shopkeepers in China and Japan who write out prices in Chinese characters, and use an abacus for adding up bills, but the numerical system is essentially no different from that of the West.[12]

The 'Culture and Cognition Paradox' has attracted much interest and controversy in recent years, although the debate has largely bypassed the realm of numbers.[13] The simplest resolution of the paradox is that propounded by Cole, Gay, Glick and Sharp (1971) as a result of research they carried out among the Kpelle of Liberia: that 'cultural differences in cognition reside more in the situations to which particular cognitive processes are applied than in the existence of a process in one cultural group and its absence in another'. This is essentially my own conclusion (in the previous section): it is no more than what one would expect, if it is accepted that 'human brains are governed by a single set of neurological principles without regard to time or place' (Paredes and Hepburn 1976). At the opposite pole is the position taken by Tsunoda (1978) in relation to the Japanese, which is that certain unique features of the Japanese language relate to a quite distinct allocation of functions between the left and right hemispheres of the brain. His argument is then extended so as to establish a unique position for Japanese culture in relation to all others.[14] The question of the different functions of the two hemispheres may be central to the argument, if only because this is often the only possible basis for experiment.

The starting point is that certain cognitive functions, which can be described as analytic, abstract, rational, and digital, belong to the left hemisphere of the brain.[15] These are pre-eminently the cognitive functions required for operating with numbers. Therefore, any culture in which numerical operations are used for solving a certain type of problem, will rely on the left hemisphere of the brain. What differs from one culture to another is simply the degree to which such operations occur in the first place. The solution of navigational problems provides an ideal comparative test-case. In the European tradition, navigation is essentially a mathematical operation, based on time-keeping combined with various forms of charts and almanacs, recording both terrestrial and celestial information – often in numerical form. Practical progress, reflected in increasingly ambitious voyages of exploration, was closely tied to improvements in the accuracy of the instruments used. A quite different approach was to be found on the other side of the world, where Pacific islanders, for hundreds, if not thousands of years, made long voyages – out of sight of land – without the benefit of any such aids to navigation. The logical basis of such navigation has been analysed by Lewis (1972:13f.) in relation to the Caroline islands, whose sailors navigate by means of a mental image, known to them as *etak*, according to which the position of the boat is known at any time, by relating the islands and reefs visible from the course being followed to the rising and setting of known stars, although in a starless night the navigator can still hold to his course by noting the direction of the wind and the waves.

Now according to Gladwin (1964:175) there is an essential difference in the logical processes applied by the European and Caroline navigators. The European navigator relies on a cognitive structure which is essentially deductive, and is based on a general, abstract principle, which means that every voyage takes place according to a pre-ordered plan – which can be represented, visually, on a chart. The Caroline navigator is concerned only with details, and his strategy is determined *ad hoc*. 'The input of information[...]and its synthesis[...]is a continuous process characteristically involving simultaneous operations' (ibid.: 176). Even today the Caroline navigators have resisted the incorporation into their system of data from outside sources, for the system is essentially 'closed', and already complete in the area in which it is applied (Lewis 1972:144). Within its limits, they have nothing to learn.

23

The question at issue is whether the traditional resources available, in some way conditioned European navigators to rely, to a much greater extent than the Caroline islanders, on left-hemisphere functions. This is the view of Paredes and Hepburn (1976:126), who

strongly suspect that as human beings become increasingly dependent on artifactual recording devices[...]standardized measuring instruments[...]and calibrated monitoring equipment[...]the less they are required to rely on right-hemisphere functions, and this may lead to a diminution of acuteness of those functions. Conversely, the less dependent each individual is on personal solutions to physical problems of survival and the greater the social segmentation of work, then (1) the higher is the societal premium placed upon supporting some individuals who devote at least a portion of their thinking time to the elaboration of left hemisphere functions and (2) the greater is the general interindividual utility of left-hemisphere-dominated cognitive processes for adaptation in the social sphere.

The question, in the terms used by Gay, Glick and Sharp (cited on page 22), is whether essential cognitive differences are to be found in context or process. The answer may indeed depend on what operation is to be carried out, but it is still instructive to consider the question in its relation to sea-navigation, since the external context cannot, of its nature, be culture bound. All one needs to assume is that the crew of a boat, on the open sea, can follow any course they choose, although the actual rate of progress will depend on wind and currents. Then, so long as their destination is not in sight, they must have some process to correct any deviation from the true course. Here the essential difference is that Caroline navigation – notwithstanding the sightings taken of stars – is based upon terrestrial points of reference, where European navigation depended on the observed positions of celestial bodies. So far, this is a difference in context rather than process. But then, where the terrestrial context is static, the celestial context is dynamic, so that even a stationary observer notes its constant change. The change is determined by an invariant numerical relationship to the lapse of time, so that for navigation to be possible the navigators must not only know the required mathematical equations, but also dispose of the necessary records, measuring equipment and calibrated monitors – such as were represented until the dawn of the electronic age by the nautical almanac, the sextant and the chronometer. All this presupposes not only a literate culture, but also one in which science has been used systematically to advance mathematical knowledge. It is no coincidence that the development of accurate chronometers followed directly the age of Isaac Newton.

All this proves is that context is culturally as well as environmentally determined. There is no need to establish, clinically, that the neurophysiology of the growing child develops along lines which are culturally determined, but only to accept that the child, in the use of its brain, is always forced to adapt to cultural constraints. It can then be accepted that certain 'contexts' only allow for the use of certain 'processes': the Caroline islanders can see the stars as well as any European navigator, but context, as it is defined by their preliterate culture, denies them the processes for making the same use of what they see. In relation to the European navigators, one notes, however, not only the extreme generality of what they observe – for, in the course of the seasons, the greater part of the heavens can be seen by most of mankind – but also of the abstract processes used to interpret the observations. The link between the two is essentially numerical. It then follows that the 'left-hemisphere' dominance, may be used, in any case as a figure of speech, to characterise European culture, even if neurophysiology offers no proof that it is pre-eminently a property of the brains of European individuals.

One must still ask whether cross-cultural neuropsychology, based as much on anthropological fieldwork as on tests carried out in the psychological laboratory, has achieved any useful results relating to the use and understanding of numbers. In fact, to judge from the work done so far, normal fieldwork methods, based on participant observation, have produced fewer useful results than the use of standard psychological tests in a fieldwork context. This was the procedure used by Cole and Gay (1967:36f.) in testing the arithmetical skills of the Kpelle of Liberia.[16] Although the methods used were those of psychology, such differences as there were in the results could almost all be explained in terms of cultural factors, often closely related to the limitations of the local language in dealing with numbers – a result similar to that reached by Lancy (1983:142) in Papua-New Guinea. Since numerals must qualify a noun or a pronoun, it is not too surprising that Kpelle can only carry out numerical operations in a concrete situation, but then, in such a case – such as estimating the number of stones in a pile – they were significantly more accurate than an American control group (ibid.: 43). Among the Americans the sophistication of certain recognised individuals in the use of number was clearly apparent, but this was not so among the Kpelle.[17] On the other hand, certain specialised operations, such as dividing the annual hut tax of 10 dollars among the individuals living in the hut, were often left to specialists such as blacksmiths and traders, who in the course of their daily life often carried out similar operations (ibid.: 50). The inability of the Kpelle to think abstractly is reflected in the fact that they have no such operation as formal multiplication, to the point that they find it no easier to count 12 dots arranged in 3 rows of 4, than the same number scattered at random. At the same time, operations involving numbers above 40 hardly ever occur (ibid.: 52), which severely limits the capacity of the Kpelle to deal with measurement, particularly of time.

Conservation of quantity experiments carried out by Bovet (1974) in Algeria and Bruner and Greenfield in Senegal (Greenfield 1966) lead to the conclusion that 'schooling plays a specific part in developing an analytic approach which results in a precise comparison of the dimensions of the objects involved' (Bovet 1974:331), although the evidence suggests that the effect of schooling is largely to improve cognitive performance selectively among the individuals taking part (Lancy 1982:124), so that differences in performance which are pronounced between children of different cultures tend to be reduced as they become adults (Greenfield 1966:332). The school is a cultural institution, which represents a fundamental change in the context in which cognitive processes take place. At the beginning of the 1980s it became clear that the lessons learnt at school do not necessarily carry over into daily life (Lancy 1983:187), but in the first instance only a few special cases illustrated this point. A study of street life in Recife in Brazil (Carraher, Carraher and Schliemann 1985) showed that children engaged in petty trading, if they were to apply the algorithms learnt at school, would only make mistakes, which were avoided by applying practical concrete methods developed in the actual work situation. In some cases growth in a particular field may be accelerated by a standard process of transmitting related skills, so that children brought up in pottery-making families in Mexico achieved comparatively high scores when tested for the conservation of substance (Price-Williams, Gordon and Ramirez 1969:769). Now Lave (1988:4) questions the whole concept of *learning transfer*, and rejects the 'conventional academic and folk theory [which] assumes that arithmetic is learned in school in the normative fashion in which it is taught, and is then literally carried away from school to be applied at will in any situation that calls for calculation'.

The fact that almost all the comparative studies have been confined to the development of conservation through the three successive stages identified by Piaget – quantity, weight, volume – would hardly seem to justify any general conclusion relating to the development of advanced numerical skills. The point is that for Piaget 'conservation[...]marks the beginning of logical thinking and the transition from a pre-operational to an operational level of thought[...]and as such, has been the subject of a number of investigations' (de Lemos 1973). What is significant, as de Lemos' own survey of the work in this field indicates, is that the experiments carried out in many different cultural contexts consistently confirm the conclusion reached by Piaget, that cognitive skills are universal. It is also significant that so many scholars, working quite independently of each other, are ready to deal with any discrepancies arising by attributing them to local cultural factors. Nor does it matter that logical skills, acquired at a later stage than those relating to conservation, are left out of account, if the basic configurations of the brain are fixed at a sufficiently early stage, which is almost certainly the case. This is the conclusion reached in the field of neurolinguistics, in which the range of experiments carried out is far greater.[18]

The more controversial question is whether there is an innate mathematical structure, comparable to the 'universal grammar' posited by Chomsky, which is 'by definition, invariant across individuals and across languages[...]ultimately to be accounted for in terms of species-specific neuronal circuits' (Piatelli-Palmarini 1980:15).[19] Chomsky (1980:243f.) has suggested that 'one curious property of the human mind is our ability to develop certain forms of mathematical understanding – specifically concerning the number system, abstract geometrical space, continuity and related notions[...]It is certainly possible to enquire into the nature of these abilities and to try to discover the initial state of mind that enables these abilities to develop as they do.' The best starting point for such an enquiry is Piaget's summary, (quoted in Piataelli-Palmarini 1980:25) of the critical period in psychogenesis:

From the ages of 2 to 7, there is a conceptualization of actions, and therefore representations, with discovery of functions between covariations of phenomena, idendities, and so forth, but without yet any concept of reversible operations or of conservation. These last two concepts are formed at the level of concrete operations (ages 7 to 10), with the advent of logically structured 'groupings', but they are still bound to the manipulation of objects. Finally, around the age of 11 or 12, a hypothetico-deductive propositional logic is formed[...]

The use of the word 'finally' in the last sentence may be taken as relating to a Chomskyan 'steady state[...]attained at a relatively fixed age, apparently by puberty or somewhat earlier' on the basis of which may be constructed 'a hypothesis as to the grammar internally represented' (Piatelli-Palmarini 1980:37–8). Now whereas in the case of language, the problem is still far from a complete solution, in the numerical case there need hardly be a problem at all. Whether or not the grammar is 'internally represented', there can be little doubt about its contents, as a system. It consists simply of the basic abstract, and completely general arithmetical procedures which the child has mastered by the time it reaches the 'steady state'. Such mastery may be no more than implicit in a culture where – whether or not for linguistic reasons – numbers can only be used in concrete situations, but it will be explicit in any culture which teaches arithmetic systematically. The difficulties in crossing from one culture to the other – such as Cole and Gay (1967) investigated in relation to the Kpelle – can be explained as the result of quite different forms of education in the period before the 'steady state'. All the evidence suggests that there is but one universal grammar of number,[20] with no doubt about the nature of its contents. No doubt if one were to start with the numerical cognition of individuals from within a given culture who had reached the steady state, one could deduce the 'internal grammar' of which this was a representation, but would the deduction produce anything more than a basic arithmetic founded on standard algorithms.[21] In an elementary numerical culture, with no means of expressing any but the lowest numbers, the grammar produced in this way might be somewhat incomplete, but it would still be a recognisable part of the more complete grammars of advanced numerical cultures. It follows that there is little need in cognitive psychology, relating to numbers, for anything comparable to Chomsky's psycholinguistics.

The problem can usefully be stated somewhat differently. For Piaget (Piatelli-Palmarini 1980:26),

[...]either mathematics is part of nature, and then it stems from human constructions, creative of new concepts, or mathematics originates in a Platonic and suprasensible universe, and in this case, one would have to show through what psychological means we acquire knowledge of it, something about which there has never been any indication.

In the terms introduced in chapter 1, Piaget plainly prefers Brouwer's constructivism to Platonism, choosing to ignore the third possibility, formalism, and confusing, at the same time, nature with culture. What he apparently ignores is the process of *Aufhebung* described on page 15, which would solve many of his problems. *Aufhebung*, which cannot take place without socialization, operates – at least in part – by replacing the child's own individual knowledge with the accumulated wisdom of the culture in which it grows up (Vygotsky 1978:39). The process succeeds, not only because of social constraints and the inherent superiority of the skills transmitted, but also because it is innate in the way in which the brain of the growing child develops (ibid.: 46). This is sufficient, in the case of mathematics, for the child growing up in a traditional culture to master – by means of Piaget's 'human constructions' – the state of the art, at whatever level it may have reached. Such development is 'alloplastic' in so far as 'we move, perceive and think in a fashion that depends upon techniques rather than upon wired-in arrangements in our nervous system' (Bruner 1964:2). If mastery, at an esoteric level, need no longer depend on the human constructions (as envisaged by Brouwer) used in the process of acquiring it, then the attainment of Plato's ideal mathematical universe represents a sort of apotheosis of the process of *Aufhebung*. It is a good question as to how Plato himself attained it, but it is not one relevant to the present argument.[22] Nor is it relevant that advanced cultures accept, and indeed depend upon very different levels of individual achievement in mathematical skills:[23] in traditional cultures such differentiation largely characterises certain trades, such as that of the Kpelle blacksmiths.

The almost inevitable conclusion from the material considered in this chapter is that the experience of mathematics, judged cross-culturally, is uniform, at least up to the levels attained in any traditional culture. The limitations to mathematical achievement are primarily linguistic, for reasons which will become clear in the following chapter. Mathematics consists, essentially, of open-ended skills, which continue to convey new information after mastery (Lancy 1983:209). Its contents can always transcend language, even though language (particularly visual language incorporating special notation, such as the Arabic numerals) is essential for representation and communication. This is confirmed by the fact that numerical institutions time and time again cross cultural boundaries; they are diffusion phenomena par excellence. Take, for instance, a game like *oware*, described in chapter 10. One has only to see the game being played to learn not only the rules which constitute it, but also the basic strategies. The conceptualisation of the game which will then build up in the mind of the observer will be based, needless to say, upon a representation in his own language – so much so, that he need not understand a single word of the language spoken by the actual players, if, indeed, they have a common language. The point is that the language, or rather the notation, of *oware*, is defined by the actual board and counters used, and dialogue consists of the successive moves of the two players. As far as development psychology is concerned, it is sufficient that the mind of the individual possesses the necessary resources for understanding the game before it reaches the steady state. Furthermore, the principle of *Aufhebung* allows us, in practice, to disregard the role played by language in developing these resources, however essential it may be. On the other hand, the fact that no cultural institution can exist in a linguistic vacuum, means that language – in the sense of a normal spoken language – must also relate, in some way, to numerical institutions. Just how this happens is the subject matter of the following chapter.

Numbers and memory

This section is hardly more than a footnote, but it is an important one. It relates to long-term memory, where 'the most important thing[...]is not storage of past experience, but the retrieval of what is relevant in some usable form' (Bruner 1964:2). This is, for instance, essential for the Caroline navigators, who must be able to recall the position of the stars which guide them, although in this case 'we are not able to recreate the conceptual framework' (Lewis 1972:132). The general principle is that retrieval is made much easier if the information stored can first be reduced to some principle of organisation – this is the function of a mnemonic, often based on a recognised 'formula' (Goody 1977:116). This is a sort of surrogate for all the reference systems used in advanced cultures, for such purposes, among others, as the recording and retrieval of large numbers – such as telephone numbers. On the other hand, the use of numerical mnemonics, such as poetic meter, is common in traditional cultures.[24]

The point to a numerical mnemonic is that it gives structure to information which is otherwise disordered. The case can be illustrated (Baddeley 1985:271) by the set of numbers:

2 9 3 3 3 6 4 0 4 3 4 7
5 8 1 2 1 5 1 9 2 2 2 6

which at first sight would seem to be difficult to remember, particularly over any long period of time. If, however, one realises that by starting with the number 5, at the left hand end of the bottom row, and then adding, alternately, 3 and 4, so as to continue the row, proceeding at its end, to the left hand end of the top row, then this principle of organization immediately solves the problem of memory. As is characteristic of any mathematical principle, this one is more general and more abstract than any particular problem illustrating its application.

Now almost any effective application of numeracy is tied up with the grasp of deep structures, and one finds that the ability to remember what are essentially numerical positions is characteristic of the best performers in any relevant area – simply because they understand what these structures are. It is largely a question of economy of effort: a coherent structure, once it is understood, contains its own mnemonic base. This explains the phenomenal gifts of a concert pianist who can play all thirty-two Beethoven piano sonatas from memory, or the chess grandmaster who can recall every move in some thousands of different games.[25] But the importance of a phenomenal memory, possessed by a handful of individuals, is probably even more crucial in a traditional culture, lacking any 'cheap and easy methods of recording information accurately by writing' (Baddeley 1985:369).[26] On the other hand, with a game such as *oware* the memory processes of a top-player will be of the same kind as those of a chess grandmaster.

The key point is that there is a special relationship between numbers and memory, based upon the endless capacity of numbers in any context – music,[27] games, commerce, cosmology – to combine according to structures of great depth. Once the structure is grasped, often by means of an 'Aha-rection', the problem of memory is largely solved, even though, as with the Caroline navigators, a great many *names* must still be remembered so as to make possible the necessary conceptualisation of the basis upon which the structure rests.

3
Number and language

The use of numbers in relation to language

The relation between number and language is complex, and any research into this relationship is bound to be full of pitfalls. To begin with it should be recognised that 'the evolution of a developed understanding of number proceeded through the growth of spoken systems' (Hurford 1987:144). Not only is no thought possible without speech, but the conceptualisation of number and numerical processes is only achieved at an advanced stage of cognitive development. In practice a child's linguistic competence is almost completely developed (Fry 1979:34) before it is capable of mastering numerical systems at even the most elementary level. Such systems do not necessarily exist in every culture, as witness the general absence of any system of numerals in Australian vocabularies (Dixon 1980:107). But there may still be expedients for conveying numerical information. Two examples illustrate this point: first 'aboriginal Australians did have ways of measuring and indicating say the number of days until some planned social event, through pointing at different points on the palm of the hand' (ibid.: 108). Second, the Wedda of Ceylon, described by Menninger (1977:33) as a 'primitive tribe with a very low level of culture', can only count a quantity of any objects by pairing them one by one with some other objects (Scriba 1973:400). This exercise is not necessarily futile. In this way, a debt, say, in coconuts, can be recorded by storing a corresponding number of tallies[1] in some safe place. The point is that although language is essential to any communication or understanding of this process, the particular language used need not contain any numerals. In short, numbers can be implicit in the use of language, without their being capable of being made explicit. At the same time, even where a given language does contain numerals – and this may be taken to be the general case – there is no general rule determining which numerals these are, nor how they are related lexically or arithmetically to each other. That is, there is no one answer to the question as to how a numerical vocabulary is constituted (Hurford 1975:1). All that can be said is that any such vocabulary must be incomplete, in the sense of being able to contain no more than a finite number of words expressing numbers, when, by force of pure logic, the series of numbers is infinite (Hurford 1987:11). On the other hand, any language, however poor it may be in numerals, will be adequate for the numerical needs of its users,[2] even though any extension of these needs may give rise to lexical problems of considerable difficulty.[3] The adaptability of language, in the face of the lexical demands made upon it in the field of numerals, varies very considerably.

The relation of numbers to language depends also upon the purposes for which numerals, or numerical processes, are used in the language domain. Two main types of use, nominative and operational, may be distinguished, each with its own demands upon language. As to the former, numerals are 'most frequently used as nominal modifiers' (Hurford 1987:157), that is, they must qualify, generally as an adjective, a noun, so that 'for instance, *five bricks* [is] logically prior to an understanding of *five*' (ibid.: 161). What five bricks represents is the intersection of the class of aggregates containing bricks, and that of collections with five members. From this point the following step is to treat numbers (as opposed to collections) as real, but abstract objects created through an interaction of people, language and the world. Number, as an abstract concept, cannot exist without numerals, in the sense of words representing different numerical quantities. In other words, a numerical lexicon is essential to any conceptualisation of number. One's intuition revolts against the idea that the words, 'one', 'two', 'three' and so on, which represent the series of natural numbers, can be dispensed with. They are in fact quite indispensable to one fundamental view of number, which in the western world is associated with the school of Pythagoras.[4] The point is that they represent much more than the series, 1, 2, 3..., as it is established by the processes of formal logic. For as Burkert (1972:43) points out, 'One learns to count and calculate in childhood, and from the beginning the numbers are appreciated as things, with certain characteristics; they preserve this peculiarity even, at an unconscious level, in the mind of the adult.'

The emphasis on counting is not misplaced, since ordinary understanding of number is inextricably bound up with counting, it is doubtful whether one can reasonably attribute understanding of particular cardinalities (above about 3) to anyone who has not mastered a counting sequence (Hurford 1987:174–5). And even if the systematic way in which the Pythagoreans related, successively, the members of the series of natural numbers to different concepts is not discernible in every traditional society, it reflects none the less a way of looking at numbers of extreme generality, with far-reaching cultural implications.

The operational use requires cardinal numbers divorced from any collections to which they may correspond, although the purpose of any such use may well relate to some specific collection, such as a sum of money occurring in a bookkeeping operation. The essence of any such use is calculation and comparison. Here the etymology of the Latin word 'calculus' is itself suggestive. The word means 'pebble', and its derivative, calculation, refers to the use of pebbles in mathematical operations.[5] At the most elementary level such an operation need be no more than the counting system used by the Wedda, but the important point is that at every level such operations provide an analogue to the actual problem confronting the operator. This is essentially no more than an instance of the well-known mathematical procedure of reducing one problem to another. The difference, here, between traditional and modern societies is epistemological. The 'modern' operator realises that the *calculi* do no more than make concrete an abstract problem, and their use provides no more than one particular instance of its solution. The 'traditional' operator is more likely to see the calculi as in some way essential to the ritual process leading to the solution of the problem, and in doing so avoids any number of conceptual difficulties.

The operational use of numbers is characterised also by the use of algorithms, that is, standard procedures to be used at different stages in the operations to be carried out,[6] playing much the same role as soft-ware in modern computers.[7] The analogy is a useful one, since the binary, numerical system of the computer is extremely elementary, particularly in comparison to the operations which can be carried out.[8] Indeed, so restricted are the purely lexical requirements arising from the operational use of numbers that, with the support of cases such as that of the Wedda, one can almost conclude that such use has no essential numerical base. It is not easy to determine just when the use of numbers becomes essential for carrying out certain familiar transactions, for once such use is possible, it tends to be applied also to transactions which had earlier been carried out without it (Murray 1978:203).

The aural representation of number

'"It's the passing bell," said Mr. Venables, "they have rung the nine tailors and forty-six strokes[...]it must be for Sir Henry."' Sayers (1959:60) here recounts what is intuitively the most obvious way of representing any natural number to the human ear. The bell tolls forty-six times to represent the forty-six years of the life of Sir Henry Thorpe. Could anything be simpler? And yet the short passage quoted raises, almost immediately, three significant points, each of which needs further elaboration.

First, the representation of numbers by the simple repetition of a single sound is not to be found in any spoken language. There is '...hardly any trace of the number 2, the crucial first step, even being syntactically complex in any way at all'[9] (Hurford 1987:102). Occasionally, the duplication of a noun may be sufficient to indicate plurality: this is sometimes possible in Japanese. But this is no basis for establishing a numerical lexicon. Second, it cannot be taken for granted that years can be counted as the peals of a bell: every language contains its own rules as to what can and cannot be counted. Third, the age of a man, at the time of his death – if it is known – becomes in a sense a fixed part of his name. This is a clear instance of the nominative use of number. The headstone of the grave, complete with the name of the deceased and his age at the time of his death, is a permanent representation of him, with parallels in many different cultures.[10]

The numerical vocabulary is the obvious starting point for linguistic analysis. At the simplest level a small collection of unrelated words may be all that a given language contains in the way of numbers. The Plateau Tonga, of Southern Africa, have numerals from 'one' to 'five', which are declined like adjectives, and also for 'ten' and 'hundred', in the form of nouns (Junod 1927:166). Although the words 'tjandjabahlayi' and 'hlulabakonti', literally meaning 'innumerable' or 'beyond the capacity of reckoners', are readily used when numbers not represented in the lexicon occur, operations involving such numbers – such as the counting of hoes for bridewealth – are quite legitimate. At an even more elementary level, the only numerals used are formed by combining the words for 'one' and 'two', as in the language spoken by the Aranda and other indigenous peoples of Australia (Gerschel 1962:695), or by including a separate word for 'three' in this process, as has been observed among certain Indian tribes in South America (Dixon and Kroeber 1907:664). The limits to such a system are obvious. These are sometimes extended by assigning to numerals words representing some other ordered series, such as the different parts of the human anatomy occurring in the span of the out-stretched arms (Ifrah 1987:25f and Barnes 1982:9).[11] This is another intuitively attractive idea occurring in the history of the lexical analysis of different numeral systems, but it is hardly more than one possible explanation of the origin of the words used for numerals. Much more commonly, particular numerals, such as the words for 'one man' used for 'twenty' in the vigesimal Mayan languages of southern Mexico, exemplify this type of derivation, while in the same language the remaining numerals have no such alternative meanings.[12] It seems to be true in every case that no gap ever occurs in a numeral sequence starting with the word for 'one', however few members it may contain (Hurford 1987:87). The only exception is that a base number, such as 10 and 100 as they are represented in Plateau Tonga, may be beyond the end of the sequence.

No part of speech is more susceptible to linguistic borrowing and cultural diffusion than numerals (Crump 1978:508f.). This in part explains not only why the lexical origins of numerals are so difficult to trace, but also why numerals tend, intrinsically, to be so little related to other parts of the vocabulary. More specifically, in any language, the word class of numerals has a fixed number of items, and the complete list is learnt during the period of primary language acquisition,[13] a property which it shares with

34

prepositions, conjunctions and pronouns (Fry 1979:33). Using the linguistic term 'morpheme' to mean any non-reducible element in a language with its own recognised meaning, then the numerical lexicon is built up out of both unbound morphemes, consisting of all non-reducible numerals capable of standing alone, and bound morphemes, consisting of those elements which can only be used in combination. In English, the unbound morphemes are 'one', 'two', 'three', 'four', 'five', 'six', 'seven', 'eight', 'nine', 'ten', 'eleven', 'twelve', 'hundred', 'thousand', and then such higher powers of ten as are represented by special words, such as 'million'.[14] The bound morphemes are 'twen-', 'thir-', 'fif-', '-teen', '-ty', and also 'and', which is always bound when it is used in numerals. The position is not affected by such obvious derivations as 'twen-' from 'two', or '-teen' and '-ty' from ten, nor by the less obvious derivations, 'eleven' and 'twelve'. In some languages, such as the many different varieties of Chinese, all numerals are built up out of unbound morphemes.

Apart from the most elementary cases, such as that of the language spoken by the Plateau Tonga,[15] the great majority of all recognised numerals are compounds of the numerical morphemes, a practice which allows a very small number of morphemes to generate a very large number of numerals. In English nineteen[16] morphemes are sufficient for every number up to a million. The systematic way in which numerals are formed, in any language, can be analysed according to a method established by Salzmann (1950), which is based upon three general structural patterns. The first of these, the frame pattern, consists simply of the class of unbound numerical morphemes, which must exist in any language containing numerals. The second pattern, known as the cyclic pattern, consists of such of the successive powers of an established numerical base as can be expressed in words.[17] In English this pattern comprises the numbers, 10, 100, 1,000, 10,000 and so on, so long as they remain expressible.[18] The third pattern according to Salzmann (1950:82), is not of the same order as the two preceding ones, but it is rather an additional working criterion, by which numerical morphemes, or groups of morphemes, are combined by the basic arithmetical operations of addition, subtraction and multiplication. The actual formation of words representing the whole series of natural numbers, on the basis of the three patterns, depends in any language on recognised grammatical rules, which may be seen as a sort of linguistic, or lexical algorithm. The simplest case, provided by Chinese, can be adopted as a general model. The numerical lexicon comprises two classes of unbound morphemes, the first class representing the numbers from 1 to 9 inclusive, and the second class representing, to a given upper limit, the successive powers of 10.[19] The two classes combined constitute the frame pattern, and the second, standing alone, the cyclic pattern. Any number not belonging to the frame pattern is then formed according to a polynomial rule, starting with the numeral

Coefficients	3		8	0	4
Frame morpheme	*sān*	*qiān*	*bā*	*bǎi* — —	*sì*
	三	千	八	百	四
Powers of 10 (cyclic frame)		10^3	10^2	10	

Fig. 2. A representative Chinese numeral (3804).

expressing the coefficient of the highest power of ten, with the process continuing through all the lower powers of 10 until the whole number is expressed.[20] This is the operative pattern for Chinese. The way it works is best illustrated by an example. Take the number 3804. Figure 2 then shows how to break it down, according to the rules of the operative pattern. The Chinese numeral for 3804 is then sān-qiān-bā-bǎi-sì,[21] with – be it noted – no mention of the powers of ten with zero coefficients.

The Chinese case is simple, since in the formation of the numerals there are no anomalous deviations – such as often represent survivals from frame and cyclic patterns belonging to an earlier stage of lexical development – in the operative pattern. The French, *quatre-vingt-douze*, for 92, is one example of such deviance, clearly derived from a cyclic pattern with a base of 20. It is impossible to list all the variants, but all known numerical systems capable of expressing the complete range of natural numbers beyond a certain relatively low threshold – which will almost certainly be less than 100 – are based upon a Chinese-type model once they pass beyond this threshold. A mathematician could devise any number of alternatives to the polynomial model, but few such alternatives occur in practice. On the other hand, the base, 10, although the most common case, is by no means universal. The vigesimal Mayan numerals are based on 20, and the sexagesimal numerals of ancient Babylon, which still survive in the measurement of time, on 60. In these cases, where the base number is relatively large, there tend to be subsidiary systems based upon some factor of it, such as 5 in the case of vigesimal systems,[22] or 10 in that of sexagesimal systems.

Any operative pattern, to be workable in practice, must be free of deviant cases when it comes to the expression of relatively large numbers. In such 'troublesome' languages as French and Danish these cases are confined to numbers under a hundred.[23] The degree of difficulty arising from the anomalous cases[24] can vary greatly, from the simplicity of Chinese at one end of the scale, to the complexity of Yoruba at the other. As I have already noted, the deviant cases often represent lexical survivals, sometimes reflecting elementary non-polynomial operative patterns suitable only for the expression of a limited range of relatively low numbers. The Japanese numeral system, which is essentially no more than a fairly straightforward adaptation of the Chinese numerical lexicon, none the less retains a series of autochthonous numerals from 1 to 10 which are based upon a binary operative pattern, so that *futatsu*, '2', derives from *hitotsu*, '1'[25] *muttsu*, '6', from *mittsu* '3', *yattsu*, '8' from *yottsu*, '4' and *tō*, '10' from *itsutsu*, '5',[26] with additional words for '7' and '9'. Therefore there are at least two alternative words for all the numbers from 1 to 10,[27] but in many common cases only one of them is likely to be correct.[28] This is still a decimal system rather than a pure binary system with a base value, 2: it seems that such systems are 'never used in the syntactic and semantic organization of spoken languages' (Hurford 1987:50).

The binary operative pattern is just one of a number of possibilities applicable to low numbers: both addition and subtraction are repeatedly used in generating new numerals from a basic frame, so that $3 = 2+1$, $5 = 2+2+1$, $6 = 5+1$, $9 = 10-1$ to cite a few instances which occur in any number of unrelated languages.[29] The range of possibilities is extended by allowing a lexical rule of multiplication, so that $6 = 2 \times 3$, $9 = 3 \times 3$, $18 = 3 \times 6$... or, to cite the familiar French case of 'quatre-vingt', $80 = 4 \times 20$. Once again, it is impossible to list all the different known cases.

The compilation of a numerical lexicon is simply the first step in solving the problem of incorporating numbers into language. The mere fact that a restricted class of numbers can be expressed in words says nothing about the way in which any member of the class (any recognised numeral), may actually be used in the language to which it belongs. This is a question of syntax, and it has no general answer. Grammatical prejudices, born out of a knowledge of one's own language, can easily lead to false generalisations and incorrect conclusions. To take one example, Hungarian has plural forms for both nouns and verbs,[30] but when the noun is qualified by a numeral, both it, and the verb it governs, must be in the singular form. Going one step further, to Japanese, the question does not even arise, since there is no grammatical distinction between singular and plural, but then, most nouns cannot directly be qualified by a numeral either. This is an example of a language incorporating *numeral classifiers* which occur, subject often to quite idiosyncratic rules governing their use, in many languages. These classifiers may as a rule represent an early stage in the evolution of language, leaving, in languages where they are not a regular part of the syntax of numerals, no more than vestigial traces – such as, in English, 'three head of cattle' (Hurford 1987:214f.). Returning to the case of Japanese, numerals can only govern a restricted class of recognised 'counters', known as *josūshi*, each relating to a given category of nouns.[31] The counter for birds, for example, is 'wa', so that three pigeons is 'san wa no hato', and three nightingales, 'san wa no uguisu'.[32] Counting days is even more complicated, since there are special compound words based on the autochthonous numerals, but in languages such as Hopi days cannot be counted at all. Can it be taken for granted, even in English, that everything can be counted? Japanese, or Hopi for that matter, may do no more than make explicit a problem which is implicit in any language. But numbers may also be implicit in words in which they are not immediately apparent. Chinese, for example, makes explicit the numeral, *wŭ*, meaning 'five', in *wŭ-yuè* for 'May' or *xīngqī-wŭ* for 'Friday'. If such use generally relates to ordinal numbers, this is probably because cardinal numbers generally lack such precise connotations.[33]

The distinction between cardinal and ordinal numbers is generally reflected by special grammatical forms, according to which the ordinal is derived by means of some recognised modification of the cardinal – which is somewhat paradoxical if it is accepted that the concept of ordinals is developmentally prior to that of cardinals; but then, 'in languages which make a morphological distinction between cardinal and ordinal forms, it is the cardinal forms which are used in the conventional counting sequence' (Hurford 1987:168). In any case the rules for such derivation are remarkably regular, particularly in comparison to those governing the formation of numbers out of the elements of the frame pattern. The only common exception is to be found in the few ordinals, such as 'first' and 'second' in English, which are suppletive, that is not related to the corresponding cardinals (ibid.: 172). The ordered sequence, implicit in the use of an ordinal, means that, whatever may be possible with cardinals, there can be no discontinuities in any set of ordinal numbers: the word 'tenth', for instance, can only mean anything if there is also a word for 'ninth'. Dantzig (1930:8) states the point too simply in saying that 'the ordinal system acquires existence when the first few number words have been committed to memory in their ordered succession, and a phonetic scheme has been devised to pass from any larger number to its successor', for this statement ignores the purposes for which ordinal numbers are used.[34] An ordinal number is deictic, or nominative, in the sense introduced at the beginning of this chapter. Friday is meaningless without the other days of the week: in any context in which the word 'Friday' is used, it implies, at the very least, 'not Monday', 'not Tuesday' and so on. The difference between an ordinal and a cardinal is that the former is a true attribute of anything it refers to, where the latter defines only a fortuitous property. This distinction can be made clear by an example: suppose that a man has five children, and the oldest three are present in a room. Then, if a fourth child enters the room, the cardinality 'three' is simply effaced, whereas the third child's rank in terms of age is quite unaffected. The cardinality 'three' does not depend upon any principle of ordering; it would not for instance be affected by the first child leaving the room, to be replaced by the fifth. Indeed the numeral 'three' may equally refer to any of the ten possible combinations of the five children.

The result is that a cardinal number has little significance unless it can be used operationally, that is in some process which combines it with or relates it to other cardinal numbers. This use is essentially syntactic, whereas the use of ordinals is semantic or paradigmatic. In other words, cardinal numbers belong to a self-contained logical system, and the linguistic problem is to relate the output of this system to the demands of other cognitive systems. The absence of any essential connection between the two explains not only the equivocal grammatical status of the cardinal numbers,[35] but also the existence of special categories of words necessary to fit them into the syntax of languages.[36] An example is provided by the Japanese *josūshi*, literally 'help number words': some hundred recognised *josūshi* allocate all nouns representing things which can be counted into a like number of separate categories. To take one example, *mai* is the classifier for flat, thin objects, so that 'two stamps' is not *ni kitte*, but *ni-mai no kitte*, just as 'two plates' is *ni-mai no sara*: (*no* is a particle required by the rules of syntax). Ordinal numbers, on the other hand, are semantic in the sense that they denote what they refer to, and paradigmatic in the sense that they are interchangeable with any other member of the open category of words to which they belong. That is, accepting that the ordinal number is an adjective, it is interchangeable with any of the other adjectives denoting attributes of the same subject.[37] Instead of referring to one's third child, one could equally refer to the child with blue eyes. The advantage of the ordinal number is in its unrivalled precision (Hurford 1987:170). One could have quite a few children with blue eyes, but never more than one third child[38] (although a man with a succession of wives might have difficulty in identifying his *third* child). The point is critical, since it leads one to look for ordinal numbers in cultures which require the specific identification of the different members of certain recognised classes, which may vary from the days in a year, through the inhabitants of a city, the pages of a book to the postal districts in a given country. In modern societies such deictic use of ordinal numbers has become so complex as to be divorced from any question of rank.[39]

In traditional societies, in contrast, the implications for rank may be so deep-seated in the local culture, that the use of ordinal numbers may have to be avoided where such implications are to be excluded. This has led to the use of alternative systems for such purposes as denoting points in time. The use, originating in China, of the *kanshi*, in which ten 'trunk' signs combine with twelve 'branch' signs to provide an ordered series of sixty compounds, as shown in figure 3, is an example of this expedient. It is significant here that the operative frame has no polynomial base: the price paid is that after reaching 60, this alternative system of numerals repeats itself.[40] This is equally true, however, of other ordinal systems – not necessarily explicit – such as the days of the week.[41] The *kanshi* system is also to be distinguished from that of the ordinary Chinese numerals in that the ten 'stems' and twelve

甲寅51	甲辰41	甲午31	甲申21	甲戌11	甲子1	天
乙卯52	乙巳42	乙未32	乙酉22	乙亥12	乙丑2	支
丙辰53	丙午43	丙申33	丙戌23	丙子13	丙寅3	順
丁巳54	丁未44	丁酉34	丁亥24	丁丑14	丁卯4	位
戊午55	戊申45	戊戌35	戊子25	戊寅15	戊辰5	
己未56	己酉46	己亥36	己丑26	己卯16	己巳6	
庚申57	庚戌47	庚子37	庚寅27	庚辰17	庚午7	
辛酉58	辛亥48	辛丑38	辛卯28	辛巳18	辛未8	
壬戌59	壬子49	壬寅39	壬辰29	壬午19	壬申9	
癸亥60	癸丑50	癸卯40	癸巳30	癸未20	癸酉10	

Fig. 3. The *Kanshi* system of ten trunks and twelve branches.

'branches' which together constitute the frame pattern all have well-established non-numerical meanings,[42] so that their use, even if it avoids denoting rank, is still encumbered with all kinds of other implications. This is precisely the point which distinguishes numeracy in traditional societies from that in modern societies, which is one reason why the present linguistic analysis is so important.

The visual representation of number

So great are the advantages that visual representation has over the aural representation of number, that there is every reason for believing that it represents no later stage in cultural evolution. If, intuitively, one rejects this belief, it is almost certainly because writing is assumed to be the starting point for any such representation. The significance of writing lies in the fact that it enables numerals to be recorded, but even then it represents no more than the most refined means of achieving this result.[43] The Ishango bone which, certainly in the part of Africa where it was discovered, predates any system of writing by some thousands of years, is marked with groups of notches, set out in three columns. While no one has been able to establish the actual use of this mesolithic artifact, it is virtually certain that the notches reflect a system of numerical notation, even though the precise significance of the numbers recorded is impossible to discover (Marshack 1972:22f.).

Long before the introduction of any permanent records, however elementary, numbers were certainly represented by the fingers, including the thumbs, of the two hands, a practice to be found at every stage of cultural evolution. The precise mode of representation may vary,[44] but the fact that the number 10^{45} is by far the most common base of any cyclic pattern of numeration encountered in spoken languages leaves little doubt about the near universal symbolic use of the fingers for the purposes of numeration.[46] They provide an instantly accessible means for applying the principle of correspondence, which is the whole basis of the cardinal numbers.

The need for visual representation of number becomes much more acute where there is a demand for arithmetical computation. It is not only that such representation crystallises[47] the essential discontinuity of the series of natural numbers, but the spatial location of the constitutive elements then becomes subject to possible rearrangement. Although Lemoine (1932) has demonstrated the extraordinary potential of the fingers for such rearrangement, for the purposes of calculation their usefulness is clearly restricted by the anatomy of the hand.[48] It is not surprising, then, that other visual aids to calculation, such as pebbles, whose manipulation is free from such restrictions, came to be used.[49] Once this practice was established, the procedures became more and more refined over the course of time, to the point that numbers, of whatever size, came to be expressed by groups of pebbles representing the coefficients of the successive powers of the number base, so that 284, for instance, would be represented by three such groups, containing, respectively, two, eight and four pebbles. The groups had to have both order (so that 284 would not be confused with, say, 428) and position (so that null groups could be represented so as to distinguish 284 from, say, 2804).[50] This need for an operational framework is realised in concrete form by the abacus, in which the pebbles, in the form of beads,[51] are threaded on fixed columns, representing, successively, the powers of ten.[52] The origins of the abacus are unknown,[53] but it is certainly one of the most perfect inventions of all time. (The electronic computer is based upon the same principle, although the numbers are expressed in binary rather than decimal form.) The abacus is however subject to the same limitation as the hand, in that its use effaces the record both of the steps taken in calculation, and of the numbers involved in it. The fact that its function is purely operational means, inevitably, that it deals only in cardinal numbers. The abacus can never tell anything about the extrinsic meaning of either its input or its output, to use modern computer terminology. Its internal 'syntax' has no basis in any spoken language, and accepting that neither the input nor the output can be conceived of by the human mind except in terms of such a language, it then follows that the abacus is only accessible by way of some process of translation.[54] (This process, which is implicit in the use of the abacus, is made explicit by the need to use special languages for access to the modern electronic computer.) At the same time, the abacus is free of the limitations of language when it comes to the representation of the numbers it deals in.[55]

The need to provide some permanent record of numbers is fundamental in the emergence and evolution of writing, for once the operational use of numbers required such a record – almost certainly for the purpose of communicating across otherwise unbridgeable gaps in time and space – writing evolved as the most perfect means of satisfying this need.[56] Writing, in this context, requires a somewhat idiosyncratic definition as any permanent visible record of information, belonging to certain established categories, and based upon a uniform code known to every member of the class to whom such information may have to be transmitted. It should be noted that this definition does not require that speech, as such, should be capable of being encoded. Accepting this definition it is but a short step to the realisation that numerical information can be encoded simply by 'writing' a series of identical marks in a form established by convention – equal in quantity to the number to be represented. An elementary instance of this procedure, by which the Lamet of northern Laos use marks made with charcoal to record the number of working days devoted to harvesting, is given in chapter 8. It should be noted, in particular, that this procedure does not even require that the numbers recorded should be capable of being expressed in the spoken language.

The most remarkable instance of such recording is provided by the knotted strings, known as *quipu*s, used for censuses and bookkeeping in the Inca empire at the time of the Spanish conquest, by a people who otherwise had no indigenous writing system (Murra 1980:159). The basic unit is a coloured two-ply cord made of wool or cotton (Ascher and Ascher 1981:11). An actual *quipu* consists of a main cord, with others suspended from it, which in

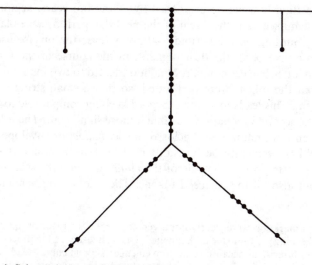

Fig. 4. Schematic example of a *quipu*.

turn may have yet further pendants – without any prescribed limit to the branching process (ibid.: 109f.). The meaning is determined by length and colour of each cord, their relative positions, the types of knots in each knot-cluster and the position of the clusters on the cords (ibid.: 15–23). The numerical system was that of place-value described later in this chapter, with units next to the free end of the cord, and ascending powers of ten coming progressively nearer to the main cord. Units were represented by a special multiple long knot, while higher powers of ten were represented by groups of single knots, all in preordained equally spaced cluster positions, so that zero could be represented by a blank position (ibid.: 29). There was often a top-cord, giving the total of the associated pendants (ibid.: 31). In figure 4 the numbers on the two pendants are 302 and 441, and that on the top cord, their sum, 743. *Quipus* contain both ordinal numbers (as labels) and cardinal numbers (as magnitudes) (ibid.: 32). In any given case there were several alternatives, on the basis of colour-coding and spatial order, for recording information systematically (ibid.: 82), but 'the placement of the cords, relative to each other – that is, their spatial arrangement – carries a large portion of the stored information' (ibid.: 56).

The way in which the representation of numbers by 'counters' – of which *quipu* knots and pebbles (or calculi) are but special cases – can lead to the invention of 'written' forms, has been established by Schmandt-Besserat (1979), working with archeological materials from ancient Mesopotamia. Small clay artifacts, in a limited number of abstract forms, discovered in archeological sites from Beldibi in western Turkey to Chanhu Daro in

Pakistan, and relating to a period of at least five thousand years, beginning in the ninth millenium B.C. at the dawn of the neolithic period, were plainly produced for accounting purposes (ibid.: 40). Whatever the precise use of these tokens may have been, the development, in the course of the fourth millenium B.C., of an urban economy, rooted in trade, led to two innovations. The first was that the tokens were perforated, so that a small string could pass through them. This leads to a type of record keeping comparable to that of the *quipus*. The second innovation was much more significant. The tokens relating to a given transaction were enclosed in clay *bullae*, or envelopes, in which they could conveniently be transmitted. The transmission was then validated by impressing on the outside of the *bulla*, not only the seal of the 'transmitter', but also all the enclosed tokens. Then, following Schmandt-Besserat (ibid.: 47),

Although the bulla markings were clearly not invented to take the place of the token system of record keeping[...]that is what happened. One can visualize the process. At first the innovation flourished because of its convenience; anyone could 'read' what tokens a bulla contained and how many without destroying the envelope and its seal impressions. What then happened was virtually inevitable, and the substitution of two dimensional portraits of the tokens for the tokens themselves would seem to have been the crucial link between the archaic recording system and writing. The hollow bullae with the enclosed tokens would have been replaced by inscribed solid clay objects: tablets. The strings, baskets and shelf load of tokens in the archives would have given way to representative signs inscribed on tablets, that is to written records.

To summarize, the earliest examples of writing in Mesopotamia may not, as many have assumed, be the result of pure invention. Instead they appear to be a novel application[...]of a recording system that was indigenous to western Asia from early neolithic times onwards. In this view, the appearance of writing[...]represents a logical step in the evolution of a system of record keeping that originated some 11,000 years ago[...]Images of the tokens[...]supplanted the tokens themselves, and the evolution of symbolic objects into ideographs led to the[...]adoption of writing all across western Asia.

There is one gap in this chain of reasoning which is, at least at first sight, difficult to bridge. The repetition of the visual symbols inherent in the written representation of numerals, so that, for instance, $92 \ (= 1 \times 60 + 3 \times 10 + 2)$ was represented in the manner shown in figure 5, was not reflected in the vocabulary of the spoken language. It was not, therefore, immediately obvious that the spoken language could be represented in writing by an analogous process. But then the first written representation of 'words' were confined either to proper names, or to such things, as measures of barley, as occurred in transactions recorded in numbers (Oppenheim 1964:230f.). Chinese is the only language in which a perfect one-to-one correspondence between the written and spoken forms of numerals ever evolved, and even in this case, the earliest written numerals did not have this property.[56]

In two cases, in which the evolution of writing led to the representation of

D • • • ᴅ ᴅ

Fig. 5. The number 92 in Sumerian cuneiform.

words by the letters of an alphabet, the process of evolution described in the previous paragraph was turned on its head, and the 'new' letters were used to represent numbers. In point of time, this happened first with Greek, which was then followed by Hebrew – this in spite of the fact that the Hebrew alphabet, as such, is older than the Greek alphabet (Menninger 1969:265). The civilisations of Greece and Israel, in making this choice, cut themselves off from the mainstream of numerical development in Babylon, so that, in the end, the development of mathematics in the Western world was blocked for more than a thousand years.[57] Particularly in the case of Hebrew, the loss was made good in the realm of number mysticism, whose supreme achievement is contained in the Kabbala. It is significant, here, that in this realm China tended to rely on alternative numerical systems, such as that of the 'stems' and 'branches' described earlier in this chapter or the hexagrams of the Book of Changes.[58]

In the time of the dark ages of Western mathematics there developed in Persia and India the place-value representation of number, which, transmitted by the civilisation of early medieval Islam, reached the West in the familiar form of the 'Arabic' numerals.[59] If the starting point for this development was the Babylonian numeral system (which represents no more than the final stage in the evolution of written numbers in Mesopotamia), the decisive breakthrough occurred when it was realised that a number could be written in the same form as it was represented on an abacus, for this is the essence of any place-value system. But before this could occur two requirements had to be satisfied. First, there had to be an operative pattern in which the same series of numerals was used in representing the coefficients of every successive power of ten. Neither the cuneiform numerals of Mesopotamia, nor the numerals which had evolved independently in Egypt (but with an identical operative pattern), had this property. The Chinese numerals, which first appeared in the fourteenth century B.C., always satisfied this requirement, but this factor does not seem to have played any part in the development of a place-value system.[60] The second requirement was for a sign to represent the vacant position, such as occurs on an abacus when a column is vacant. (The numerical example given in figure 2 makes this clear.) The fact that in the present version of the Arabic numerals this is no more than the zero-sign, '0', does not mean that the vacant[61] sign must also represent a true zero.

In the development of Arabic numerals, the first Brahmi prototypes of the 'digits' from 1 to 9, dating from the third century B.C., are to be found in the Buddhist inscriptions of Nana Ghat in India, but the principle of position did not yet apply. The first known use of these digits, applying this principle, is to be found in the *Lokavibhaga*, a Sanskrit text from the year 458 A.D., in which, needless to say, a sign for zero occurs. The place-value system, as represented in this text, could not be more perfect as an operative pattern. The actual form of the Arabic numerals, after their introduction into the Western world in the tenth century, evolved in line with the evolution of handwriting, until the invention of printing, some five hundred years later, led to the fixed forms which are still in use today.[62]

The literate culture of medieval Europe, with its suspicion of all that was not Latin, was not favourable to the acceptance of Arabic numerals, and they did not become generally used until the fifteenth century. 'Formal schooling-teaching in the new arithmetic[...]was at schools separate from those which taught reading and writing.[63] So a man could learn to reckon without ever learning to read and write in the ordinary way' (Murray 1978:169). In the end the success of the Arabic numerals was partly due to the fact that the board abacus used in western Europe was much more cumbersome in use than the frame abacus used in the east. The efficiency of the frame abacus may help to explain why the Chinese numeral system is still, after three thousand years, in daily use, not only in China, but in Japan and Korea also.

Finally, where the old world followed, over some thousands of years, its tortuous path to the realisation of a perfect place-value system, the Maya civilisation of central America needed no more than a few hundred years to get the answer right for the new world. The definitive use of a sign for 'zero' to establish a place value system occurred at about the time of the *Lokavibhaga*, but the journey was much shorter. The vigesimal Maya system represents the digits from 1 to 19 by a combination of bars, expressing multiples of five, and dots, expressing units, with a special sign for zero. The system had, however, a curious defect, in that the base of its third place was 360 (18×20), and not, as it should have been, 400 (20^2).[64] This meant that the adding of a digit for zero did not effect a multiplication by the numerical base, 20. In practice this may not have mattered, since the most important use of numbers, which was for calendrical purposes, did not require this operation. It is once again significant that while the use of numerals, which constantly occur in Mayan texts, has long been understood by archeologists, the decipherment of the ideographs representing other words in the same texts is still far from complete. This justifies, in a quite different context, Murray's (1978:169) leitmotiv in his study of the European middle ages, that the paths of numeracy and literacy are distinct.[65] The implications of this fact, in the realms of culture, religion and society, politics and economics, are the theme of the next two chapters.

4

Cosmology and ethnoscience

The rule of order

Archaeologists maintain theories of what happened from the number of steps in each pyramid – mathematical computations that lead to a human sacrifice or a struggle between rival cults[...]The mathematical sense seems to have run riot – everything is symmetrical; it is important that the Pyramid of the Sun should be sixty-six metres high and have five terraces, and the Pyramid of the Moon be fifty-four metres high and have – I forget how many terraces. Heresy was not an aberration of human feeling[...]but a mathematical error. Death was important only as solving an equation[...]One expects to see Q E D written on the great court – the pyramids adding up correctly, the number of terraces multiplied by the number of steps, and divided by the square metres of the surface area, proving – something, something as inhuman as a problem in algebra   *Greene 1982:82–3*

Graham Greene's description of Teotihuacan, if certainly a parody of a traditional cosmology, none the less reflects a common enough judgment of modern, supposedly rational, man. The point is simple enough: modern western man is brought up to accept a disjunctive view of the universe. As Needham (1969:26) has noted, 'from the beginning of their thought history, Europeans have passed continually from one extreme world outlook to another, rarely finding any synthesis[...]Theological spiritualism and mechanical materialism maintained perpetual war.'[1] The universe is pre-eminently a physical rather than a metaphysical construction. The result is that the realm of numbers is defined largely by the use of mathematics in the so-called 'exact sciences', so that music[2] and even such sciences as medicine and agriculture are excluded from it. The result of this approach, to paraphrase Needham (ibid.: 14), is that European mathematics is mathematics; all other mathematics is anthropology. That explains why this other mathematics belongs to what has been called ethnoscience,[3] and also why this book is written by an anthropologist (albeit one who started his scientific career as a mathematician).

The idea of a 'cosmology' is the best starting point for understanding the 'scientific' use of numbers in any culture, traditional or modern. 'Cosmos', in its opposition to 'chaos', means order. Accepting Gellner's (1972:172) view that 'no society has succeeded in devising a style of life based on the assumption of chaos', the idea of cosmos – or better 'cosmology', in the sense of some rule which orders the universe, is essential. If, in a traditional society, acceptance of such a rule may require an act of faith, where in a modern society it is based upon recognised scientific axioms, it must lead – in either case – to representations which transcend the actual cases to which it applies. This requires a level of abstraction for which the use of numbers is ideally suited. One cannot say that such use is 'necessary', since there are many recorded cosmologies without any numerical base. But equally, there are many other cosmologies, traditional as well as modern, which reflect the view that we live in a mathematical universe.[4] Numbers, in a variety of different interpretations and combinations, do seem to be a 'sufficient' base for a viable cosmology, as the historical and ethnographical evidence, considered in the second part of this chapter, abundantly confirms.

The difference between traditional and modern cosmologies, is essentially the same as the difference between astrology and astronomy, or alchemy and chemistry. But what is this difference? It is easy to recognise in particular cases, but more difficult to describe analytically. The rule that the weather on St Swithin's day, whether wet or fine, decides that for the following forty days plainly belongs to traditional, rather than modern meteorology: the statistics now recorded would almost certainly prove it false. In any sort of popular historical analysis, the difference between traditional and modern is seen in terms of 'scientific method'. This means that any mathematical representation of natural phenomena is acceptable only so long as it accords with the facts disclosed by experiment and observation. According to this view, the way in which the scientific community carries out its activities is essentially mechanistic. Scientific advance has its own internal logic, to which practising scientists are subordinate. Carried to the extreme, this leads to a vision of a world free of politics, with no room for value judgments.[5] There is, perhaps, a refraction of such a world in the community of pure mathematicians, where the rule seems to be that every member of it is free to pursue his own esoteric research, whose results, devoid of any practical application, will only be intelligible to a small circle of colleagues working in the same field.[6] On the other hand, this world, almost by definition, admits neither experiment nor observation. Nor does it allow for any but the most incidental practical applications.

Any cosmology belongs essentially to the world of applied mathematics. Here, if a distinction is to be made between traditional and modern cosmologies, the former tends to emphasise the applications, where the latter emphasises the mathematics. In a traditional cosmology the applications are sacrosanct (which is what the whole trial of Galileo was about).[7] It does not matter that the mathematics is trivial, and in any case this is no more a judgment of the modern world. We can see the results of this approach particularly in traditional approaches to time and space, as described in chapters 7 and 11. The Balinese calendar (page 84) or the Kyoto temple of

Sanjūsangendō (p. 135) reflect a use of numbers which, although extremely involved, is mathematically quite elementary. It could hardly be otherwise. Once the message is established in mathematical terms, these are deprived of any inherent autonomy: if this were not so, the content of the message would itself be open to doubt. This explains the extremely permanent form in which such institutions are cast: if *soi-disant* professional mathematicians were allowed to work on the numerical basis of Sanjusangendo, all the labour of building it might prove to have been in vain. The mathematics of Sanjusangendo is impregnable, and whatever factors may have caused changes in the use and meaning of the building over the course of the centuries, they are not numerical.[8]

There is thus a finality in a traditional cosmology which would be objectionable to modern science. This explains why the focus is largely on those elements of culture that transcend the natural order: this is one possible definition of religion, so that the religious applications of numbers will be considered further in the second part of this chapter. But traditional cosmology also comprehends such applied sciences as agriculture and medicine: as to the former, the cycles of cultivation, in their relation to the ordering of time, are maintained according to numerical principles. Wet rice cultivation, in Bali and Japan, well illustrates this process.

Animal husbandry is a somewhat different case: here numerical principles are more likely to govern the size of the herds, as is illustrated by the case of the Nuer cattle, described in chapter 5. In both cases, however, the choice of the numerical principles to be applied is subject always to local ecological factors, and judged in the light of such factors the mode of application may well be counter-productive. This is essentially an economic judgment, of only incidental importance in the present context.[9]

If medicine, according to the intuitive judgment of the modern world, is hardly a science based on numbers, it is often otherwise in traditional cultures. Once again time is a factor, particularly where the condition of the patient is subject to a timetable imposed by nature. Here the most obvious case is the woman's reproductive cycle, which by the regular occurrence of menses, or the fixed duration of pregnancy,[10] lends itself to numerical interpretation and prescription. In Japan, a sash known as *iwata-obi*, is still worn by a majority of women from the first day of the dog[11] occurring during the fifth month of pregnancy: this comes usually from a temple or shrine noted for its efficacy in childbirth (Ohnuki-Tierney 1984:182), but the obstetrician in charge will also write on it, in red, the character for 'happiness'. It then 'signifies not simply that the woman is pregnant, but also that the pregnancy is stabilized and that childbirth is more or less assured' (ibid.: 182).

Traditional Chinese medicine, from which Japanese medicine is largely derived, extends the application of numerical principles much further. The

49

basic system was known as *wŭ-yùn liù-qì*, or 'five elements, six spirits': in combination with the opposing forces of Yin and Yang, the former corresponded to the ten *trunk* signs, and the latter to the twelve *branch* signs used in figure 3, leading to the same sixty possible combinations. *Yùn-qì-xué*, that is the science of the elements (*yùn*) and the spirits (*qì*), which provided the underlying principle, contained several basic ideas.

One was that no life, no growth, no disease, nor recovery, could come about if the cooperation of[...]heavenly and earthly forces was lacking. The celestial *thien* [*tiān*] and the terrestrial (*ri*) [*dì*] had to combine their powers; and in this system it is noteworthy that the five elements operated from the heavens while the six *chhi* [*qì*] were those of the earth. Another idea was that the affairs of health and sickness proceeded according to a number of subtle rhythms, which, for effective intervention had to be caught at the right times and moments. Then again there was the conviction that man was not isolated from Nature, indeed mirrored in himself the whole, so that cyclic astronomical, meteorological, climatic and epidemiological factors mattered enormously for physiological and pathological processes[...]The dominance of this proto-science[...]was a turning point in the history of Chinese medicine, for in it abstraction triumphed over empiricism and practical experience

Lu and Needham *1980:141*

Abstraction is the essence of any mathematical model: the process is essential for establishing any general principle, in modern as well as in traditional science. But as already noted, the abstractions of traditional science are sacrosanct: indeed they are not even recognised as being abstractions, an error almost unthinkable in modern science.

Chinese medicine shows the same approach in the context of acupuncture, a form of treatment based upon a spatial model of the human body. One of the earliest texts, the *Nei Ching* (which means no more than 'Book of Corporeal Medicine') refers to 365 acu-points, for placing the needles, relating this number not only to the 365 days in the year, but also to the 365 degrees in the celestial circles (Lu and Needham 1980:15). The distribution and location of the acu-points was conceived of according to a modular diagram, of which figure 6 is an example. The model basis is entirely general, and the plan of the Rin'ami house in Japan, given in figure 16 shows how it was also applied in architecture. Similar models were also used far outside the Chinese culture area.

This holistic approach is a common characteristic of traditional science. Once a general concept has been accepted, the field of application tends to be extended to the whole of life. As Needham (1980:305) observes, 'the very success of the Aristotelian synthesis at imposing reason and coherence upon most of man's concerns over two millennia gave it a strength which could be overcome only by that total confrontation which we call the Scientific Revolution'. It is no wonder that the Inquisition put Galileo on trial, but Aristotelian cosmology (which was the basis of the Church's thinking) was based on the principle that since 'mathematics[...]dealt with perfect and

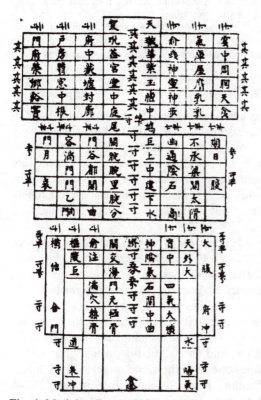

Fig. 6. Modular diagram of acupoints.

eternal bodies and their relations, it could only be applied rigorously to astronomy, for nothing below the orb of the moon was perfect and eternal' (ibid.). This equation of cosmology with an unattainable perfection, if it accords well with Christian theology – which associates perfection with a future state in another world[12] – is not a cultural universal, and the Chinese case points the contrast. The distinction may lie in the fact that 'in the West the influence of the planets was direct; but in China it is perhaps confusing even to use the word "influence", for the relation was one of correspondence' (ibid.: 227). Its numerical basis, together with a number of applications – in Japan as well as China – provide the starting point for the following section.

The mystery of numbers

It is tempting to believe that mystics lack intellectual clarity, and that they easily confuse one thing with another. It is the symbolism they use which explains this mistaken view: a careful reading of the writings of the saints dealing with their visions, shows that once the transition is made from the tangible to the symbolic world, they never mix their images, but consistently adhere to the proportions which they have chosen. Why is this? The answer is that these images are the exact representation of the truth which they contemplate. In fact no-one is more precise than a mystic, and the mystic is not a dreamer.   Green *1972:41*

Julien Green, in writing the above passage was thinking of Christian mysticism, but what he has to say is equally true of the symbolic basis of any cosmology, and particularly of one based on numbers. The emphasis on precision is extraordinarily apt.[13] The result is that numerical systems are accepted as the model of transactions to which they have no inherent relationship. The point has already been made above, in relation to Chinese medicine, but it will now be worked out in greater detail, first for China, and then extended to other cultures.

The basis of Chinese applied numerology is to be found in three institutions, (i) Yin–Yang, (ii) Wǔ-yùn ('The Five Elements' and (iii) the *I Ching* (*The Book of Changes*). The first of these is the basis of any binary system of classification.[14] All natural phenomena are governed by the rhythmic alternation of the fundamental forces of Yin and Yang (Ronan and Needham 1981:327), which can be represented in the form of the sine wave in figure 7. The connotations of Yin and Yang are almost endless: basically the former represents the negative, and the latter, the positive principle in nature. Yin is a feminine principle connoting the moon, night, winter, shade, secrecy, where Yang is a masculine principle connoting the sun,[15] day, summer, light, and openness. It is best to see the two principles in symmetrical opposition, without making any value judgments about the relative merits of what they connote.

The five elements are wood, fire, earth, water and metal. Their relationship to Yin and Yang can be read from figure 7. Earth then represents Yin and Yang mixed in equal proportions, fire pure Yang, water pure Yin, metal a mixture with Yin > Yang, and wood a mixture with Yang > Yin (Needham 1980:157). Where Yin and Yang represent the sun and the moon, the five elements represent the five planets known to the ancient world, so together they are the seven heavenly bodies – which in Japanese provide the names for the days of the week (Crump 1986b:68).[16] Now the five elements, even if capable of being derived from Yin and Yang in the manner given above, can still constitute an independent system, with endless connotations of its own relating to 'every conceivable category of things in the universe that it was possible to classify in fives' (Ronan and Needham 1978:153). Of these some,

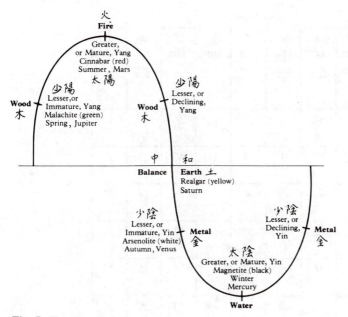

Fig. 7. The Yin–Yang cycle.

though by no means all, are essentially numerological, while others are seen as such simply by virtue of their being incorporated in the system.

The five elements were also related to each other in different recognised cyclic orders. Of these the Mutual Conquest Order – wood, metal, fire, water, earth – is particularly significant in the context of this chapter, since it was used in explaining the course of history (Ronan and Needham 1978:151). The logic of this order was that every element was capable of conquering its predecessor – water, for instance, conquers fire, because it can extinguish it. In any situation the order of the five elements is likely to be at least as important as the quantities present.

The *I Ching*, or *Book of Changes*, is more than two thousand years old: it probably originated from compilations of omens used by ancient Chinese peasants, but its distinctive form – based upon eight trigrams, and 64 hexagrams, as illustrated in figure 8 – led to its being regarded as a scientific treatise (Ronan and Needham 1978:183). The basis of the *I Ching* is to be found in the eight trigrams, since these can be combined in 64 different ways, to constitute the hexagrams, each of which in turn derives some of its attributes from the trigrams comprising it. The trigram is built up out of three lines, each of which may be either unbroken, or firm, or broken, and yielding: the former are Yang, and the latter, Yin lines (Blofeld 1968:49).

Table of Numbers

Upper Trigram → Lower Trigram ↓	1 qian	4 zhen	6 kan	7 gen	8 kun	5 sun	3 li	2 dui
1 qian	1	34	5	26	11	9	14	43
4 zhen	25	51	3	27	24	42	21	17
6 kan	6	40	29	4	7	59	64	47
7 gen	33	62	39	52	15	53	56	31
8 kun	12	16	8	23	2	20	35	45
5 sun	44	32	48	18	46	57	50	28
3 li	13	55	63	22	36	37	30	49
2 dui	10	54	60	41	19	61	38	58

Fig. 8. *I Ching* trigrams, hexagrams and associated numbers.

The same principle is extended to the hexagram simply because each hexagram comprises two trigrams. Each trigram, or hexagram, has a *guà* or name, which is a Chinese word summing up its attributes. In the case of the hexagrams, 45 out of the 64 *guà*, deal with some aspect of time or space, which may explain the readiness of Chinese scientists to incorporate the *I Ching* into their cosmology (Ronan and Needham 1978:184). In the present day the *I Ching* has reverted to its original use, as a book of omens, and as such it has also become popular in the West.

The *I Ching* is used to provide a cryptic commentary on the proposed course of action. The basic question (Blofeld 1968:60) is: 'If this or that is done, what will be the result?' Such an inquiry is put in an approved ritual context, and the answer is provided by the repeated use of 49 divining sticks: the same basic procedure must then be repeated six times, because each line of the hexagram is separately determined. The result will not only give the complete hexagram, but also indicate whether there are any 'moving' lines,

1	Name in *Rōmaji*	Naka -	mura	Take -	shi
2	*Kanji* equivalent of 1	中	村	武	子
3	Number frame	A	B	C	D
4	Number of strokes	4	7	8	3
5	*Yin-yang* of 4	yin	yang	yin	yang
6	Binary equivalent of 5	0	1	0	1
7	*On*-reading *Rōmaji*	chū	son	bu	shi
8	*Katakana* initials of 7	チ	ソ	ブ	シ
9	8 according to the 5 elements	fire	metal	water	metal
10	Quinary equivalent of 9	3	2	5	2

Ten signs under five heads	Total	Sign
First head (*tenchi*): A greater/less than B		−
Second head: literal meaning of name		+
Third head: totals from stroke count		
A + B (*ten-i*) inherited traits	11	+
B + C (*jin-i*) acquired traits	15	+
C + D (*shonen*) first years of life	11	+
A + B + C + D (*chi-i*) last years of life	22	− −
A + D (*fuku-on*) qualifies first four totals	7	+
Fourth head: *yin-yang*		+
Fifth head: (rank) two middle numbers		−
(destiny) all numbers		+

Fig. 9. *Seimeigaku* or Japanese 'full-name science'.

whose sign is then changed so as to provide a second hexagram. This is the essential 'change' which gives the book its name.[17] The book will then provide a general commentary, not only on the two hexagrams, but also on the moving lines. The art is then to relate the commentary to the specific question posed. In the Far East mastery of this art has provided a livelihood for any number of fortune-tellers.

The principles of Yin–Yang, the five elements and the *I Ching* are all applied in the Japanese 'full name science' or *seimeigaku*, which is concerned to determine the choice of proper names. The procedure is to be found in any number of popular paperbacks, sold in local super-markets. The distinctive form of the Japanese proper name provides the starting point. Every individual Japanese, almost without exception, has one family name followed by one given name, chosen by his parents. The common written form for both names – which provides the basis for applying *seimeigaku* – consists of two *kanji* (that is, characters of Chinese origin), so that the full name consists of four *kanji*, as in the example given in figure 9. The first two *kanji*, which form the common Japanese name of Nakamura, are fixed, since this is the name of the family. The last two *kanji* form one of the possible spellings of the popular boy's name, Takeshi.

The principles of *seimeigaku* govern the choice of this name. Their application requires the written form of the name to be analysed according to three different criteria. The first, given in line (4) of figure 9, is the number of strokes in each of the component *kanji*. The second, in line (5), is the Yin--Yang equivalent of line (4), on the basis that even numbers are *yin* and odd numbers, *yang*. The third criterion is more elaborate. It requires first that the general autochthonous form of the Japanese be rendered in the alternative Chinese form, which is given in line (7). (This conversion from the so-called '*kun*' to the '*on*' reading is an essential part of the process of learning *kanji* in the six years of primary school.) The *on*-reading resulting from the conversion is then represented by the appropriate characters from the traditional fifty sounds (*gojūon*) of the *kana* syllabary,[18] as shown in line (8). To each of these characters corresponds, according to a table included in every manual, one of the five elements: this is shown in line (9).

It will be noticed that to every proper name correspond three sets of numbers, given in lines (4), (6) and (10) of figure 9. The numbers in line (6) are binary, and in line (10), quinary, but in either case they are ordinal, not cardinal numbers – that is, they denote, but do not count. What is important is their cyclical order, so that the numerical representation in lines (6) and (10) is not only inessential, but also potentially misleading.[19]. The numbers in line (4) are a different case. These must be combined to produce the five totals, $A + B$, $B + C$, $C + D$, $A + B + C + D$ and $A + D$, which in the example given are, respectively, 11, 15, 11, 22 and 7.

The final result is that line (4) produces five different numbers, while line (5) and line (9) each produce a combination of numbers. The fortune and character inherent in the name are then determined under five different heads, and for any one of these the result can be either positive and auspicious, or negative and inauspicious – or in Japanese,'*yoshi*' or '*kyō*'. The first head, *tenchi*, meaning 'heaven and earth', depends simply on whether the number of strokes in the first character is greater or less than that in the second: according to figure 9 this asks simply whether A is greater than or less than B in line (4). The second head simply interprets the actual name according to the meaning of the characters comprising it. This in practice is often the starting point for the choice of a given name. In the example given in figure 9, Takeshi is a particularly auspicious boy's name, since the common reading of the first character means 'brave', while the second means child. The third head comprises the five totals, based on stroke-count combinations, given at the end of the previous paragraph. Their meaning is given in figure 9. The fourth head is Yin–Yang, and the fifth, the five elements.

Now as figure 9 illustrates, the first, second and fourth heads each have a positive or negative sign; the five combinations falling under the third head each have four possible signs, for certain numbers are defined as doubly positive or doubly negative. (This corresponds to the *turning points* of the sine wave in figure 7, used to relate Yin and Yang to the five elements in traditional Chinese science). The fifth head assesses rank according to the two middle characters (which in figure 9 form an inauspicious combination), but judges the name as a whole according to all the characters.

The complete assessment depends, therefore, on ten signs, positive or negative, each with different connotations. A change in the given name may change any of the signs, save the first. It would be difficult to choose a name which would score positively in every instance: the problem is to decide which are the more important, given the predilections of the family. This can be done simply by consulting any one of the popular manuals, but the forthcoming advice is bound to be equivocal, and thus a potential source of discord within the family home.[20] The answer is to consult a fortune-teller, or '*ekisha*',[21] who will in practice use the same rubric as that contained in the popular manuals.

Seimeigaku can also be used to determine whether a girl can be considered as a prospective wife for a son of the family. Indeed concern with the correct choice of name is perhaps greater with women than with men. One of the new Buddhist sects, Risshō Kōseikai, which has a particular appeal to married women, started by emphasising the need to have an auspicious name, in relation to the proper worship of the ancestors. New adherents were allowed to choose a new name, according to well-established principles of *seimeigaku*, as adopted by the sect. If this is now somewhat played down, Risshō Kōseikai still distributes its own manual (Kobayashi 1951) to new converts.

Finally, it is worth noting how similar, in spirit, the choosing of a name is to the observance of the agricultural cycle in Japan described in chapter 7. The numerical precision of the rules applied is in pronounced contrast with external factors which are both conflicting and uncertain. At the same time the numerological system, however elementary mathematically, is conceptually extremely complicated. This is essential, not only for allowing different interpretations of the results of applying the system, but also for revising, with the benefit of hindsight, advice already given, and acted upon with contradictory results. The *ekisha* are continually, and inevitably, wise after the event: if it were otherwise they would not stay in business. In any instance of *seimeigaku*, they can also correct previous advice by suggesting that the positive signs were interpreted too optimistically, while too little regard was paid to the negative signs.[22]

The numerical interpretation of the written language, which is the essence of *seimeigaku*, is also the basis of the Kabbala, a form of Jewish mysticism, which is concerned with 'the problem of re-uniting a perfect and unified creator with a fragmented and disharmonious creation' (Weiner 1969:101). But whereas *seimeigaku* applies numerical formulae to determine the fortunes of an individual, the Kabbala seeks to provide a means of relating a human community to the infinite. At the present time, the Hasidim, the best-known community embracing the Kabbala, are to be found in many different parts of the world as a distinctive ultra-orthodox Jewish sect. The concern of the Kabbala is with the Jewish law, or Torah, such as it was laid down by Moses in the first four books of the Pentateuch (Ginsburg 1955:84) – the fifth book, Deuteronomy, being left out for essentially numerical reasons. The principle is that the Torah has two meanings: the first is simply that obtained by reading the text; the second can only be obtained by treating the Torah as a code, which can be broken (Weiner 1969:116). The process of deciphering is essentially mathematical, and is based on a principle known as 'gematria', by which each Hebrew letter is assigned its numerical value. Furthermore, as I argue in chapter 9, in relation to Psalm 119, the principle is already apparent in the Old Testament.

The Kabbala has its own sacred text, known as the Sohar, which is supposed to have originated with Moses, to be communicated to the outside world by Rabbi Simon ben Jochai at the time of the destruction of the Temple in Jerusalem by the Romans in 70 A.D.[23] Because of certain implicit historical references,[24] the content of the Sohar suggests a much later date – so much so that many scholars regard it as a thirteenth-century pseudograph (Ginsburg 1955:175).

The basic problem of the Sohar is to provide a link between the infinite – or *En Soph* – and the finite world. The link takes the form of ten 'intelligences', or *Sephiroth*, each with its own characteristics. The role of the *Sephiroth* is essential, for the real world, being 'limited and not perfect[...]cannot directly proceed from the En Soph[...]which still[...]must exercise his influence over it, or his perfection would cease. Hence the Sephiroth, which, in their intimate connection with the En Soph, are perfect, and in their severance are imperfect, must be the medium' (Ginsburg 1955:177). Furthermore, 'all bodies have three dimensions, each of which repeats the other (3×3); and by adding thereunto space generally, we obtain the number ten. As the Sephiroth are the potencies of all that is limited, they must be ten' (ibid.: 178).

The three triads of the *Sephiroth* are respectively dominated by the Intellectual Word, the Sensuous World and the Material World. The first two elements of each triad, are respectively male and female, and combine to produce the third element – the whole succession originating with the union between wisdom and intelligence (Ginsburg 1955:91). This is the same binary principle as that of Yin and Yang in Chinese mysticism.

The number ten, which is also the basis of counting, is fundamental, as are the twenty-two letters of the Hebrew alphabet. Both the numbers and the letters can be classified in different sub-groups, so that the number of members in each has its own mystical significance. The letters in particular, although small in number, 'by their power of combination and transposition, yield an endless number of words and figures, and thus become the types of all the varied phenomena in the creation' (Ginsburg 1955:154).[25] The underlying principle of the Kabbala is that the combinations and permutations of letters occurring in the scriptures is determined not only by the demands of the text, as a written narrative, but also by scarcely perceptible numerical signs (Ginsburg 1955:181). These are supplemented by the use of any number of acronyms, anagrams and other word-plays, which fall outside the scope of gematria. Indeed 'the whole system of Kabbalistic imagery might be looked upon as a system of co-ordinates of the kind a mathematician would use for drawing a graph; it is simply one of the many symbolic ways of describing relationships. By working out these relationships, expressed through patterns of psychic movement, kabbalists believe they can come to a greater understanding of man and the world, the laws of physics, or the insights of psychology' (Weiner 1971:116).

The understanding of numbers implicit in the Kabbala is that numbers have two sorts of meanings. According to the first, they represent ideal constructs, combining with each other according to the rules of pure mathematics. The second meaning requires that numbers relate to concrete experience: they must count or order recognisable phenomena.[26] This characteristic neo-Platonic approach is also that of the Kabbala, in which the *Sephiroth* provides the means of relating the sorts of meanings to each other, for as Rabbi Steinsalz has said (Weiner 1971:108):

The goal of Jewish mysticism is the effort to come close to things, a yearning for identification[...]with the innermost aspect of everything – the divine. Mysticism, therefore, is the desire to remove the outer covering of things which hide their inner quality[...]It is possible to perceive two processes at work in mysticism. First an activity which is mainly speculative – that is, the intellectual effort to remove the shells of reality. Secondly, the activity by which, after removal of the outer coverings, one binds oneself to this truth. These two processes make up, respectively, the philosophy and practice of mysticism.

This statement is almost equally apt to apply to modern mathematical physics, where numbers also represent the ideal state. In the modern world, the West has somehow given up the idea of the mystical significance of numbers, but this is no more than a symptom of the popularly accepted divorce between religion and science, which is still far less pronounced in the Orient. In the Christian tradition, St Augustine was fully conscious of the mystical significance of numbers,[27] as were his successors in the Western Church, even up to the time of the Counter-Reformation, more than a thousand years later.[28] This brings us back to the point made at the beginning of this chapter, that the Western world sees the universe as a physical rather than a metaphysical construction: if then, mathematics, as one of the exact sciences, belongs to physics, it has no place in metaphysics, for as Needham notes, there is no synthesis between the two.

5

Economy, society and politics

Numerical models and structures

This chapter is concerned with numerical systems whose operation is constantly tested against the pragmatic demands of everyday life: indeed their whole rationale is to satisfy these demands. The starting point is the proposition that the economy, society and politics of any defined human population are dynamic systems – although they may be in equilibrium. The totality of any such system may be called its structure, which, conceptually, consists, not so much of all the bits and pieces which would be revealed by any attempt to dismantle it, but of the interactions which take place between them. The investigation of structure in this sense is part of any ethnography – that is the scientific process of establishing the empirical basis of any economic, social or political institution. Such investigation does not, however, answer the questions as to how and why the system works, or is seen to work by those involved in it, which is not necessarily the same thing at all. Answering this latter question is another part of any good ethnography: it is what establishes the cognitive basis of the institutions being studied. The answer to both questions takes the form of a model. In the one case it is 'the anthropologist's hypothesis about "how the[...]system works"' (Leach 1964:8), in the other, it is the local community's understanding of the same question. In the former case the model may be general, and in certain cases expressed in numerical terms[1] (which is after all the real point at issue in the present study), while in the latter case the model will be local and specific, and, at least in the general experience of cognitive anthropology,[2] not be capable of being expressed in such terms. The interesting question is whether such experience always accords with reality, and if not, what are the special features of the exceptional cases.

It is convenient to start with Gudeman's (1986:37) 'central assumption that humans are modellers[...]but a social model as opposed to models of the natural or physical world has a reflexive quality, for it is both derived from and applied to social activity[...]the term "local model"[...]describe(s) this circular and self-referential process. As a way of searching, coping, adjusting and making sense of things, local models represent an exercise in human control and a form of public communication. They are made by humans for specific communities[...][the] working hypothesis is that securing a livelihood, meaning the domain of material "production", "distribution" and "consumption", is culturally modeled in all societies.' The question asked at the end of the previous paragraph can be rephrased, so as to ask whether these 'cultural models' can ever be numerical, and if so, under what sort of conditions.

The difficulty – which may be more apparent than real – is that a numerical model requires a distinctive two-stage process, with the first stage being what in the context of a modern society would be called 'scientific', but in that of a traditional society viewed from outside, 'cognitive', with the second stage being essentially political. This somewhat involved point is made much clearer by Gudeman's (1986:48f.) discussion of Ricardo's 'An essay on the influence of a low price of corn on the profits of stock', which according to Robinson and Eatwell (1973:11) 'probably represents the first time a model was explicitly used in economics' – a conclusion which any anthropologist, let alone economic historian, must view with some scepticism.

Ricardo's model is essentially numerical (Gudeman 1986:52), and the process by which he reached it, scientific. His object in establishing it was political, that is to persuade the British parliament to repeal the tariffs on the import of corn – which would change not the model, but its parameters, in a direction which Ricardo thought desirable.[3] These factors are not only historically, but culturally determined. In particular the institutional context in which Ricardo worked has few, if any significant parallels in traditional societies. The economy with which he was concerned was 'disembedded', with material activities being organised in distinct institutions, in contrast to the general case of the traditional 'embedded' economy, in which 'the processes of livelihood are arranged through kinship, religious or political institutions[...]because it has no existence apart from these other relationships' (ibid.: 44).

But is there any reason why Ricardian insights, in a comparable numerical form, should not be a part of the cognitive domain of a traditional society, and then be accompanied by the same will to act, politically, upon any conclusions which follow from them? The whole lesson of chapter 4 would seem to argue the contrary, at least if there the political aspect were not so marginal. The question can best be answered by means of concrete examples, which are given below (pp. 63ff.). First, however, one must look, from the perspective of 'structure', more closely at the distinction between society and culture, which are essentially two different logical types (Russell 1920:135f.).

Starting with Bateson's (1958:25) definition of 'cultural structure as a collective term for the coherent "logical"scheme *which may be constructed by the scientist*, fitting together the various premises of the culture', with a premise defined as 'a generalised statement of a particular assumption or implication recognisable in a number of details of cultural behaviour', one notes first that if the words in italics are omitted, the definition is entirely acceptable from the perspective of the cognitive domain of the local culture. Then, the fact that the elements of the structure are 'assumptions' and 'implications' means that it is not directly tied to the 'ecological' factors implicit in the definition of economic, social and political structure given at the beginning of this chapter. One is left with a disembodied structure, in which there is much greater freedom to incorporate any desired interactions. The different numerical systems considered in chapter 4 are of this kind.

The fact that the premises of a culture 'in many cases may only be stated in symbolic terms' (Bateson 1958:25) leaves the way open to state them in terms of numerical relationships. That this is so is made clear by any number of specific instances of music, poetry and dance, or art and architecture. To take the example of the temple of Sanjusangendo, described in chapter 11, nothing in the structure of the Japanese economy, society or politics prevented the construction of a temple with 32 or 34 bays, in place of 33: it is only that such a building could not possibly have had the same meaning.

In the case of a purely cultural structure, the two stage process required by the Ricardian model, is turned on its head. Tradition establishes, at one and the same time, not only the meaning of the model, but also what it is supposed to achieve. The model is expressive rather than instrumental; one cannot say that Sanjusangendo as such incorporates any policy (although its construction, in the year 1164, by the Emperor Goshirakawa, did represent an attempt to bring about peace by spreading Buddhism throughout Japan). The constricting historical parameters of the Ricardian model are therefore eliminated – at least so long as the cultural model does not need to be brought down to earth.[4] The question then is, is this ever necessary for the model to be effective in its own terms?

The point is that 'with every kind of technical action, there is always the element which is functionally essential, and another element which is simply the local custom, an aesthetic frill[...]it is precisely these customary frills[5] which provide the social anthropologist with his primary data. Logically, aesthetics and ethics are identical[6][...]In origin the details of custom may be an historical accident; but for the living individuals in a society such details can never be irrelevant, they are part of the total system of interpersonal communication within the group. They are symbolic actions, representations' (Leach 1964:12).

The necessity then is to establish the parallel between cultural structure, which is concerned with the interaction of details of behaviour, and social structure, which is concerned with the interaction of individuals, linked together into different groups. If as Bateson suggests (1958:26), it is true that 'in the two disciplines, we shall to a great extent be studying the same phenomena, but looking at them from two different points of view', the problem is largely solved.

The following two sections, which are based on a number of specific cases, consider this problem under two heads, one relating to models based on cardinal numbers, and the other on models based on ordinal numbers. This division is a natural one, since the specific problems arising under the two heads will prove to be quite different.

Distribution and the use of cardinal numbers

The use of cardinal numbers is inherent in any economic system in which undifferentiated inputs or outputs are allocated to participants, whether these be individuals, or some form of group. Such allocation may be related to money (which by definition is undifferentiated),[7] either as a unit of account, or even as the actual means by which it is effected, but this is a special case. In the general case, such allocation can take two forms: the first is based on division into equal parts,[8] the second, on the transfer of fixed quantities.[9] The difference between the two forms is that the first may require only the number of participants to be counted, whereas the second requires counting for each separate allocation[10] – and counting is pre-eminently a process relating to cardinal numbers.

Although the model basis of the different cases to be considered in this section is essentially economic, the structure maintained by the process of distribution is also, in almost every case, social and political: such integration is indeed characteristic of traditional societies. In the Inca empire at the time of the Spanish conquest, numerical information of interest to the state, recorded on *quipu*s by a special hierarchy of bookkeepers known as '*quipu camayoc*', provided the basis of social, political and economic integration. The information recorded included the number of citizens liable to *corvée* in any given area, the number of llamas grazing on each state pasture, the quantities of maize, wool and cloth in a given warehouse, and anything else likely to interest the policy-makers (Murra 1980:110). As the area of responsibility grew, the *quipu camayoc* became in increasing measure full time specialists, who had passed through a long and laborious apprenticeship during the third and fourth years of study in an elite school for royalty and the bureaucracy. In this process, 'the neophyte had to learn not only the system of color, strings and knots in use in his branch of the service, but had to familiarize himself with past records. The kind of skill and feats of "memory" mentioned by the early Europeans came only from long practice and full time dedication to the task at hand' (ibid.: 159f.). Since the only information now available is provided by a relatively small number of *quipu*s recovered from cemeteries in remote corners of the Inca empire, together with such matters as the contemporary Spanish chroniclers thought worth recording, it is impossible to tell to what extent, and in what way, *quipus* provided the means of controlling and directing the Inca political economy. The significant point, in any case, is that such means were purely numerical – no-one has ever suggested that the *quipus* had the potential of developing into a means of recording and transmitting the spoken word, and for this purpose the Incas had no alternative system.

On the other side of the world, the Hindu caste system is another prime example of an integrated social and economic structure, which contains in the institution of *jajmani* – effectively the economic dimension of caste (Beidelman 1959:6) – one of the best-known and most comprehensive models.

For present purposes the essence of caste is the division of the local community into a number of discrete, endogamous groups, with a specific and recognised hierarchical order. Although the difference between the groups is generally conceived of in ritual terms, closely related to the permissible forms of contact if pollution is to be avoided, the *jajmani* system is concerned with the allocation of goods and services between the different castes. The basis of the system is the specialist occupations of the numerous different castes: in general, the lower castes render services, in return for agricultural produce distributed by the higher castes, who will tend to monopolise the ownership of land. More specifically, *jajmani* is 'a system of prescribed hereditary obligations of payment' – generally in kind – 'and of occupational and ceremonial duties between two or more specific families of different castes in the same locality' (Beidelman 1959:6).[11]

This conception of the system is based on a division of the local community into two power groups, the *jajmans*, who are dominant, and the so-called '*kamins*', who are subordinate. In general every *jajman* is related to individual *kamins* from a number of different castes, according to the traditional services required at any time: in the same way a *kamin* will provide the traditional services of his caste for any number of different *jajmans*, and even *kamins* from other castes.

It is difficult to establish any general rule about the way payments are to be made under the *jajmani* system. Since almost every village in India is organised on the basis of the caste it is not surprising that there are endless variants in the system of *jajmani* allocation. The basis must, however, still be that reported for the District of Gonda in Uttar Pradesh some hundred years ago (Bennett 1878). Then the village servants received some fixed payments and some proportional payments from the common village grain-heap after harvest, a system assuring a basic minimum of subsistence in poor years, and a share in the general prosperity in good years. This applies to both forms of allocation stated in the first paragraph of this section.

In the terms introduced in the first section to this chapter, *jajmani* is a social structure imposed, separately, upon every village community in India, each with its own specific variant of the general model base. The Gonda prototype allowed everyone in the village a claim on its produce, but with no room for bargaining over payments, nor any payments for specific services. It took no account of the possibility that certain castes might be over-represented: in short all economic and demographic factors were left out of the reckoning – not surprising seeing that *jajmani* is, in principle, a religious institution.[12] From a cognitive perspective, therefore, *jajmani* must be seen as a cultural rather than a social structure. The question then is, how has it been able to adapt to the social and economic reality of the Indian village?

The answer is only relevant to the numerical basis of *jajmani* in so far as it shows what sort of expedients can be adopted so as to preserve its integrity. First, *jajmani* need not embrace all the castes actually present in the village; second, the occupations of under-represented castes may be taken over by others which are over-represented; third, some distributive arrangements, such as sharecropping tenancies, are outside the system; fourth, the principle of allocation may in practice be modified to take economic factors, whether on the input or output side, into account. In the result an economic system whose form is, in principle, entirely general, survives by continually adjusting itself to external factors.

The analysis of the present section, while remaining within the Indian caste system, now shifts from the general case of *jajmani*, to the idiosyncratic case of the Benares funeral priests, which has a quite different model basis. The funeral priests, known as '*mahabrahman*', over a period of some eleven days following the death of any one of the thousands of pious Hindu's who come to die in Benares, handle 'all the rituals up to the point where the marginal soul is converted into an ancestor, and [...] accept the prestations associated with this function' (Parry 1980:91). This particular instance of *jajmani* exemplifies also its original religious function. The traditional gift, or 'sajja dan', consisting of a year's supply of grain, household goods and a lump sum in cash, is conceived of as offerings to be received by the deceased in the next world (ibid.: 96). In practice it is commuted to the largest possible lump sum in cash which the *mahabrahman* can extract from the mourners, who represent the *jajman*.

The cremation *ghat*, where the *mahabrahman* receive the corpses, is divided into two parts, one for city families, and the other for families from outside. The rights to officiate, known as *pari* for the city, and *pachchh* for the countryside, are each allocated by tradition and inheritance, on a time basis. The charter rights were based on the principle of five *mahabrahman*, operating a five-day cycle for *pari*, and a five-fortnight cycle for *pachchh*. These are the putative ancestors of all the present *mahabrahman*, who, by reason of partible inheritance in the male line operating over several generations,[13] must each be content with no more than an aliquot share of the original *pari* or *pachchh*. As a result of successive binary division, the *pari* of an individual *mahabrahman* recur at 40-, 80-, and 160-day intervals, while the *pachchh* recur at the rate of one day in $2\frac{1}{2}$, 5, 10 months, and so on – with the possibility of holding different sets of rights by virtue of lines of succession combining, or sales and mortgages between the *mahabrahman* (Parry 1980:98). The same principle applies to the *karinda* servants whose help, together with that of the barbers, is indispensable to the *mahabrahman* actually officiating (ibid.: 100).

The remuneration of the *mahabrahman* in Benares hardly relates at all to any *jajmani* prototype. The chances of an individual *mahabrahman* depend entirely on the amount of money which can be extracted from the generally impoverished *jajman* falling within his *pari* or *pachchh*. Although occasional windfalls occur with the death of a rich man, the *mahabrahman* can maintain his family at only a modest level, particularly after taking into account the cut taken by the *karinda*s and the barbers (Parry 1980:101). Indeed many pursue other occupations on the side (ibid.: 102), which commonly occurs with the operation of the ordinary village *jajmani*. It is to be noted that the numerical base is the consistent element in both variants.

The two examples given of the working of the *jajmani* system illustrate the practical difficulties in the way of organising an economic institution on the basis of a prescriptive model defined in terms of fixed quantities or proportions. The success of such models must depend either upon their operating in an extremely stable society, or upon their application being marginal, or at least intermittent, in the general economy. These conditions have been satisfied, historically, by a wide range of African societies in which a fixed quantity of cattle are transferred on the occasion of a marriage, or as compensation for homicide. The payment of bridewealth[14] requires the transfer of a fixed number of cattle from the lineage of the bridegroom to that of the bride, often with a prescribed allocation among the bridegroom's kin of the contributions required, and among the bride's kin of each individual's entitlement.[15]

Since the amount of bridewealth is generally far beyond the normal resources in cattle of any individual herder, the institution is bound to involve wide categories of individuals, whether they are defined in terms of kinship, or pure credit. In this sense the obligation to make the payment serves to create, maintain and reinforce social relationships, but equally the actual payment may put the recipient in the position to dissolve such relationships. The system is in any case dynamic, and requires liquidity in cattle to be maintained at a higher level than would otherwise be necessary. To some extent this can be achieved by simply increasing the rate of circulation among successive owners, in which case the aggregate size of the herds need not be affected, the same being true, a fortiori, for their productivity, whether in milk or meat. On the other hand the demands of liquidity may be met by increasing the size of the herds to a level which, judged economically, is counter-productive – with overgrazing leading to poor quality stock, if not exhaustion of the land. One could start, in a case such as that of the Nuer of the Southern Sudan, (Evans-Pritchard 1940:217f.), for whom a fixed number of cattle is prescribed both for bridewealth and many cases of blood money for death, with a sort of Ricardian model in which the aggregate productivity of the cattle was related to the amount of this number, but in fact there seems to be no mystery about the actual number prescribed: in principle the only requirement seems to be that it remains constant.[16] It remains true, however, that the prescribed number is far from optimal according to any economic model. It only remains to ask whether it has any cultural significance,[17] but nothing in the literature relating to African pastoralists suggests that this might be so.[18]

This want of cultural significance, somewhat surprisingly, would seem to be true also of the numerical basis, not only of the *jajmani* system – in any of its applications – but to the whole generality of numerical institutions relating to ordering an economic system, and by extension the society and polity in which it operates.[19] Chapter 8 will also confirm this conclusion in relation to money. Only lack of space has prevented the discussion of the many other cases which would support it: judged cognitively, the role of cardinal numbers in mediating social relations, where it occurs, is somehow subordinate, indeed prosaic, however rich the cultural context. The quite different role of ordinal numbers is the theme of the next section.

Ranking and the use of ordinal numbers

Ordinal numbers are essentially adjectives whose effect is to rank the substantives to which they apply: the process often creates a proper noun, or name, sometimes in a form in which the numerical component is no longer explicit. Ordinal numbers have, therefore, no meaning or function outside a specific context: one cannot simply talk about 'the fourteenth', without at least meaning 'the fourteenth something', so that, for instance, a statement such as 'I am coming back on the fourteenth' implicitly refers to the fourteenth day of a month – the actual month being implicit in the context. In mathematical terms, the series of ordinal numbers, is always of the form $f(1)$, $f(2)$, $f(3)$ ... $f(n)$, so that the general form is $f(k)$, with k being an integer, and 'f' a function defined by the context. The variable 'k' can itself define no numerical relationships (such as are fundamental in the use of cardinal numbers – as the previous section illustrates). It would be absurd – even for the Chinese who number the months of the year – to suggest that 'March squared plus April squared equals May squared', on the basis of the fact that $3^2 + 4^2 = 5^2$.[20] Indeed the general algebraic form of the Pythagorean equation[21] cannot possibly be related to any of the properties of ordinal numbers. Finally, the general 'ordinal' function, 'f', given above, is monotone, in the sense that some recognised non-reflexive transitive relationship holds between successive values. If this relationship is expressed by the mathematical sign ' > ', then, all that is being said is that if j > k, then f(j) > f(k). It is this property which establishes the 'ranking' function of ordinal numbers, according to any given criterion, such as, for instance, age. This is what gives a meaning to a sentence like 'my son is the third oldest boy in the class'. On the other hand, ordinal numbers, in everyday use, often constitute a finite closed set, like the months of the year, or the days of the week, which then repeats itself endlessly. A statement such as 'March comes before April' is, according to the monotone property, no different from 'January comes before December', but intuitively one is inclined to accept the truth of the former statement much more readily than that of the latter. It is no answer to this dilemma to say that ranking is not of the essence of cyclical systems: indeed, as the Japanese game of Janken, discussed in chapter 10, shows, such a system, without ranking, can be completely meaningless. What this dilemma does indicate is that the explicit linguistic use of the cardinal numbers, to derive the ordinal numbers, can be, in the cyclical case, extremely confusing. On the other hand, the cyclical case, in the context of the present chapter, is relatively unimportant.[22] A single illustration, taken from Bali, will suggest why this is so.

One of the names given to any Balinese child, even a stillborn one, is taken from an ordered cyclical set of four elements. As explained by Geertz (1973:370f.), 'the most common system is to use Wayan for the first child, Njoman for the second, Made[...]for the third, and Ktut for the fourth, beginning the cycle over again with Wayan for the fifth, Njoman for the sixth, and so on'. These names are used for addressing and referring to children, and young people without offspring, coupled, where necessary for avoiding ambiguity, with the family name. They 'have no literal meaning in themselves (they are not numerals or derivatives of numerals)' nor do they 'indicate sibling position or rank in any realistic or reliable way'. Their role is cultural, rather than strictly social, for they convey a message of 'an endless four-stage replication of an imperishable form. Physically men come and go as the ephemerae they are, but socially the dramatis personae remain eternally the same'. This is hardly a model for any form of social organisation, nor could it become such by means of any sort of transformation. The reason, it seems, must be that any such organisation – even at the elementary level of age-sets[23] – if it is based on ordinal numbers, must be strictly hierarchical. Although at first sight the Balinese name system would seem to have this potential, in practice it can never be realised. This does not matter either, since Balinese society is not based on any principle of primogeniture.

Japan provides a good example of the organisation of hierarchy on the basis of ordinal numbers. Taking the principle of seniority, in the literal sense of the word, as starting point, this means no more than that age, in the absence of other overreaching criteria, determines hierarchy: this rule applies for instance in Japan, and is based on the antithesis of *semmai/kōhai*, whose actual meaning is simply senior/junior. The moral basis of the precedence of the elder over younger (*chō-yō-no-jō*) originated in China, and is reflected in the first instance in the precedence of siblings of the same sex, which is an important structural principle within the family.[24] It now extends to establish precedence in any number of different groups, which would otherwise be homogeneous, on the basis of age, years of service or date of graduation (Nakane 1973:28). Where such a group must act on the basis of consensus, it is supplemented by a 'bottom to top form of leadership called the *ringi* system' (Reischauer 1977:188) which allows the most junior member of the group to have the first word (Smith 1983:54).

The principle of order becomes much more explicit in institutional contexts in the field of religion, education and sport. A large notice-board at the local temple will list the donations made to it, the amounts given being calculated according to the '*kotōhyō*, the acknowledged social and economic ranking of all the households in a village community' (Nakane 1973:95). In education and sport, examinations and competitions are focussed upon establishing class (*kyū*) and rank (*dan*), each having its own explicit numerical order, whose precise form is determined by rules specific to each separate activity, which may be flower-arrangement (*ikebana*), calligraphy, *go, sumō*-wrestling, or whatever.[25] The general principle is that one proceeds through the successive *kyū* simply by increasing one's own proficiency, measured according to fixed numerical standards. The *dan*-ranking,[26] on the other hand is competitive and cumulative, so that a high ranking depends not only on having won against other high-ranking players, but also on having maintained one's position over a period of time sufficiently long to enable the requisite number of points to be accumulated. This principle, a sort of compromise with the principle of strict seniority, often means that the current top players do not have the highest *dan*.

The classic example of ranking based upon examination and competitive success is the traditional Chinese bureaucracy based on the 'idealised administrative system elaborated by Han scholars and handed down to us as the Chou Li' (Needham 1956:337), based upon nine ranks of officials (*jiǔ pǐn*) and six departments of state (*liù bù*), the latter related to the 'tremendous filing system of the *I Ching*' (ibid.: 338), discussed in chapter 4. In their final form, which in the Ching period determined the content of education throughout China, the examinations involved three main stages. Candidates successful in the first stage, the district and prefectural examinations, were exempt from labour service and corporal punishment. Then at provincial level, second stage examinations qualified the successful candidates for the third stage, comprising the metropolitan examination for the *jin shì* degree,

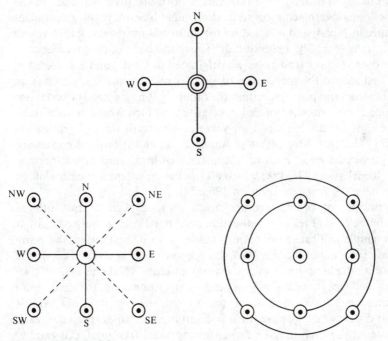

Fig. 10. The *mandala*.

whose results were confirmed by an examination in the Imperial Palace. Second and third stage examinations were triennial, and effectively recruited some hundred new officials every year, of which something under a half would come from families with no official connections (McMullen 1982:131). Finally, it is perhaps significant that the hydraulic conservation works, which were the basis of bureaucratic power because of their control of the life-blood of the economy, have a typical step-structure corresponding to the Japanese cases discussed in the previous paragraph.

An even more perfect model of government is provided by the '*mandala*', which is a model of what Tambiah (1976:102) calls 'the galactic polity' established in many parts of south-east Asia. The *mandala* (as figure 10 illustrates) is in the first place an ideal geometric or topographical construction comprising a core (*manda*) and a container (*-la*). The core is unitary whereas the number of units comprising the container, which is subordinate to it, is always a power of 2. A compass-card, with the pivot as the core, and the cardinal points comprising the container, is an elementary example, which can be extended by including the lesser cardinal points, to any degree. A more complex model, has a succession of containers, like a set of Russian dolls, the number of units in each being increasingly higher powers of two.[27] This may be termed the 'complex' as opposed to the 'simple' *mandala*. In a number of different representations, it is the basic model of the temples of Angkor Wat and Borobudur, but the present context is concerned with its political applications. Indeed, 'the kingdom was a miniature representation of the cosmos, with the palace at the centre being iconic with Mount Meru, the pillar of the universe, and the king, his princes, and ruling chiefs representing the hierarchy in Tavatsima heaven' (ibid.: 109).

The 'best expression of this model is the 32 *myos*[28] of the medieval Mon kingdom and the subsequent '37 *nats* of the Burmese pantheon[29] [...] the 32-*myo* pattern, or its variants, was a blueprint, which was sought to be implemented, in the belief that it intimately affected the well-being of king, polity and people. This is the formal aspect of the system, and its archetype supposes a king ruling over a circle of subordinate princes' (Tambiah 1976:108, 111).

The traditional polity, which saw the state 'as a *mandala* composed of concentric circles, usually three in number', is a clear representation of the devolution of power from the centre, with the capital being also laid out as a *mandala*, with 'the palace at the centre surrounded by three circles of earthen ramparts, with four gateways at the cardinal points' (Tambiah 1976:112).[30] Numerically the structure consists of hierarchical ordering of cyclical sets, of which that consisting of the four cardinal points can be taken as the basic prototype. The *mandala* was acceptable as a model basis, since the actual definition of its components, as also of the boundaries between them, in terms of local ecological and political factors, was extremely flexible:[31] the best parallel in the western tradition is probably to be found in the Byzantine empire, which over a period of more than a thousand years was also to adapt an apparently rigid structure to the demands of *realpolitik*.

In conclusion, it is worth noting that the *mandala*, seen numerically, incorporates aspects of both cardinal and ordinal numbers. The former are essential for counting the number of components according to its arithmetical form as a polynomial to the base '2'. The successive terms of the polynomial, with co-ordinates which can only be 0 or 1, determines its structure as a hierarchy, on the basis of ordinal numbers expressed in binary form, so that, for instance, the 37 of the 37 *nats* becomes 100101. Finally it should be emphasised, once again, that this chapter only deals with the *mandala* as the model of a political system, and even then the treatment is too summary to be entirely adequate.[32] The extremely elementary, abstract nature of the model base, which can be encoded as a single binary number in any actual application, gives it an astonishingly wide range of application, so that it must constantly recur in any structural study relating to the many parts of the world to which it applies.

71

6

Measurement, comparison and equivalence

Function and cognition

Wherever the command of numbers has developed beyond the simple level attained by the Plateau Tonga of southern Africa or the Aranda of central Australia, it is tempting to assume that the incentive for such development is the need to use numbers for the purpose of measuring quantity. This essentially intuitive assumption is misleading. An author such as Stevens (1958:383) who contends that 'early mathematicians did not readily discern the difference between measurement and mathematics' and that 'man was usually more interested in empirical measurement than in mathematics' can only base such an argument on certain special historical cases, such as that of Egypt in the time of the Pharaohs. Generally, the process of constructing a measurable continuum is only mastered at an advanced stage of cognitive development.

Measurement of quantity is an operational use of number, whose function must be defined largely in economic terms. Not every economy needs this function, because the need for it is determined by the existence of other socioeconomic institutions. In relation to measuring quantities of food, Richards (1939:206), in her study of the Bemba of Zambia, states the point very clearly: 'the incentive to measure food supplies depends largely on whether it is intended that they should be exchanged, or used as a means of assessing wealth, status or some other attribute valued in the particular society'. The fact that such operations played no part in the daily life of the Bemba, in contrast to that of many other Bantu populations in the same part of Africa, does not necessarily explain why they never had any but an extremely rudimentary numerical system. The institution of measurement must have 'utility' before one may expect to find it in any given culture, so that Davis and Hersh (1983:84) are justified in their contention that 'computations which refer to counting, measuring and pricing constitute the bulk of all mathematical operations at the level of common utility'.[1] This allows neither such utility, nor the use of numbers which it may require, to be taken for granted. In truth, 'the mere existence of a verbal number system

72

is no warrant in itself for inferring that the adult members of that culture have an operational grasp of number[...][for] ideas of number and measurement[...]depend for their development on the kinds of problems that have to be solved and the means available for their solution' (Hallpike 1979:278–9). The point is that systematic measurement defines just one class of problems, which can, however, only be solved with the help of a sufficiently advanced numerical system.

The question is much more profound than appears at first sight. It is easy to be trapped into the sort of cultural determinism characteristic of, say, Malinowski, and so forcefully criticised by Sahlins (1976:81).[2] No consideration of the functions of measurement is possible without some understanding of its cognitive basis. This basis must be defined in terms of two concepts, number and measure. Measurement, by its own definition, is the application, generally for purposes of 'common utility' of number to measure. The cognitive basis of number has been explored in chapters 2 and 3, but what about measure?

Measure is best defined as the conceptual means by which two different entities can be compared in numerical terms. Once established, this means provides a unit in terms of which a numerical coefficient can be assigned to every member of the class to which the measure is applicable. This implies that some abstract property is recognised as being common to all members of the class.

The above definition is best illustrated by an example. The ounce, as a measure, is applicable to all entities which have the property of weight, and provides the basis for placing any particular instances on a scale marked out in successive units. (In terms of length, a ruler is an example of such a scale.) This exercise is futile, at least in practical terms, unless there is some reason why these instances should be compared in terms of the measure being used. Shoes, and ships, and sealing-wax can all be weighed, but unless their weight is significant, the matter is of no interest. Nor does the recognition of weight, as a property of concrete objects, require that it be measured on a scale. In the first instance, such a property tends to be used as the basis of metaphor. The expression 'as light as a feather' does not imply, either logically or intuitively, the use of any sort of weighing-machine. The conservation of weight is intuitively difficult to grasp, as one sees from the familiar conundrum, 'Which is heavier, a pound of feathers or a pound of lead?' Even so, the conceptualisation of properties such as weight is not a part of every culture. To give one example, the Kpelle of Liberia, do not think of length, weight or size as independent realities (Gay and Cole 1967:60).

It follows that the concept of a 'measure' requires in turn some concept of dimension, in the sense that a given measure applies to a class of objects having the same dimension, so that an ounce, for instance, applies only to objects sharing the dimension of weight. The recognition of dimension is by no means sufficient to define a unit of measure applicable to it. If experience, in almost any culture, teaches that objects may be hot or cold, it provides no clue as to how to measure temperature (a technological problem which was only solved in the modern age). Indeed the idea of scale implies that the measure of something, in any dimension, must be transformed into some form of visual representation, in order to be 'read'. In the case of temperature, therefore, physicists had first to establish a 'linear' relationship between temperature and the expansion of metals for any such representation to be possible. This provides the reason why the measurement of temperature is not an accomplishment of any traditional culture.

A study of traditional systems of measurement, in terms of the dimensions recognised by modern physics, reveals, first, a proliferation of different units, within a single dimension,[3] and second, considerable confusion about the relationship between different dimensions. As to the first point, the choice of the appropriate unit will depend not only upon the category, recognised in the local culture, to which the quantity to be measured belongs, but also upon the purposes for which measurement is required.

This point can be illustrated by the different corn measures used by the highland Indian populations of the state of Chiapas in southern Mexico. To take one particular case, that of the Chamula, there are 4 cuartillos in a kilogram, 4 kilograms make a cuarto, 4 cuartos a litro, 12 litros a fanega, and 10 fanegas a tonelada. The cuartillo is the usual measure for retail sales within the Indian community, while the kilogram is used in dealing with outsiders, generally Spanish-speaking Ladinos. The cuarto, and even more the litro, measure the grain used for sowing, the fanega measures the harvest, and the tonelada is used in bulk sales to government stores (Crump 1978:515). This is merely the Chamula variant of a system common to the whole highland area, if not the whole of Mexico. The immediate neighbours of the Chamula, in Zinacantan, use a different measure, the almud, in place of the cuarto and litro (Cancian 1965:65).[4]

The above information tells us a surprising amount, not only about the cognitive basis of the Chamula economy, but also about the functions of the different units used for measuring corn. The different operations relating to the economics of corn, whether agricultural or commercial, each have their appropriate unit. The arithmetical relationship between successive units on the scale is unimportant: the Chamula farmer will simply think in terms of the unit appropriate to the operation being carried out. It does not matter that some of the units measure weight, and others volume, because he knows, implicitly, that there is a fixed relation between the two – that is, in physical terms, he is dealing with matter whose density is more or less constant. This is the factor that renders the whole system inappropriate for anything but corn. At the same time the Chamula farmer will not be conscious of any abstract relationship between volume and length in terms of the physical dimensions, although he will almost certainly relate the yield of the harvest, measured in fanegas, to the area under cultivation.[5] This in turn can be related to time, in terms of the labour input, just as the English acre was originally defined as the area which could be ploughed in a single day. Other contexts relate the units to money, so that the tonelada relates to wholesale, and the cuartillo to retail sales. At this level time and money have the clearest identity as separate dimensions, which is one reason why they have their own chapters (7 and 8) in this book.

The specific numerical relationship between different units within the same 'dimension' – although it may be known to those who use them[6] – is much less important (Hallpike 1979:254) than maintaining a constant relationship between quantities in different dimensions. The basic cognitive principle is that no variation is allowed for in the yield of a given field, or the price which it will realise in the market. This explains the conservatism, often observed among traditional cultivators, in the face of new agricultural technology – however much it may increase the productivity of land or labour – as much as the problems they have in dealing with inflation (Crump 1986a:99). Time, however, tends to be left out of these equations, probably because it is based on ordinal, rather than cardinal numbers, and the latter provide the basis of measurement.[7] This means that velocity can only be conceived of as a separate dimension (Piaget 1972:78) in which it is generally observed in purely relative terms – so that everyone knows that the hare moves faster than the tortoise, without necessarily being conscious of the mathematical paradox which this fact gives rise to.

The confusion about categories, described above, makes it extremely difficult to apply any general abstract principle, or to conceive of numbers other than the series of integers. The first difficulty is well illustrated by the Pythagorean triangle, with sides in the ratio 3:4:5. One need not know any proof of the well-known theorem of Pythagoras, nor even that there is such a theorem, and that it can be proved, to realise that this is a right-angled triangle. The difficulty lies in conceiving of it as a general case, applicable on any scale, small or large. The realisation that this is so represents a major advance in scientific understanding. This does not prevent the use, in special cases, of some elementary surveying instrument – consisting, say, of a string loop, with twelve (3+4+5) evenly spaced knots – based on Pythagoras' theorem. The fact is that the use of units of measure, in all their multiplicity, must have been a major factor in inhibiting the development of abstract mathematical thinking. The remarkable achievements of Chinese science followed the adoption of the principle that the units used in any dimension – other than time – being based on successive powers of ten, were but special instances of the general system of counting. In the cognitive domain, the realisation of this principle led to great clarity of thought.

The second difficulty mentioned in the previous paragraph arises in connection with fractions and irrational numbers. The use of a multiplicity of different units makes it possible to reduce not only the need for large numbers, by using larger units of measure, but also that for fractions, by using smaller units. Fractions, in particular, are cognitively difficult for anyone using a language which has no means of expressing them. It is possible to realise that there are 16 ounces in a pound, without having the concept of 'a sixteenth'. Indeed, the more diverse the numerical relationship between successive units on a scale, the less is the practical need for fractions. Taking the case of the Chamula, the only word in their own language, Tzotzil, expressing a fraction, is '*Polol*', meaning 'a half', and this is not subject to the special rules of syntax governing the use of ordinary integers (Crump 1978:506). Irrationals are even more difficult. The fact that the hypoteneuse of a right-angled isosceles triangle has 'length' which can not be measured as an integral multiple of the units measuring the two other sides is well outside the cognitive domain of many traditional cultures. It is better to use a rule of thumb, where necessary, than to try any general approach to this intractable problem.

There is here a quantum leap in thought from a cognitive domain in which the idea of dimension implies measurability in terms of an integral number of constant units, which can always be given concrete expression, to one in which dimension is a general, abstract property, whose true character is determined, not by any considerations of utility, but by the physical nature of the universe. The only exception is money, a cultural, not a natural phenomenon, which but for utility, in one form or another, would not exist. It is not surprising, therefore, that traditional numeracy is often closely tied to the use of money.

Standardization and compatibility

It is a lesson from the previous section, that in any context in which a system of measurement is applied, internal consistency is much more important than compatibility with systems used in other contexts, however these may be defined. It does not matter that these other contexts may be defined in terms of precisely the same physical dimensions. Whatever the context, measurement must have a 'standard' in terms of which its results can be stated. The standard is the link between the numerical coefficient and the substance being measured. In the many languages, such as Japanese, which require a special 'counter', linking a numeral to the noun it qualifies, standard units of measure belong to this class.

All this suggests that the process of measurement must be conceived of as one of iteration, that is of repeating the same unit steps, until one has covered the interval to be measured (Hallpike 1979:238). As Hallowell (1942:66) has pointed out, 'naively, distance is measured in terms of activity' so that 'processual units of various kinds as measures of distance are extremely common'. The elementary measure is then simply the number of steps taken, ascertained by counting, in which case the practical problem is simply to define the unit step. This is all very well if one paces out the length of a field, but longer distances, such as are involved in travel, can often only be measured in terms of the time taken – and even then the measurement of time is not always easy. Before the invention of modern surveying techniques, such as triangulation, measuring instruments were however too elementary for measuring distances beyond the field of view.

There is none the less a cognitive distinction between 'counting' and 'measuring', and the relation between the two requires further examination. The real essence of measurement is comparison rather than counting. 'What measurement implies is simply this: For quantities of magnitude based upon naive discrimination it substitutes the operation of matching as a determinative technique' (Hallowell 1942:63). The Kedang of Indonesia have a word '*ka*' which 'means the coinciding of an object with a point in or on a countable sequence, and it is used both for measuring spatial length and also for durations' (Barnes 1974:20). The problem is then to establish the countable sequence in terms of a basic step, or unit, and if necessary to devise some instrument which can be used in applying it.

An example of the way this problem is solved is also provided by the Kedang, who require a standard for 'determining quantitatively bridewealth responsibilities, for setting the worth of objects, and for relating the relative value of objects of different kinds' (Barnes 1982:7). In this case the context is one of social exchange, so – according to the norms of western monetary theorists – the standard will essentially serve to measure 'value' according to the Kedang understanding of this quality. But it is doubtful whether the Kedang have ever approached the problem in this way: after all they can hardly have been expected to have read Adam Smith, let alone Keynes. It is sufficient that their standard, known as '*munaq*', is seen to inhere in all the things to which they need to apply it: in cognitive terms it defines its own category. It does not matter that by derivation the term is really only appropriate for measuring elephant tusks, which are in turn measured according to different measures occurring in the human body (ibid.: 9). Needless to say, the 'Kedang have no department of weights and measures which stores a standard munaq in polished ivory. They establish and maintain the position of the munaq as a measure only through constant use. The munaq does not permit further gradations[...]A tusk is arbitrarily assumed to be precisely divisible by this unit, and any remainder is implicitly rounded off' (ibid.: 12–13). When it comes to value, this is stated in terms of tins of rice, but these are essentially extrinsic to the category defined by munaq.

Definitions such as that of the Kedang munaq belong, essentially, to a closed circuit, but it is one which, in any particular context, is difficult to escape from. Most forms of measurement have no inherent standard, but time and money do. This explains the practice, almost universal among the Indian populations of South America (Bennett 1963:603) and commonly encountered elsewhere, of measuring distance in terms of time, or quantity in terms of money. In the former case only the Inca, who had adopted the pace, or 'thatkiy', as a basic unit of length, is cited as an exception. In the latter case, the use of money as a standard certainly implies the purposes for which things are measured, but it may well be that things only need to be measured when they are to be involved in monetary transactions. The great advantage of money is not only to be found in its clear and distinctive identity, as mentioned in the previous section, but also in its essential countability. The problem of comparison hardly arises.[8]

Implicit in the imposition of a standard which transcends the demands of particular local contexts is a degree of abstraction which, almost inevitably, must be in the direction of the dimensions of classical physics, for this is almost the only practical way of attaining the necessary generality. The advance in learning, which this case requires, has only occurred where language has a written, as well as a spoken form. Because a written language has always proved essential for the diffusion of abstract standards of measurement, there is in practice a clear distinction between literate and pre-literate cultures in the use and understanding of measurement – although there is no reason why systems of both kinds should not coexist, or even be combined.[9]

In all this, the classic case is provided by China. The logographic form of the written language meant that it was not tied to any one of the many, mutually unintelligible versions of spoken Chinese. In socioeconomic terms, the class defined by mastery of the written language was the bureaucracy, whose authority derived from the emperor. It was the prerogative of the emperor to define the standards of measurement, and the bureaucracy provided the means by which they were established throughout the empire, so that they provided a uniform basis for fiscal and commercial administration.

The Chinese, for their standards of measurement, pursued the ideal of abstraction to the point of establishing a single unit, known in Mandarin as '*fēn*' – with 分 as its written form – as the common basis of almost all of them. The cognitive principle is simple. As a verb *fēn* means to divide:[10] as a noun it means the smallest unit into which something can be divided. As such it has not only the general meaning of 'part' or 'fraction', but also such particular meanings as units of length, area, weight, money and time – in this last case meaning, simply, a 'minute'. Moreover, in almost every case – but not that of time[11] – this unit has been for more than two-thousand years the basis of a decimal system of measurement (Ronan and Needham 1981:37), so that 'nowhere else in the world was the decimalisation of weights and measures so early or so consistent' (ibid.: 337).

The idea behind a single unit standard is remarkably sophisticated – so much so that it really only became established in Europe, less than two hundred years ago, with the introduction of the metric system. The obstacle in the way of a unified system is simply the difficulty of realising, let alone proving, that nature provides the means for establishing a constant fixed relationship between different physical dimensions. It is, for instance, far from obvious that there is any natural expedient available for relating units of weight to units of length. This requires not only the knowledge that substances of constant density do occur in nature, but the identification of at least one such substance. It is easy to say that water, or any number of other chemical substances have this property – subject to other physical factors, such as temperature, being kept constant – but this pre-supposes a degree of scientific knowledge far beyond the range of any traditional culture. The Chinese did at least grasp the correct principle, and found a remarkably sophisticated means of applying it.

The Chinese solution was based upon the standard bamboo pitch-pipe, whose pitch was based on that of the yellow bell, described in chapter 9 (Page 105). The governing principle was that the length of the pipe should be ten times its circumference, with its length at standard pitch, 9 *tshūn* (*jūn* in Pinyin), and its circumference 9 *fēn*. (A *tshūn* is something more than an inch, and comprises 10 *fēn*.) The standard pitch-pipe is therefore approximately the size of a treble recorder. If filled with millet, it will hold exactly 1,200 grains, each weighing one *fēn* (Faber 1873:326).

The Chinese case is unique not only because of its numerical sophistication, but also because of the high standing of the Imperial Offices entrusted with the control of the standard upon which everything depended. The maintenance of this standard ensured the compatibility of all measurements throughout the empire, an important consideration for a highly centralised administration. This case, judged historically, is no more than the first step in establishing a uniform system of weights and measures. Much time elapsed before the idea arose of fixing terrestrial length measures in terms of astronomical units (Ronan and Needham 1981:337). A far more stable standard unit of length could have been established by the many devices invented for determining the day of the summer solstice. As early as the second century A.D., the Gnomon Shadow Template was used to measure the shadow cast by a fixed pole to achieve this end, but this, and similar instruments, never provided a standard unit. From the eighth century the Imperial Astronomer groped towards the principle of a unit of length based on the shadows cast, at different latitudes, at the time of the summer solstice, but the mathematical problems involved were much more difficult than could be realised at that time, and the results were inaccurate by modern standards.

None the less, 'the mathematics for analysing the evidence was very advanced for the time, and there was absolutely no inhibition about discrediting the beliefs of the scholars of past ages, an enlightened attitude which no contemporary European would have thought of taking' (Ronan and Needham 1981:339). In such a case, one can hardly speak of tradition: the correct conclusion is that a uniform system of measurement, based on universally accepted standards, is a characteristic only of modern societies. The truth of this is not altered by the fact that the Chinese took the first step on the way to modernity more than a thousand years ago.[12]

7

Time

The experience of time

Our experience of time is conditioned by the constant use of the calendar and the clock, both of which count time in fixed, universally recognised units. Traditional societies, in the sense conveyed in this book, do not necessarily use any calendar, and in most cases know nothing of mechanical timepieces.[1] This denies them the conceptual framework within which we conceive of time. What time does require is the sense of 'the intrinsic character of an event' Whitehead (1932:160). This, being more than just an instantaneous moment, allows time to be conceived of as a succession of intervals, each lasting long enough to comprise the event which defines it. So long as events are chosen so that the intervals do not overlap, this provides the basis for the notion of time as a 'discontinuity of repeated contrasts', which Leach (1966:134) sees as 'probably the most elementary and primitive of all ways of regarding time'. Here the notion of earlier and later must be taken as a primitive, irreducible concept, – a sort of axiom of time (Whitrow 1961:288.[2])

The succession of events is not necessarily continuous: indeed experience of events is essentially discontinuous, as exemplified by the succession of days, with night separating each day from the next. The continuity of time is an abstraction, no more than an indirect deduction from experience. What is essentially continuous is something immanent in ourselves,[3] as is reflected in the fact that the person who wakes up in the morning is essentially the same person who went to sleep at night. The conception of the conservation of time is not a human universal, but varies greatly between different cultures.[4]

Intuitively, at least, the fact of succession implies the possibility of systematic order, with a numerical basis. In the context of time, succession implies a series of events, each one of which, at least in principle, can be assigned an appropriate ordinal number. In terms of cognition, this must be the first stage in establishing time as a numerical phenomenon.

The potential for order is extremely difficult to realise in terms of a workable system. The difficulties are of two kinds. First, it is necessary to

81

decide upon the category of events which must provide the basis for the ordered system. Second, a point in the series of events must be chosen as its 'co-ordinate'[5] origin. As to the first point, it is extremely difficult to place in order any series of non-uniform events, even if it were clear, in relation to any two of them, which was earlier and which later. Part of the problem is that this need not always be clear, for events do occur, or at least are seen to occur, simultaneously. And if such events are bundled together in discrete classes so as to provide the basis for an ordered series, there are very real problems in defining these classes.[6]

What then are the uniform events that meet the demands of an ordered system? Social factors in part determine the possible answers to this question. In a small community the natural life cycle in terms of birth and death, combined with the different stages in the process of growing old, can determine an ordered series of events useful for naming and identifying individuals – a process exemplified by the Balinese birth order names considered in chapter 5 – or classes of individuals, such as age-sets, each with its own name.[7] It does not matter that time, on this basis, is not a continuous mathematical parameter (Whitrow 1961:58). Nor does it matter if, in certain systems, such as that of the Balinese birth-order names, the series consists of a small fixed number of members, which repeat themselves in a continuous cycle. There are any number of cognitive systems known to anthropology, in which essentially non-repetitive events – such as every stage in the life cycle of a given individual – are treated as if they were repetitive. Leach (1966:125) may well be right in saying that both classes of events are treated as 'aspects of "one thing", time, not because it is rational to do so, but because of religious prejudice. The idea of Time, like the idea of God, is one of those categories which we find necessary because we are social animals rather than because of anything empirical in our objective experience of the world.'

In the end, the physical universe is far better at providing a regular succession of recognisable events than any purely social institution. The succession of days, phases of the moon, or years, contains its own order but makes no suggestions as to how this can be reduced to a workable cognitive basis. The idea of a calendar is not inherent in anyone's experience of the physical events which mark the passage of time. This is in contrast to the social institutions considered in the previous paragraph, which by the very fact of their existence structure time in terms of the local culture.

The problem of finding an origin is acute in this case. In the experience of society, the intuitive choice of origin is the present moment, which separates the past from the future. As Whitrow (1961:295) puts it: 'The past is the determined, the present is the moment of "becoming" when events become determined, and the future is the as-yet undetermined.' The problem is that any system based on the present moment, or rather on some recognised interval – such as a day – containing the present moment, must constantly be recalibrated, as one such interval succeeds another. Such a system is therefore only useful in the context of immediate discourse. 'Yesterday's *Times*' causes no difficulty in today's conversation, but is useless as a reference in a scientific treatise.[8] The choice between context-bound and context-free references to time necessarily demands a somewhat sophisticated, and by no means universal, experience of time. The ability to see 'a year ago' as – at the time of writing – '1987' must be seen as a late product of human cultural evolution (Whitrow 1961:310), for the existence of the second alternative is only possible if the problem of a co-ordinate origin has been solved. The difficulty is that any solution is completely arbitrary according to any natural or cosmic criteria, and unless the local culture provides a solution, none will be provided from any other source.

The point is important in considering time in any traditional society, since, in the cultures which have solved this problem, time may be experienced objectively, and this in turn is essential if time is to be seen as an essentially numerical phenomenon.

The measurement of time

The measurement of time embraces two different concepts, one essentially linguistic, and the other, arithmetical. The conjoint systems of ordinal and cardinal numerals provide the link between the two. The linguistic system is concerned to name different, and possibly recurrent, points in time, whether these be days, years or whatever, whereas the arithmetical system measures the lapse of time, again in different units, according to the end in view. The former is characteristic of 'traditional' time, where it is above all important to begin the harvest or observe a festival at the correct time. The latter is pre-eminently an institution of the modern world, in which the use of accurate clocks has enabled time to be equated with other numerical factors, such as distance or money.[1]

The result is that the relation of numbers to time, in traditional societies, must be seen as essentially Pythagorean – even where the name of Pythagoras is unknown. The measurement of time is then part of a numerical cosmology based on the non-mathematical associations of numbers. Numbers are important for their connotations, which have to be established extrinsically. If Pythagoras said that all things were numbers (Russell 1946:53), it is better to interpret this in the sense that all numbers are things (Crump 1986a:89). It follows that in any system of measuring time, based, as it must be, on a succession of 'events', every such event must have its own name. The names may be provided by a system, such as that of the sixty Chinese *kanshi*, where there is in every case a clearly recognised non-numerical meaning. Even so, any true system of measurement must be able to correlate with the series of ordinal numbers, in a way of which figure 3 (illustrating the *kanshi* system) provides one example. One could for instance always refer to the date by using the Christian calendar of saints' days, with all that this connotes in the right cultural background, but one still cannot escape from the fact that St Matthias' Day is the 5th day of the year.[10]

The events most suitable for the measurement of time are those which are determined by the position of the world in the configuration defined by the other heavenly bodies – the sun, the moon, the planets and the stars. It does not matter how any particular culture explains or understands the succession of night and day, the seasons or the phases of the moon, nor that the length of certain periods, such as that of the solar year, is not precisely known.[11] All that is needed is that the observed movements of the heavenly bodies provide the basis for whatever system is used for measuring time. At the most elementary level, that of one day succeeding another, such observation is quite superfluous, but the problem then arises as to, how, and indeed why, the succession of days should be counted in the first place. Even it were possible to establish an origin, why should one then want to count the days indefinitely from this starting point. In practice the mere counting of days, without reference to any other period, can only take place on a cyclical basis, such as is to be found in the seven days of the week.[12]

This provides the starting point for a system of numeration based on the mathematical theory of congruences, which has been used for counting different units of time – from hours to units comprising several years – in many quite unrelated cultures. An elegant example of this system, and the purposes which it can serve, provided by the native culture of Bali, is described in Geertz (1973:392f.):

The permutational calendar[...]consists of ten different cycles of day-names[...]The longest contains ten day-names, following one another in a fixed order, after which the first day-name reappears and the cycle starts over. Similarly, there are nine, eight, seven, six, five, four, three, two and even[...]one day-name cycles. The names in each cycle are also different, and the cycles run concurrently[...]Of the ten cycles only those containing five, six, and seven day-names are of major cultural significance[...] [and their] interaction[...]means that a[...]day with a particular combination of names from all three cycles will appear once in every two hundred and ten days, the simple product of five, six and seven.

Mathematically Geertz's explanation is slightly misleading in that the length of the longest cycle built up in this way is not necessarily the product of the numbers of days in the component cycles, but their lowest common multiple. The *kanshi* cycles based on the ten heavenly stems, and the twelve earthly branches, which the Chinese use to count years, months, days and hours[13] thus repeat themselves after sixty combinations. This process can be endlessly repeated by combining different cycles; for example, the classic Mayas regularly worked with a fifty-two year cycle compounded out of the *hab* of 365 days and the *tzol-kin* of 260 days, with the latter being composed of cycles of 13 numbers[14] and 20 named days. There is no limit to the length of cycles, so that the Maya recorded dates separated by hundreds of years, but in the end every such system must repeat itself.[15] The Maya were however unique in establishing a cycle so long that in the historical span of their culture it was never repeated, but then, even if the system assigned a unique date to every recorded event,[16] it still provided no means of calculating the length of time between any two such dates.[17]

In practice no system, not even that of the Maya, ever confined itself to the counting of days. The question then arises as to what kind of observation of nature or the cosmos allows longer periods to be established. The answer is not as obvious as it seems at first sight. The simplest observation, that of the phases of the moon, is also the most misleading, for any calendar based on it inevitably gets out of step with the seasons. The duration of the synodic month, measured from one full moon to the next, is some twenty-nine and a half days, and no multiple of this duration is even approximately equivalent to that of a solar year. The twelve months that we know are not only unequal in length, but with the exception of February, longer than a true lunar month, but this is a necessary expedient if they are to be fitted into a solar calendar. Taking the case of the Chinese Almanac, which dates from 2256 B.C., when the Emperor Yao 'commanded two groups of officials to correlate the lunar and solar dates and to advise the ordinary people' (Palmer 1986:14), there is still no doubt about the priority of the lunar calendar, in spite of the difficulties in using it for any practical purposes.[18]

Determining the length of the solar year, by observing the movement of the sun, is remarkably difficult, particularly in the sub-tropical regions where many of the earliest calendars first came into use. One can determine the day when the sun reaches its highest point in the sky, which explains the many different rituals prescribed for midsummer day, but in the tropics the sun reaches its zenith, directly above the observer, twice a year. In practice it is simpler to take advantage of the fact that the apparent revolution of the heavens, as manifested by the stars to be seen at any given time, occurs according to a timetable, changing slightly with every night of the year, but repeating itself from one year to the next. This enables time to be measured according to such phenomena as the heliacal rising of a star, such as Sirius, which occurs on the first day that it is to be seen in the night sky, just before dawn. The accurate observation of the night sky, based on a detailed record of hundreds of named stars, explains the saying of the Confucian Scholar, Kan Sazan, that 'there is no other use for astronomy than the determination of time' (Nakayama 1969:158). The fact that the calendar was used largely to give the right date for religious events explains also why, in China and Japan, the mathematics used by the court officials entrusted with regulating the calendar had far higher status than that used in the computations of clerks and traders (ibid.:14.)[19]

A number of factors complicate, but also extend the range of the astronomical observation of time. One such factor is the deviant movement of planets, which appear to be otherwise no different from stars, across the night sky. The Mayas observed that after a cycle of 2,920 days – exactly equal to eight 365-day years – Venus returns to the same place in the sky, and fitted this observation into their calendar (Aveni 1984:161–2).[20] Eclipses are a knottier problem. In China and Japan, because they were believed to coincide with cosmic events, they could not just be left out of account. Since, however, their occurrence depends upon the alignment of three heavenly bodies, of which two, the earth and the moon, revolve, with different periodicities, in plains set at angle to each other, accurate prediction is hardly within the scope of any traditional mathematical astronomy (Palmer 1986: 22f).[21] For the hapless astronomers, comets were even worse than eclipses. They were ominous simply because they were so unpredictable, but for this reason they played no part in calendrical mathematics.[22]

The establishment of a solar calendar combines well with a permutational system for counting successive years so long as every instance of two, or more, particular components coinciding, can be uniquely designated by some other, independent factor. The Chinese sixty-year cycle, introduced on page 39, can be combined with the name of the current emperor, to provide a definite and unequivocal date for any year, so long – at least – as no emperor reigns for more than sixty years.[23] It is not surprising then that in China, 'One of the constant major marks of Imperial authority and power was the right and ability to produce an accurate yearly calendar. By ordering and assisting agriculture, by giving warning of eclipses and movements in the heavens, the Emperor showed he was a true 'son of Heaven', ruling by and with the supreme authority of Heaven' (Palmer 1986:15).[24]

The observation of the stars also provides the means for dividing the day – or rather the night – into fixed units of time, by choosing fixed stars, spaced at equal intervals across the sky, as reference points. This is easier said than done, simply because the sky changes every night, so that for much of the year many well-recognised stars are simply not visible. So, also, the view of the night sky changes from one physical location to another.[25] The problem this posed to traditional astronomy could be solved by combining the available mathematical resources with constant observation of the night sky. This led to the development, in Egypt, of the prototype for the 24-hour day,[26] and it was the Egyptians also who first used the sundial, in the fifteenth century B.C., to tell the time by day (Macey 1980:22): in this case also, the fact that the path of the sun changes from one day to the next, makes accurate calibration impossible. In practice, before the modern era, almost all systems of dividing the day into hours, or any other small units of time, allowed their duration to vary according to the respective durations of night and day in different seasons of the year. In Japan this practice was given up barely a hundred years ago.

There are very few reliable alternatives to the astronomical measurement of time. In Egypt, although 'the sun was the right eye of Horus, and the moon his left[...]the Nile was the real ruler' (Krupp 1984b:187), and provided the names of the seasons – inundation, planting and growth, harvest and low waters.[27] The use of astronomy was still very sophisticated, so that the heliacal rising of Sirius was used to recalibrate the solar and lunar calendars.

Finally, it is worth asking the question whether it is possible for there to be a cultural institution, which, on the basis of the constant repetition of some established ritual, itself provides for the measurement of time. This reverses the usual order, in which time, measured according to natural or physical phenomena, itself determines when rituals are to be carried out. Instances of such reversal are difficult to find, but de Coppet's (1970) study of the way in which money circulates in the course of the protracted funeral rites of the 'Are 'Are of the Solomon Islands does suggest that such a regime is possible. It seems as if one of the most important functions of the circulation of money is the way in which it measures the passage of time.[28] It is difficult to believe that this is an isolated case, but similar cases are certainly difficult to find in the anthropological record.

The use of interpretation of time

The named instances of time, as they occur in traditional cultures, according to the rules given in the previous section, 'don't tell you what time it is; they tell you what kind of time it is' (Geertz 1973:393). Geertz's study of Bali shows how the units of time occurring in the two calendars, could not be counted, but instead, by virtue of their different names, provided the means for formulating the social, intellectual and religious significance of each separate day. In this way the days of celebration, called '*odalan*', are determined for each of the many different kinds of temples, of which there may be more than 20,000 in all. This carries to its ultimate extreme a sort of taxonomy of time, but similar use and understanding of time can be found in many parts of the world remote from Bali.

The Balinese case may suggest that taxonomic time provides no more than the basis for activities and events of quite secondary importance, but this is simply the impression made upon the outside observer who has no interest in how the Balinese themselves interpret and control the world they live in. The world of taxonomic time is, by our own culture-bound standards, a world turned upside down. In Bali 'mass ritual was not a device to shore up the state, but rather the state[...]was a device for the enactment of mass ritual' (Geertz 1980:13), and most rituals took place at a time determined by the calendar.

The Spanish conquest of Mexico in 1519 illustrates the far-reaching political consequences which can occur where time is allowed to be the master of events. In this year, 'One Reed' in the fifty-two year cycle, Quetzalcoatl, the second principal god of the Aztecs, was expected to return from the east, dressed in black, on his personal name day, '9 Wind', and drive out the first principal god, Tezcatlipoca. On this very day, 22 April in the western calendar, Cortes landed, wearing a black suit – because it was Good Friday – and also the sort of hat which Quetzalcoatl was expected to wear. The terror that this caused to the Aztecs, and particularly to their ruler, Montezuma,[29] paved the way for Cortes, with a handful of soldiers, to conquer a vast empire in the name of the King of Spain.

It is easy to say that history is ruled by coincidence, but the point is that it is almost an inherent property of the systems of traditional time that the necessary coincidences must occur. This, indeed, is their whole *raison d'être*, and if, as in the case of Cortez and Montezuma, two quite unrelated systems combine to produce a coincidence not inherent in either of them, independently, the cognitive base of either system is more than adequate to explain and interpret the chain of events which then follows. In the months following that fateful Good Friday, or 9 Wind, depending upon how one looks at it, both Cortez and Montezuma did not doubt that everything that happened was preordained.[30] That, in the order of time, the same events appeared to the two protagonists in a quite different light, is a matter of perspective. What one sees always depends upon the point from which one sees it, and this is doubly true of a time and cosmos defined not by nature, but by an indigenous culture. What Cortes and Montezuma believed in was only remotely determined by what we would now call ecological factors.

If all this seems to lead to the conclusion that calendrical events play little part in the purely economic order, the conclusion is largely correct. In the agricultural economies sustaining the cultures which reckon, systematically, with time, nature can be relied upon to provide the necessary signals, quite independently of the calendar. Such signals may well not fit in with the rigid programme of a calendar, simply because the timing of the seasons varies from one year to the next. Judged in terms of time, the intervention of nature is stochastic, so that on a time-scale measured in days it will be too random for any sort of co-ordinated programming. It does not matter that a farmer starts sowing a week later than his neighbour, or a week earlier than in the preceding year, so long as he interprets the weather and other natural factors in the right way. It may even be advantageous that the busy period of one farmer does not coincide with that of his neighbour, for then they will be able to help each other out.

On the other hand, certain systems of agriculture require a high degree of temporal co-ordination: here wet-rice cultivation is a prime example, for once the water available for irrigation is allowed to flow, it will determine the agricultural cycle for all who use it. Once again the temple cults of Bali provide a supreme example of how this works. Taking as an example the 'kingdom' of Tabanan, the flooding of the terraces, took place in stages, beginning with those at the highest level on the slopes of the sacred Mount Agung. The whole process began in December, with the 'opening of openings' on a fixed day in the solar calendar, with rites carried out at Batu Kau temple, 'which dominates the Tabanan area both physically and spiritually' (Geertz 1980:81). In the following months, similar calendrically defined ceremonies were carried out at subsidiary 'water-opening' temples lower down the mountain, until the lowest terraces, nearest to the coast, received their share of water some time in April. Judged by an outside observer the system has the merit of ensuring the correct period of irrigation for all the terraces: it works because it coincides, accurately enough, with the annual rainfall pattern, which is sufficiently constant and reliable to ensure, in every year, all the water needed by users.

Here again the rites are seen as pre-eminent, and exemplify the comment of the second-century Chinese Record of Rituals (cited Geertz 1980:82) that 'rites obviate disorder as dikes prevent inundation'. To argue that they happen to work because they fit in with the natural order of the seasons, in its relation to the local agricultural cycle, is simply to miss the point. It should be noted also that although the succession of water-openings necessarily defines for each level a period of flooding of a fixed number of days, this is not part of the cognitive numerical basis of system as a whole. The days are not counted during this or any other period in the cycle of cultivation. The opening ritual is a signal to start the work appropriate to this stage, on the implicit assumption – justified by hundreds of years of past experience – that it will be completed in time.

The agricultural cycle can also provide a model for the life cycle of the individual. Here the Japanese case provides a particularly good illustration, in that it shows how numerical structures derived from one context can be imposed upon another. It is useful first to make a distinction between nature and cosmos, and then to explain how any given culture – in the present case that of Japan – can discover a numerical structure in both of them. From a cognitive standpoint, nature comprises everything which occurs in the direct environment of any individual but as a result of forces not originally created by man. It comprises the weather in all its manifestations, the differing states of land and water, and all the changes – sudden or gradual – which may occur in them, all animal and plant life, and finally man himself as a living being with the capacity to pass endlessly through the cycle of birth, reproduction and death. Nature is earth-bound, and provides for the continued existence of all its creatures,[31] save man, who, though dependent upon its bounty, must still provide by his labour for his own survival. This means not only that man can interfere with nature, and direct it, at least in part, to his own ends, but that he must do so if he is to survive at all. This is what makes the interaction between man and nature fundamental in any culture.

Cosmos is that part of the environment beyond the reach of man: he can observe the phenomena which occur and draw any number of conclusions from his observations, but he cannot interfere,[32] whatever he may believe to the contrary. Not only will experience of the cosmos vary from one part of the world to another – at least in part according to the experience of natural phenomena, such as the weather – but so will the interpretation of the cosmos vary from one culture to another. None the less, the theme of the present chapter, is that the concept of time provides an almost universal basis for such interpretation.

Now, in terms of time the cosmos is ordered, while such order as occurs in nature (in the seasons of the year, for instance) is generally imposed by cosmic events. Chaos may be defined as nature deprived of cosmic order. Any culture concerned with time is almost inevitably involved in an attempt to impose a higher degree of cosmic order upon the course of nature: this is at the heart of any system of agriculture. At the same time, the signs of apparent cosmic disorder, such as an eclipse, or the appearance of a comet, are highly disturbing.[33]

In Japan the annual cycle for the cultivation of rice can be seen as beginning with the spring, and ending with the autumn equinox, thus comprising the part of the year in which the days are longer than the nights. The year, so defined, is seen to begin with the birth of the grain-spirits, but this is preceded by a series of preparatory rites or *yoshūku*. The first three months of this year, up until the middle of the summer, start with the planting of the seedlings, with the young plants being transplanted at the next stage to the irrigated rice-fields, which are then gradually flooded, so that the water always remains level with the tops of the plants. In this period the rice-fields must be continually weeded, and insect pests brought under control. Each phase of this busy period is precisely timed for every agricultural community, by being made to coincide with rituals occurring at definite times in the lunar calendar. At the end of the period the water is let out of the fields, and the first ripe ears of grain are offered in the *hokake* festival.

The first three months of the cultivation cycle are critical. Every stage, both ritual or agricultural, must occur at the right time, if the grains of rice are to mature: the process is seen as inherently unstable. For the second three months success is, in a sense, assured: the grain is there to be harvested and later threshed, and the ritual programme is much less intensive. The six months following the autumn equinox divide up into two periods according to the same model, with the important difference that the events which occur, as the cycle of cultivation proceeds on its way to the beginning of the next new year, are hidden from view, with only their ritual counterparts being manifest at fixed dates in the calendar.

Just as a cosmic order, defined in terms of the lunar calendar,[34] is 'copied',[35] so as to structure the cultivation of rice, so also is the timing of events in the cycle of life and death of the individual 'copied' from the agricultural cycle. The cycle again begins with birth, although there is some ritual preparation in the course of pregnancy.[36] Events in the ritual life of the new-born child occur after the lapse of prescribed numbers of days, and later at the time of its third, fifth and seventh birthdays.[37] These rites, which take place in the local Shinto temple, correspond to the mortuary rites carried out in a Buddhist temple, which take place according to a similar timetable, in the thirty-three years following death.[38]

For the individual, living in this world, the first series of rites ends with marriage, which is absolutely essential if, at the end of the thirty-three year period after death, the *shiryō* – or spirit of the departed – is to become an ancestor god. There is thus an exact correspondence between the *tomurai-age*, the final mortuary rite, and *kekkon-shiki*, the marriage ceremony. (This may help to explain why the Japanese find it so important to marry at just the right stage in life.) In both cases, also, the appropriate ritual terminates a period of uncertainty, just as it does in the yearly cycle of cultivation. After marriage the future of the individual is assured,[39] in this world and the next. Of the years remaining until death some will be *yakudoshi*, that is subject to ill omens, at least in the absence of the appropriate ritual precautions (Miyako 1980:122f. and Norbeck 1955:109f.). Once again, the sixty-first year, known as 'kanreki', must reckon with the 'return to the calendar' of the sixty-year cycle. In this period, however, the appropriate rituals are domestic, and the local Shinto temple plays no part, the religious life of the individual being governed by Buddhism (Miyako 1980:121, fig. 10). The corresponding period, after death, is governed by Shinto, so that the *tomurai-age*, which closes the series of Buddhist mortuary rituals, actually takes place at a Shinto temple.[40]

Two final comments are appropriate. First, where Buddhism is a religion of the cosmos, Shinto is one of nature. The cosmic order of Buddhism provides the essential basis of the order which Shinto, as a cultural system, imposes on nature, whether in the timing of the cultivation of rice, or in the timing of the life-cycle of the individual. Second, because the basis of this order is numerical, any deviation from it will always be noted. Punctuality becomes the supreme virtue, and *hamideru* – literally, 'sticking out, pro-jecting', the supreme vice, creating a profound sense of *haji* or shame in the offender. Losing face is, more than anything, the consequence of making an arithmetical error. This explains the almost Pythagorean respect for numbers as the basis of the moral system.

91

8
Money

The cognitive basis of money

In the world of number, money is a complete contrast to time. Where time is part of the experience of every man, money is something man creates, although just how and why remains a problem.[1] A population can live without money, if necessary by resorting to alternative means for dealing with the problems money solves. In the cognitive domain money provides the supreme model for elementary arithmetic, with its fundamental concern for operations involving cardinal numbers. There is hardly any problem about the measurement of quantity. Money measures not only itself, but almost anything else which can be quantified. Money, in its broadest definition, is 'the means for comparing – in quantitative terms – two unlike things on a scale which is common to both of them. The reason for making such a comparison depends upon its institutional context, in which there must be, in any case, a recognised common "standard of value"' (Crump 1981:10), applicable to different categories of things. This abstract concept has no natural basis. The different categories brought under one and the same 'umbrella' are a matter determined by cultural factors, provided one recognises that the cognitive domain defined by this concept, in any particular case, may bridge any number of separate cultures that are otherwise quite unrelated.[2] The categories can be as disparate as 'shoes and ships and sealing wax, and cabbages and kings' as long as they possess the elusive quality of 'value', measurable according to a single yard-stick. In arithmetical terms, money is a sort of 'common denominator', which 'reifies' value in terms of recognised units. The 'denomination' of money is thus no more than the name given to the units in which money is represented in any particular case. In purely formal terms this step does not essentially change anything. One per cent can be equated with one pence, even if the former represents a common denominator, and the latter a monetary denomination.

At first sight, a standard of value would seem to have no purpose in the absence of a system of reciprocity in which the things measurable, or 'denumerable', in terms of money could in some way be exchanged with each other. Thus money, at least as a standard of value, only makes sense in the context of a sphere of exchange defined by the different things which may be transacted on the basis of a recognised standard. This leads one to conceive of a system of barter in which the rate of exchange between different categories is determined by a common standard of value. The difficulty is that the concept is more theoretical than real, for it is practically impossible to find any actual instance of such a system based upon a purely abstract standard. In practice, in such traditional barter economies as that of precolonial Mexico, the Congo basin in the late nineteenth century, or the Siassi Islands off the north coast of New Guinea in the mid twentieth century, there was one particular good which was always accepted in exchange. This was the role of cocoa-beans in Mexico (Katz 1956:58), cloth in the Congo Basin (Vansina 1973:297) or pigs in the Siassi Islands (Harding 1967:35).

Once such a particular role is recognised the definition of money must be drastically revised. Taking for instance the case of the Siassi Islands, pigs there function not so much as a standard of value, but as a universal means of exchange. This is a much more familiar function of money, and the one preferred by economists, such as Professor Clower,[3] in establishing any basic monetary theory. Although, intuitively, there would be obvious practical advantages in money having the same denomination both as a means of exchange and as a standard of value, this is not in fact essential, and it would not be too difficult to find cases in which the two were not the same.

In any culture the essential representation of money in numerical terms must have an acceptable cognitive basis. A number, as a purely abstract concept, is not generally acceptable. The strength of money, as a cultural institution, is derived from its capacity to represent quantity in the most abstract and general terms. In the many different languages whose rules of syntax allow numbers to qualify only a limited class of general classifiers or measure words, such as the Japanese *josūshi* (see p. 00), the classifier for money is almost always in a class of its own: indeed, in Yoruba, there is a separate classifier for money, while all other nouns are grouped into one general class. Now one might suppose, after looking at such cases as that of the Siassi Islands pig circuit, that the common lexical derivation of the money-classifier would be from a word denoting the most actively transacted good in the money sphere of exchange. For instance, in the Siassi Islands the word for money should be related to that for pigs. This line of reasoning, however much it might appeal to theoretical economists, is not borne out by the facts. The Siassi Islanders are perfectly well aware of the fact that they can exchange pigs for many other things (and make a profit out of the transaction), and it would not perhaps cause them too much difficulty to conceive of pigs as a universal means of exchange, even though they have never heard of Professor Clower.[4] But whatever their conception of pigs may be, it is not a conception of money.[5] The question is, why are such conceptions hardly ever the same, not only for the Siassi Islanders, but for almost any other society, traditional or modern?

The answer is that the most distinctive characteristic of money is not so much that it is exchanged, nor even that it somehow represents the elusive quality of 'value', but simply that it circulates among a recognised class of transactors. In doing so, it defines the class, which, as a whole, disposes of a stock of money, consisting of a sufficient number of identical units distributed among the transactors. The key to understanding money is that it is a dynamic system: money has no function unless the pattern of distribution is continually changing as a result of transactions known as 'payments'. Payment is simply the transfer from one person to another of a quantity of money. Its result so far as the money used to make it is concerned, is to put the payee in what, before the payment, was the position of the payer. Whatever functions money may have, the payee, is, by virtue of the payment, put in a position to perform them, and – this is the key point – he can do so only by making a further payment. It is of the nature of money, therefore, to be used in an indefinite succession of payments, that is to circulate, without being subject to any loss of function (Crump 1981:3–4). Money is a numerical phenomenon because the meaning and consequences of any payment are directly related to its amount. This purely quantitative attribute distinguishes money from circulating systems, such as the well-known *Kula* ring[6] described by Malinowski (1922), depending upon objects each with their own separate identity, and whose meaning must be judged qualitatively.

Once the focus of investigation shifts to circulation, it is no longer necessary to insist that the payments maintaining the system must represent one side of an exchange transaction, with all that this implies in the way of a contractual basis being essential to any monetary system. The fact is that exchange, understood in any such terms, is hardly ever more than marginal in traditional societies.[7] Contract, in relation to the use of money, is a characteristic of the modern age, just as clocks are in the relation to the use of time.[8] Indeed, a pure exchange system would be as difficult to find as a system based exclusively on gifts carrying no obligation to give anything in return. And because the reason for any payment is always extrinsic to it (Crump 1981:4), money is no more than 'an extreme and specialized type of ritual' (Douglas 1966:69). For this reason anthropologists, as opposed to economists, prefer to define money as a 'means of payment' rather than as a 'means of exchange' (Melitz 1974:8f): the anthropological definition does not confine research into the phenomenon of money to a narrow range of essentially modern institutions.

Once we appreciate that the correct focus is on the circulating system, in its most general form, we can understand why the forms taken by monetary

94

denominations are so heterogenous that 'the classification of money according to the allusions implicit in the words for it[...]is almost completely meaningless' (Crump 1978:511). It is perhaps significant to note that the character for the Japanese yen, 円, connotes 'circularity',[9] a meaning shared with that of 'kula', but these are no more than special cases. The position may change when a workable system of keeping records enables monetary transactions to be effected by means of bookkeeping entries. Such systems, which are recorded in regions as diverse as Kenya (Zaslavsky 1979:94) and Peru do not necessarily record monetary transactions. More significant are the records kept of loans and deposits of grain in ancient Babylonia (Bogaert 1966:59), which provide an early prototype for money as a unit of account, but such cases are still hardly evidence of monetary denominations based upon the most frequently transacted goods. The abundant lexical evidence still points conclusively in the other direction.

Finally, the fact that a true money must be capable of circulating indefinitely among those who use it, imposes considerable limitations upon the physical substance out of which a viable money can be made,[10] the more so, indeed, if this substance is to have a distinctive identity as such, so that it has no significant use for non-monetary purposes. A denomination connoting, however indirectly, anything else involved in the sphere of payment, would give rise to endless misunderstandings. In truth, the substance which we call 'money', such as the coins in our pockets, is not really the essence of money, but a representation of it, no better and no worse than a bookkeeping entry.[11] In reckoning with this chimerical characteristic of money, it is best to avoid all possible use of metaphor in monetary denominations. The universe of money, according to the linguistic school associated with the name of Jakobson, belongs to the metonymic order, in which all designations are no more than a form of mathematical notation, appropriate to 'a combination of signs which has space as a support' (Barthes 1967:58). The aptness of the words cited is apparent in any text in monetary theory written by a modern economist.[12] The lexical evidence provided by the language of traditional monetary systems suggests they are hardly less apt to describe these systems. The essential point is that money, as an arithmetical system, is one in which the denomination, whatever it may be, cancels out on both sides of the equation.[13] This being so, it is prudent to ensure that the presence of the denomination (which is a cognitive essential for all practical money users) cannot lead to any sort of metaphorical confusion. This means, once again, that money, in any tangible form, must be no more than a counter, recognisable as such, and as nothing else.

The principle of reciprocity

Reciprocity is the principle upon which the circulation of money is based. Its general meaning is that for every benefit conferred by one person upon another, something must eventually be given in return. In the context of money, either the original or the return benefit must take the form of a payment. At the same time there is no essential restriction on the form of the non-monetary benefit, although in any particular society the range of such benefits will be limited, and the form taken by them well recognised. Neither is there any need for the two reciprocal benefits to be coincident in point of time. This, the case of the self-liquidating transaction, is exceptional, particularly in any traditional society.[14] It follows that the constant flow of benefits, both original and return, maintains a network of reciprocal obligations. Once this point is reached it is possible to maintain such a network exclusively by means of monetary payments, so that any such payment may serve to create, extend or dissolve a link in the network. This may add up to no more than an established pattern of gift-giving, for as Mauss (1968:194) demonstrated in his classic study, the acceptance – in any traditional society – of any gift, automatically implies the acceptance of any number of well-recognised social obligations which go with it. These make a positive virtue out of the circulation of money, in successive stages of being given and returned (ibid.:24). This makes it essential to maintain both the circulation of money and the prevailing social relations. Indeed each supports the other. This explains the peculiar significance of the state which the Tangu of New Guinea call '*mngwotngwotiki*', a word which connotes a particular field of relations in which the individuals concerned are temporarily unobliged to each other (Burridge 1969:1).[15]

Because other 'valuables' are often incorporated into systems of reciprocity, it is not so easy to find a case in which the role of money is clearly pre-eminent. Of the many recorded cases, one of the richest in its numerical and monetary aspects, and also one of the best documented, is that of the 'Are 'Are funeral cycle, described by de Coppet (1968, 1970). It is important in the present context, not so much for its ethnographic content, but for its insights into the way in which money is conceived of in at least one traditional society.

The 'Are 'Are, a Melanesian people who occupy a part of the island of Melaita in the South Pacific, use a money consisting of strings of pearls of varying lengths (de Coppet & Zemp 1978:116).It is used primarily in a system of balanced reciprocity, in which ordinary transactions in consumer products play hardly any part (de Coppet 1968:47). The circulation of money, which takes place only among individuals, is concentrated on various recognised stages in the protracted 'Are 'Are funeral rites. For those men who die a natural death, leaving descendants to survive them, the amount of money presented on the platform where, several years later, the final consummation of the funeral rites takes place, determines their status and rank as ancestors.

At the opening stage of the money circuit the officials in charge of the funeral rites – who will have been closely related to the deceased – stand upon a platform where they receive gifts of money from the individuals present who have chosen to participate. Every such individual, as he makes his gift, names either one of the officials or one of the gravediggers.[16] In the former case the official, once this stage is completed, will lend the money to those friends and members of his family who helped with the funeral preparations. In the latter case the money is handed over to the gravedigger at the end of the day, with the officials at the same time announcing the total amount given. The gravediggers carry the greater part of the economic burden of the funeral – in the material sense – but they share it with others in their home village, among whom they then divide the money given to them. The recipients are free to use this money in any way, but they are obliged to repay an equivalent sum two or three years later, when the gravediggers, in the final stage of the funeral rites, themselves must repay the same officials as gave out the money at the end of the first stage. In either of these two cases, therefore, the officials ultimately receive the money given by the individual participants.

These, in turn, will sooner or later become officials or gravediggers at other funerals, and when this happens they are entitled to repay every sum freely given by them at earlier funerals. It follows that much of the money given by individuals at the first stage of a funeral is in fact paid in satisfaction of pre-existing obligations. On the other hand the system can only be maintained by individuals choosing, at some stage in their life, to make such a gift freely. This is in fact no more than the first step in the 'Are 'Are prestige race, in which the winners become the recognised 'big men'.[17]

The 'free' gifts would seem to ensure a steady increase in the total amount of money involved in the funeral circuit. This is counteracted by two factors. First, there is a third category of gift, made by the officials at the final stage of the funeral, so as to repay the gravediggers for the considerable amount of food provided for the festivities. Gifts of this category do not have to be repaid in any way. Second, an old man destined to die without issue, will bury all his money at the grave of his ancestors, and then patiently await his own death (de Coppet 1970:37). Even if the loss of money then arising is made good from external sources,[18] it will not immediately be absorbed into the funeral circuit.

The 'Are 'Are regard the monetary system maintained by the endless succession of funeral rites as autonomous. All social relations are dependant upon the flow of money. De Coppet (1970:34) emphasises that the whole social life, and the work of everyday, revolve around the countless funeral celebrations which in every year involve the living in the moneys of the dead of yesterday and always[...]Money [ibid.:39] is the most general attribute of all human acts, and in their interpretation represents the highest level of abstract thought. Money is omnipresent, since it measures the lifespan of every individual, from birth to death, and in all his relations with others. Money [ibid.:35] has a supernatural power to attract money not only to funeral celebrations, but to marriages and the festivities of young people[...]Money, if it is not to destroy its holder, must circulate incessantly, passing from hand to hand, from ritual to ritual, from ceremony to ceremony, for, as is commonly said in Melanesia [ibid.:39], all moneys are to be identified with the dead.

Inevitably the above analysis is based upon a much simplified version of de Coppet's rich ethnography. Nothing has been said about the payments made outside the autonomous funeral system in satisfaction for death by homicide.[19] But sufficient has been said to establish, at least in the case of the 'Are 'Are the extreme generality of money as a numerical phenomenon.

all social facts[...]once measured in monetary terms, become comparable. The ritual prolongs their effects beyond the moment of time, to integrate them in both the past and the future. The circulation of these moneys is subject to precise rules, so that, together with men, women, children and other goods recognised in the local culture, they form a system of exchanges which maintains and perpetuates the established patterns of social organization. The implicit immortality of the society, as such, is thus maintained by the mortality of the people and goods which momentarily cross its path. Both the living and the dead combine in the eventual destruction of all things, so that in the end nothing remains but these strings of money, and the unceasing ballet which they perform. These moneys, the tangible supporters of the law, are all that remain of the ancestors, and such they are the all powerful accomplices to the processes of time   *de Coppet 1968:116.*

If this is how the 'Are 'Are see their own society, we may see them as playing a game with money.[20] There is little uncertainty about the rules, which – as in any game – decide who may play, and who the winners are. It is a serious game of life and death, for the whole organisation of society, including the distinctive roles of the big men, depends upon it. It also establishes the place of the ancestors in the life after death. But any ranking system has an essential numerical basis,[21] and in providing for the money given at different stages in the funeral ritual to be counted, and credited to the different participants, living or dead, the 'Are 'Are have ensured that their monetary system meets the demands which they make of it. The case is extremely instructive, because it shows the cultural limitations of our own understanding of money. It exemplifies also the observation of Lévi-Strauss (1969:32) that 'the system of the scarce produce[22] constitutes an extremely general model'.

The above description of the 'Are 'Are monetary system allows three important points to be made. The first is that a monetary system can be maintained simply by the circulation of money according to the rules governing the system. That is, if any payment is reciprocated, it is simply by another payment.[23] The fact that payments continue to be made leads to the second point, which is that every payment relates to a relationship of indebtedness between the payer and the payee. The dynamic flow of payments takes place in the context of a network of debts, which it may extend or contract, but never leave unchanged.[24] The continued existence of this network, which as Mauss (1968:198–9) points out, can as readily be seen in terms of outstanding credits, provides the necessary impetus for the payments to be made. Because payments are only made at a series of instants of time, the debt/credit network can be seen as essentially static, and enduring over time, even though every instant payment changes its structure. The 'Are 'Are would readily accept Keynes' (1936:293) statement that 'the importance of money essentially flows from its being a link between the present and the future': indeed the 'Are 'Are see this, if anything, more clearly than modern users of money. Because of the profound difference in the numerical character of time (as presented in the previous chapter) and of money (as presented in the present chapter) the problem to be resolved in relating the two is best considered in a special section.

Time and money

Combining time with money is about as easy as mixing chalk and cheese. Time, as an ordered series of intervals, is continually effacing itself. The problem of reducing it to numerical order is by no means simple, nor is a solution necessarily essential. The concept of time as a dimension, measurable in recognised units on a fixed scale, is the product of an advanced stage of cognitive development. But measurement in such units is essential if time is to be related to money. And as I have already noted in the case of the 'Are 'Are, the endless circulation of money may be seen as providing the means for measuring time, although in the general case the measurement of time is independent of money. The situation to be considered is one in which both money and time, being 'measurable' according to the sense given above, are related to each other by some established rule.

In the simplest case time would simply provide the basis for a unit of account in a system of reciprocity, of which the component elements – whether represented in terms of the benefits conferred, or the obligations then arising – were measured purely in terms of time. The benefit would then consist, according to circumstances, of so many hours, days or years of what may loosely be called 'service', with the obligation then arising taking the form of a reverse-benefit to be conferred at some later time. If, for instance, in one week, A works for 20 hours in B's garden, then, at some other, perhaps unspecified time B will have to work for 20 hours in A's garden. The case seems simple enough, but in spite of any number of instances recorded in the ethnographic literature of mutual help between households, it is extremely difficult to find any instance in the elementary form given above, and such instances as there are prove to be no more than one component in a complex system.

Subject to this limitation, the Iban of Sarawak maintain an institution known as 'bedurok', a 'labour-exchange system[...]based on strict reciprocity' (Freeman 1955:85). In this society, the basic family economic units, known as the 'bilek', provide the constituent elements of any instance of the *bedurok*.

Thus if *bilek* family A sends two women to weed on the farms of families, B, C and D, these three are each required, in return, to send two women to the farm of family A when its turn falls due on the rota; or, if it is not possible on that day, then on some subsequent occasion. This principle of exact reciprocity is rigorously followed, so that if family A sends only one woman to work on the farm of family B, family B will only send one woman in exchange[...]In general, therefore, a *bilek* family with two women available for weeding will try to *bedurok* with other families having two women available. Again, a *bilek* family is entitled to drop out of a *bedurok* group as soon as all the work on its own farm has been completed. This situation often arises – the area to be weeded per head varying considerably from *bilek* to *bilek   Freeman 1955:85*.

The critical question is, why need this system be quite so elementary? It contains the kernel of a zero-sum bookkeeping system based on the unit of one individual's day's work, capable of indefinite extension. Stating the position in the most general terms, there could be any number of *bilek* families, each involved in a different set of *bedurok*, and each having – at any given time – its own balance of account, which could be either positive or negative. Adapting a simple mathematical notation, the families, f_1, f_2, f_3...would each have, respectively, b_1, b_2, b_3...*bedurok* units, subject only to the zero-sum condition that $b_1 + b_2 + b_3 + ... = 0$. This would be no more than an elementary sphere of credit (Crump 1981:67) such as forms the basis of any system of 'scriptual' money (ibid.:93). But in fact this is not the way the Iban, or any other system, has developed. The Iban system has a built-in tendency towards *mngwotngwotiki* (page 96). The system returns to zero at the end of every one of the four stages in the yearly agricultural cycle (Freeman 1955:82). This may be because the prescribed tasks – felling, sowing, weeding and reaping – which belong to each stage, cannot be equated with each other, but more important, for the general case, is the confusion and ambiguity which would arise in a system which made no explicit distinction between the units of time and money.

There is, in any case, no evidence of insurmountable bookkeeping objections. If the question hardly arises in the context of the *bedurok* system, which is extremely elementary, the Lamet of northern Laos, who also make use of help in agriculture, note the number of working days devoted to harvesting by means of charcoal marks on the rafters of their houses

(Izikowitz 1951:293). The fact that no less than 43 such marks could be counted in a single house suggests a more complicated system than the *bedurok*.[25] The essential difference would seem to lie in the fact that the Lamet recognise a definite correspondence between the time worked and the amount produced of a single commodity, rice. Although the actual equation is never precisely formulated, it is none the less real. It is significant that in the case of bridewealth, a one-to-one correspondence between years of service – to be rendered by the bridegroom to his father-in-law – and buffaloes (which are the prescribed means of payment) is well-established (ibid.:100f.). The significant point in both cases is that time is reduced to something tangible.

The critical objection to the use of time as a 'denomination' has already been stated at the beginning of this section. The real problem is that time, in the language of the medieval Church, is 'fungible', in a sense that distinguishes it from any 'denomination' used in practice. This is inherent in the definition. 'Fungibles' lose their identity in, or are destroyed or transformed by use, where 'non-fungibles' are not destroyed or transformed by use (Viner 1978:86).[26] In practical terms this means that five working days, beginning on Monday morning in any given week, have on Friday evening gone for ever. Those five working days can never be returned, and even if, on some other, later Monday, a new period of work is begun, in return for the first period, the two periods are not the same. What does endure is the non-fungible product of the way time is 'spent'. For the Lamet, a quantity of rice, or for that matter a wife, have an enduring identity, which time, in any real instance, never has. It is possible, conceptually, to transact with rice or buffaloes – or even wives – in a way which is impossible with time.

If, in the context of money, time can be 'reified' by means of labour, objections in principle can still arise. The equation is simple enough, as has already been shown. One need only establish a linear relationship between so many units of money, and so many hours of work. If this is fundamental in all modern economic thinking, it is by no means self-evident in many a traditional society. One sees this in the conflict of principle apparent in the New Testament parable of the labourers in the vineyard (Matthew xx:1–16), who all received the same reward although some worked only the last hour, and others the whole day. Whatever the correct theological interpretation,[27] there is a clear case of conflict between different cultural norms. Even today there are traditional societies, fully acquainted with the use of money, but in which labour, and land also, are excluded from the monetary sphere of exchange.[28]

Finally, the institution of interest relates money to time in a way which is quite independent of any actual use of money. The basis of the institution is simply that a debtor can pay for the money lent to him at a rate fixed in terms of time. There is, of course, no inherent relationship, of this form, between money and time, so the rate of interest is quite arbitrary. In purely arithmetical terms it does not matter if it is so many per cent per hour, per week or per year. In practice wherever money is lent out at interest, convention confines the rate within quite narrow limits. The economic ideal is that interest rates, like wages, are sticky (Crump 1981:251).[29] Traditional societies are likely to miss this point, for lending at interest – or 'usury' – is, if anything more obnoxious than employment at a fixed wage.[30]

9

Music, poetry and dance

The two structures of music: inherent and imposed

Music, in any form, is a purely cultural institution, with a distinctive numerical base. It is not essentially related to any of the so-called 'sounds of nature', although, as Lévi-Strauss (1974:296f.) has shown, such a relationship, in relation to elementary musical instruments, is a fundamental assumption in any number of different cultures. Indeed, 'music[...]must be appreciated for what it is: it is intended to be heard as human organised sound' (Blacking 1968:313), even though the instruments used in the production may be thought of as 'being made to cry'. The principle of organisation is always numerical. One may compare the cases considered in chapters 7 and 10, of which the former shows how the calendar is the means for ordering time, and the latter, how the rules are the means for ordering play in the form of a game. In both cases the parallel can be drawn still further. Music has its own special world of virtual time, to which we are transported away from the world of culturally regulated actual time. Or as Stravinsky has said, 'Music is given to us with the sole purpose of establishing an order in things, including, and particularly, the coordination between man and time' (ibid.: 314). As for games, the intrinsic game (introduced on page 116), with both a deep, hidden structure, governing strategy, and a superficial, open structure, defined by the constitutive rules, may be compared to music, also with its intrinsic numerical structure, upon which different instances are imposed. By applying the analytical methods of chapter 2, it is reasonable to conclude from the analysis of music, in all its different forms, that – just as in the case of language – the brain of each individual has an inherent propensity to deal with sound on the basis of some deep structure. Seen in terms of neuropsychology, this is an innate biological property, common to all individuals, if only at a sub-conscious level (Spencer 1985:10). This deeper structure, which defines the organisation of sound, outside the domain of language, as music, is essentially numerical.

The point becomes clear when music is analysed in terms of the four basic properties of pitch, timbre, volume and rhythm (Cohen and Katz 1979:101).

Defining music in terms of the sound vibrations reaching the ear, pitch is the frequency of each individual note. Although, for practical purposes, air is always the medium through which any sound is transmitted, including the sound of music, not every musical instrument operates directly by imposing the desired frequency among a given mass of air. This is the defining property of wind instruments, in which wind, generally created by the player blowing into some kind of mouth-piece, causes a column of air, of a length determined by the pipe in which it is contained, to vibrate. Stringed instruments, however, operate by causing a string of pre-determined length to vibrate, by means which differ according to the instrument being played. Now, in these two cases, if the other physical properties (such as the tension of the string) are kept constant, the pitch will vary according to the vibrating length, which determines the basic design of the instrument, as well as the way it is played. (In non-linear cases such as gongs, bells and drums, pitch must depend therefore on other physical properties. The human voice is, needless to say, a very special case.)

In the linear case, the fundamental rule is that every time the length is halved, the frequency of vibration is doubled, so that the pitch is raised by exactly an octave, as is well known to the player of any stringed instrument. But what then is an 'octave'? In an anthropological study it can only be defined as the basic aesthetic element in any individual's sense of pitch, and in any musical culture. 'The octave is the most perfect consonance, so perfect that it gives the impression of duplicating the original tone, a phenomenon for which no convincing explanation has ever been found[...]it is the only interval common to practically all the scales ever evolved, regardless of the number or pitch of the intermediate steps' (Apel 1970:589). Any music no matter how it is produced, if transposed, up or down, by any whole number of octaves, retains its original character in a way which no other interval allows for. This may be taken to be a defining property of music.[1] The important point is that an octave, even if it is a subjective element in music, still has a precise and elementary numerical base.

There are further problems arising from pitch, but they must be left to the discussion of 'imposed' structures later in this section. We can now extend the analysis to apply to the definition and explanation of timbre. Taking as the starting point a vibrating line, between two points or nodes, timbre is a phenomenon of the physics of sound that the same line will resonate, to a greater or lesser degree, at every integral fraction of its length. Any actual note produced by an instrument will comprise not only the frequency of the whole vibrating length, but that of a half, a third, a quarter, a fifth, and so on, of that length – so that the note itself contains elements, known as 'harmonics', of every integral multiple of its basic frequency.[2] Since, however, the amplitude, essentially the measure of volume, becomes smaller with every succeeding 'harmonic', the pitch of the note is still defined by its basic frequency. None the less, it is the amplitudes of the successive harmonics, in their relation to each other, which distinguishes a violin, say, from a trumpet.[3]

The basis of rhythm is the repetition, according to an established measure, of notes of fixed duration. Just as, in relation to pitch, the human ear is uniquely sensitive to the interval of an octave, so also is it responsive to rhythm with a binary basis. In the absence of any other pronounced rhythm, music tends to be heard in measures of two or four beats of equal duration. This is the most natural temporal frame in which to produce music. The rhythm of music can then be defined in terms of a standard note, say a crotchet, recurring at a constant tempo, and accentuated, in some way, at fixed intervals. In modern notation this form is expressed by the time signature, which indicates both the chosen unit of measurement and the number of such units comprised in a measure. In the most elementary case music would consist only of such units,[4] but in practice notes of both longer and shorter duration are used. In general, however, they are still in a binary relationship to the basic unit, so that two crotchets is a minim, two minims a semibreve, or half a crotchet a quaver, half a quaver a semiquaver, and so on. Three commonly replaces two in some musical traditions, to give a distinctive rhythm to certain types of music, but the process seldom goes any further.[5] Essentially rhythm is independent of the speed of music, although this is certainly a factor in determining the character of music in any cultural context. Within limits, the speed of music can be varied without disturbing the rhythm, and this is often done to achieve special effects.

Such is the inherent structure of music, but the bare bones of this structure must be clothed with flesh and blood before any actual melody[6] can be produced. Before this is done, a basic pitch must in some way be established by being anchored to some standard, corresponding, say, to the modern concert pitch. With instruments that can be tuned *ad hoc* – including, in this case, the human voice – such a standard may be otiose, but in practice it is a fairly constant preoccupation of any musical culture, particularly where there is any tradition of orchestration. Possibly as early as the sixth century B.C., the Chinese established the principle of a standard set of twelve bells, dominated by the *Huang-Chung*, or yellow bell, which were used both for giving the pitch and starting the music (Ronan and Needham 1981:372). This corresponded to a 'yellow-bell' pitch-pipe (Picken 1957:95), for which every new emperor could set his own standard.[7] By the third century A.D., the Office of the Grand Revealed Music of the Han had a tuner in the form of a seven-foot long string, which was used to tune bells by resonance.[8] The case is the more significant in view of the fact that the Imperial Court took the measures of musical pitch as the basis of establishing standards of length, capacity and weight (Ronan and Needham 1981:300).

The next step is to establish a division of the octave into notes on a scale,

105

but there are many different ways of doing this. Acoustically the simplest starting point is to bring the first two harmonics not equivalent to octaves within the compass of the fundamental octave, based on the so-called 'tonic' note. Because these harmonics have frequencies three and five times that of the tonic, this result can be achieved by lowering the former by one octave, and the latter by two, to produce frequencies, relative to the tonic of 3/2 and 5/4 – a phenomenon noted in Greece by the school of Pythagoras as early as the sixth century B.C. (Apel 1970:419) and by the Chinese not much later.[9] The intervals which then arise are simply the fifth and the major third. The Chinese, using only the ratio 3/2, and its inverse, 2/3, which produces the descending interval of a fourth, established a scale based on twelve bamboo tubes with 'lengths calculated by alternately subtracting and adding one-third of the length of the preceding tube' (Picken 1957:94), producing in this way a succession of twelve intervals which, if arranged in ascending order of pitch, produce the note sequence, F, F #, G, G #, A, A #, B, C, C #, D, D #, E (ibid.: 95) – in which a 'semitone' separates the successive notes. The only thing wrong with this process is that the next following note is not a perfect octave of F, and although the process can be continued indefinitely, it will never achieve a perfect octave, for the simple mathematical reason that no power of three can ever be equal to a power of two. In fact the Chinese gamut of pitches did not even include an octave (Ronan and Needham 1981:373f.). Indeed, as McClain (1979) has shown, the Chinese pursued the process of cyclical tuning, numerically, to quite extraordinary lengths, but although the deviation could be reduced to an interval which the human ear cannot discriminate, it can never be eliminated.[10] In Greece the Pythagorean school worked with the fifth and the major third in a parallel attempt to establish a scale of twelve notes, but this was equally doomed to failure. As long as this problem remained unsolved – and it still presents major problems in establishing the pitch of wind instruments – it was impossible to move from one key to another. In Western Europe the problem was solved by the tuning known as Equal Temperament, which first appeared about 1600, and received its greatest publicity in the *Wohltemperierte Clavier* of J. S. Bach, while in China Chu Tsai-Yu produced a solution in 1584 (Ronan and Needham 1981:385). The principle is simple enough: the octave is simply divided into twelve equal intervals, but then there are no perfect fifths, or indeed any other intervals corresponding to harmonics not based on powers of two. This introduces, inevitably, an element of *dissonance* which the sensitive ear may well detect.

No musical tradition makes equal use of the twelve notes defined by the processes analysed in the previous paragraph.[11] The character of any traditional music is largely defined by the 'scale'[12] of notes chosen as the basis of the melodic line. The most common scale is the 'pentatonic', based on five notes, C, D, F, G, A.[13] This 'occurs in the music of nearly all ancient cultures – China, Polynesia, Africa – as well as that of the American Indians, Celts and Scots' (Apel 1970:653). The diatonic scale which has long been standard in the western world is based on seven notes, with the eighth note completing the octave. Its most simple representation is the scale of C.[13] Melody restricted to the notes of a scale is a characteristic common to almost all traditional music. Subject to this restriction as many *modes* can be chosen as there are notes in the scale, simply because any note may be the 'tonic'. The mode chosen will then have its own aesthetic, although in much traditional music one mode tends to be preferred above all the others. In contrast, key is hardly an element of traditional music,[14] for the transposition of music, either up or down, which is inherent in the use of different keys, is really only possible with instruments tuned by equal temperament.

Rules of consonance and dissonance govern the choice of intervals between notes, particularly when two or more notes are played at the same time, whether on the same instrument, or by different members of an ensemble.[15] Since at least the time of Pythagoras there have been theories about the numerical basis of consonant intervals, but in the end consonance is a matter of culturally conditioned subjective impressions. Each culture chooses, implicitly, its own numerical basis for defining consonance[16] and the wide range of possible choices largely explains the apparent *foreign* quality of music from another culture. Consonance, so defined, may be taken to be the last step in imposing a culture-specific structure on the use of pitch. Consonance then represents the normal element in music, so that dissonance – arising as a result of ignoring the normative rules – represents 'the no less important element of disturbance and tension' (Apel 1970:201).

Just as there is an imposed ordering of pitch, in the manner described above, so also is there an imposed order of time in its relation to music. One basis for this is to be found in 'modules[...]little entities that could be counted in finite numbers[...]manipulated to make music' (Jones 1975:310). The principle applies in many other fields besides music, as is demonstrated by its place in architecture. In music, however, the *module* has the dimension of time, not space. It is an essential element in any ensemble in which the different parts follow each other in a fixed temporal order, such as occurs – in English folkmusic – in rounds and catches. 'Three Blind Mice' is an elementary example. A modular structure may also be imposed by outside factors, such as the need to set a poem to music, or to provide music for a dance in which the same combination of steps is executed, in turn, by different dancers.[17] More generally, a modular structure is at least inherent in the measures, or bars, of any isometric music, and it often provides a frame for analysis in terms of units of longer duration.

The application of the structural principles, presented in this section, can be illustrated by one single case, that of the change-ringing of church-bells in England, with a history going back to the sixteenth century.[18]. The basis is

Course Bell	1	2	3	4
	1234	1234	1234	1234
	2143	2143	2143	2143
	2413	2413	2413	2413
	4231	4231	4231	4231
	4321	4321	4321	4321
	3412	3412	3412	3412
	3142	3142	3142	3142
	1324	1324	1324	1324
	1342	1342	1342	1342
	3124	3124	3124	3124
	3214	3214	3214	3214
	2341	2341	2341	2341
	2431	2431	2431	2431
	4213	4213	4213	4213
	4123	4123	4123	4123
	1432	1432	1432	1432
	1423	1423	1423	1423
	4132	4132	4132	4132
	4312	4312	4312	4312
	3421	3421	3421	3421
	3241	3241	3241	3241
	2314	2341	2341	2341
	2134	2134	2134	2134
	1243	1243	1243	1243

Fig. 11. A full touch of four bells.

simple and the mathematical theory not too complicated. There can be any number of bells in a set, or 'peal', and together they comprise a scale according to the definition given on p. 106. Each bell has its own ringer, and the basic module consists of all the bells being rung just once, in a sequential order that always changes from one module to the next. There is thus never any ensemble. The object is to ring the bells through every possible permutation, so that none is repeated, to return, finally, to the original starting point, usually consisting of a simple scale descending from the top, or 'treble', bell. The example given above in figure 11 is a full peal of four bells, rung through all possible 24 permutations (24 is simply 'factorial 4' or $4! = 4 \times 3 \times 2 \times 1$). These are the basic modules. In this peal every bell 'hunts', and the treble bell – 1 – never leaves the hunt, as is shown by the line drawn through the number 1 in every successive sequence. Now the simplest *method* – or *algorithm* in the language of logic – would be to keep all the bells in the hunt, but in this case the permutations in the first eight rows would merely repeat themselves, so that those in the second and third sets of eight rows would never occur. This offends against the basic object of change-ringing, as it is stated above. The solution in the present case is to allow the two 'behind' bells to dodge, that is to change places, whenever the treble comes back into the leading position. This occurs, regularly, after every eighth peal. The result is that a method containing only two 'changes' is sufficient to ensure a complete peal.[19]

The fact that there are more than 10^{23} possible permutations of the 24 peals given above shows that there is ample scope for alternative methods. The minimum number of changes required by the simplest method increases slowly with the number of bells, and the art consists of using, and devising methods (not necessarily always the simplest possible) which define consonance in numerical terms.[20] Although none of the various notations used is anything like a score, the structure of change-ringing, with its clearly defined numerical basis, perfectly illustrate the points I have made in the present section.[21]

Poetry, song and dance

As means of communication, poetry, song and dance transcend many of the limitations of the music. Poetry, being based on language, always has a *communicative* content, however allusive it may be. On the other hand, any paraphrase would destroy half the meaning of a poem. The transformation, in the presentation of a message, which poetry requires, is essentially numerical, for metre, the defining characteristic of poetry, is a numerical principle. The result, in traditional oral poetry, is that standard phrases, which are easily memorable and satisfy the principle, are at a premium.[22] There are alternative principles, such as alliteration[23] and rhyme, but in common with metre, they require that the language used in poetry be *measured* in numbered units, so as to determine the incidence of the characteristic *markings* of the particular oral culture. The recognition of poetry is not just a matter for those who recite it, but also for the audience,[24] who can be relied upon to spot any fault, such as that of 'The Young Man of Milan':

> There was a young man of Milan,
> Whose poems, they never would scan;
>   When asked why it was,
>   He said, 'It's because
> I always try to get as many words into the last
> line as I possibly can'.

One does not need to count to know that there are far too many syllables in the last line, to satisfy the rule that the five lines in a limerick should count 8, 8, 5, 5 and 8 syllables. This last line conveys its message twice over, first numerically and then linguistically: the point would be made even to someone who spoke no English, provided he was familiar with this verse form.[25] The idea behind poetry is that rhythm, which is an essential property of music, can be imposed upon speech, but the principle can be extended so as to define poetry as any declamation, which both to those who declaim and

109

those who listen, is ordered according to some recognisable numerical principle. This does not mean, for instance, that all those who belonged to the culture in which the Homeric epics first appeared were ever concerned to analyse them in terms comparable to those of modern classical scholarship, but simply that the correct form itself was immediately recognisable. Furthermore, the actual performers must have been conscious of the linguistic requirements of this form, which is one reason that the familiar phrases – 'rosy-fingered dawn', 'swift-footed Archiles' and so on – were constantly repeated. Once again, these requirements are essentially numerical.

Song is most simply defined as poetry set to music, but we must then recognise that what music gives to a poem is melody, and that, sometimes, at the cost of its ordinary spoken rhythm. According to the numerical analysis of the previous section, pitch comes to play a dominant role. So much is this the case that some musical settings make song out of what would otherwise be prose: an example is the plainsong of the medieval Church.[26] Sometimes the process can go even further, so that the human voice is used to produce a melody, not based on any sort of text. In such a case, which can be extended to include humming, and even whistling,[27] the voice is used almost as a musical instrument. This is also its primary role where song is used to accompany some other activity, such as work[28] or dancing.[29] Of course song may itself have an instrumental accompaniment, but this is probably more usual in an advanced culture.

An extrinsic numerical pattern may also be imposed upon both verse and song: in Western culture this appeals particularly to children, who can recite 'One, two, buckle my shoe' or sing 'The twelve days of Christmas'. A much more elaborate case is the 119th psalm, in its original Hebrew version: this consists of 22 eight-lined *stanzas*, so that in every stanza each line begins with the same letter, in the order of the Hebrew alphabet. A part of the psalm is shown in figure 12, which also shows how the Hebrew letters are also used as numbers. This case is significant, not only because it is an early example of the use of numbers in a religious context, but also because it represents the beginning of a tradition, which some hundreds of years later with the Kabbala – led to an extremely involved mystical use of numbers.

Just as the spoken word provides the link between poetry and music, so also is the link between dance and music provided by the *structured* movement of the human body. However this approach is not sufficient to define 'dance', for in the s̈ame way as the human voice can be used to produce a succession of *structured* sounds, which are neither poetry nor song, so can the human body move in any number of *structured* ways which no one would describe as dancing. Gymnastics, acrobatics and marching, to mention only a few possibilities, are clearly different from dancing, even when they are accompanied by music,[30] although it is only in the case of

PSALMI 119. קיט

#		
11	בְּלִבִּי צָפַנְתִּי אִמְרָתֶךָ	לְמַעַן לֹא אֶחֱטָא־לָךְ:
12	בָּרוּךְ אַתָּה יְהוָה	לַמְּדֵנִי חֻקֶּיךָ:
13	בִּשְׂפָתַי סִפַּרְתִּי	כֹּל מִשְׁפְּטֵי־פִיךָ:
14	בְּדֶרֶךְ עֵדְוֹתֶיךָ שַׂשְׂתִּי	כְּעַל כָּל־הוֹן:
טו	בְּפִקּוּדֶיךָ אָשִׂיחָה	וְאַבִּיטָה אֹרְחֹתֶיךָ:
16	בְּחֻקֹּתֶיךָ אֶשְׁתַּעֲשָׁע	לֹא אֶשְׁכַּח דְּבָרֶךָ:
17	גְּמֹל עַל־עַבְדְּךָ אֶחְיֶה	וְאֶשְׁמְרָה דְבָרֶךָ:
18	גַּל־עֵינַי וְאַבִּיטָה	נִפְלָאוֹת מִתּוֹרָתֶךָ:
19	גֵּר אָנֹכִי בָאָרֶץ	אַל־תַּסְתֵּר מִמֶּנִּי מִצְוֹתֶיךָ:
כ	גָּרְסָה נַפְשִׁי לְתַאֲבָה	אֶל־מִשְׁפָּטֶיךָ בְכָל־עֵת:
21	גָּעַרְתָּ זֵדִים אֲרוּרִים	הַשֹּׁגִים מִמִּצְוֹתֶיךָ:
22	גַּל מֵעָלַי חֶרְפָּה וָבוּז	כִּי עֵדֹתֶיךָ נָצָרְתִּי:
23	גַּם יָשְׁבוּ שָׂרִים בִּי נִדְבָּרוּ	עַבְדְּךָ יָשִׂיחַ בְּחֻקֶּיךָ:
24	גַּם־עֵדֹתֶיךָ שַׁעֲשֻׁעָי	אַנְשֵׁי עֲצָתִי:
כה	דָּבְקָה לֶעָפָר נַפְשִׁי	חַיֵּנִי כִּדְבָרֶךָ:
26	דְּרָכַי סִפַּרְתִּי וַתַּעֲנֵנִי	לַמְּדֵנִי חֻקֶּיךָ:
27	דֶּרֶךְ־פִּקּוּדֶיךָ הֲבִינֵנִי	וְאָשִׂיחָה בְּנִפְלְאוֹתֶיךָ:
28	דָּלְפָה נַפְשִׁי מִתּוּגָה	קַיְּמֵנִי כִּדְבָרֶךָ:
29	דֶּרֶךְ־שֶׁקֶר הָסֵר מִמֶּנִּי	וְתוֹרָתְךָ חָנֵּנִי:
ל	דֶּרֶךְ־אֱמוּנָה בָחָרְתִּי	מִשְׁפָּטֶיךָ שִׁוִּיתִי:
31	דָּבַקְתִּי בְעֵדְוֹתֶיךָ	יְהוָה אַל־תְּבִישֵׁנִי:
32	דֶּרֶךְ־מִצְוֹתֶיךָ אָרוּץ	כִּי תַרְחִיב לִבִּי:
33	הוֹרֵנִי יְהוָה דֶּרֶךְ חֻקֶּיךָ	וְאֶצְּרֶנָּה עֵקֶב:
34	הֲבִינֵנִי וְאֶצְּרָה תוֹרָתֶךָ	וְאֶשְׁמְרֶנָּה בְכָל־לֵב:
לה	הַדְרִיכֵנִי בִּנְתִיב מִצְוֹתֶיךָ	כִּי־בוֹ חָפָצְתִּי:
36	הַט־לִבִּי אֶל־עֵדְוֹתֶיךָ	וְאַל אֶל־בָּצַע:
37	הַעֲבֵר עֵינַי מֵרְאוֹת שָׁוְא	בִּדְרָכֶךָ חַיֵּנִי:

הקם

Fig. 12. Psalm 119 in the original Hebrew.

dancing, that musical accompaniment is essential (Brinson 1985:208). This does not mean that dancing adds nothing to the numerical structure of the music that accompanies it. The intricate rule governing the dance-steps to be taken successively, by individual dancers, in such familiar forms as square-dancing and highland reels, is not reflected by anything in the musical accompaniment, which is likely to go on repeating itself until every dancer has performed individually. In this sense, dance music can be compared to the case of a song, where the music repeats itself with every verse: it would, for instance, be difficult to compose a musical accompaniment for Psalm 119 such that listeners would recognise a numerical structure isomorphic to that of the Hebrew words.[31] Yet there is an inherent difference between dance and song in the fact that the act of dancing, in contrast to that of singing, does not and cannot produce music that is in any sense complete in terms of the four basic properties introduced at the beginning of this chapter.[32] As part of its play, a child may imitate a dance, in recognisable form, but as an adult it will put away such childish things. Consequently dance is necessarily more of a performance than verse or song, which may make up for the fact that the elements of dance, in the form of the different steps and gestures, have not the same inherent power to communicate. True there are songs without words (Spencer 1985:13), and dances, such as the Indian 'mudras' which 'can relate an entire narrative, with gestures that act as nouns, verbs and modifiers' (Blacking 1985:71), but they are not the general case. There are also interesting special cases, such as the choreographed speeches of the Tonga (Kaeppler 1985:102), in which the structural elements of dance and verse are combined in such a way that the message transmitted in part describes the action taking place – an instance of double articulation comparable to that of *The Young Man of Milan*. In this case, at least, the description is not in numerical terms.

Aesthetics and meaning

In any culture the individual must learn both the emotional and the intellectual response to music and dance. Blacking's (1985:65) assertion that 'Discourse about dance, as about any nonverbal communication, really belongs to metaphysics, because it is strictly speaking, an unknowable truth' is equally true about music. If, for the anthropologist, 'what is[...]interesting about dance and music is the possibility that they generate certain kinds of social experience that can be had in no other way, and[...]constitute a link between the behavioural and cultural aspects of movement and the social and cultural aspects of ritual', in the present context the important question is how the essential numerical base of music and dance is related to the properties stated by Blacking. We can ask the same question of song and verse. It is important to note, first, that the meaning attributed to numbers

112

is also metaphysical, unless they have a clear physical basis, such as is relatively seldom encountered in traditional cultures.[33] If, then, any such meaning comes across in music and dance, then it is a case of one metaphysic imposed upon another. But does this ever happen in practice?

It is easier to answer this question in relation to poetry, where the use of numbers in both form and content is more immediately apparent. With poetry, numerical formulas are important for indicating genre. An example is the 'terza rima', in Dante's Divine Comedy (Candler 1910:20),[34] which determines the mechanical pattern of both metre and rhyme throughout the entire work. In Dante's time the basic numerology was an essential part of poetic 'technique; it was not an imposed doctrine but a thoroughly practical aid to planning and executing the writing of a poem, and the symbolism of numbers they used added another dimension of meaning to their readers' understanding' (Anderson 1980:117). The parallel with musical forms was also deliberate. The *canzone* form, which Dante also used, (though not in the Divine Comedy), corresponded to a song-form based on two repeated melodies, in opposition to each other, but in a form determined according to numerological principles. Where Dante's formulas were adapted for use in works of epic length, the Japanese, on the other side of the world, developed the analogous forms of the *haiku* and the *tanka* for the composition of highly stylised epigrams. The former comprised 17 syllables, divided 5-7-5 into three lines, and the latter, 31 syllables, divided 5, 7, 5, 7, 7 into five lines. In either case, the number of syllables, and the way they are divided between the lines, are a signal that an example of the related verse form is being recited, so that the listeners have certain definite aesthetic expectations. The form is that of the musical recitatif: in Japanese, 'uta', the normal word for both song and verse, blurs the distinction between the two. The point is that all language has both a paradigmatic and a syntagmatic axis (Milner 1971:254), with the content or meaning of any given verse defining the former, and its form, the latter, with or without musical accompaniment. The two are related: once the form is apparent, the content must satisfy certain aesthetic principles.[35] It follows that 'as we listen to a message along its syntagmatic axis, paradigmatic messages, more or less deeply embedded in our memory, which contrast or agree with what we are now hearing, are continually reaching us' (ibid.: 255). The numerical basis of the form does not necessarily connote other contexts, governed by the same numbers, but it may do so. This is almost certainly true of almost any of the poetic works of Dante, but not, apparently, of the *haiku* or the *tanka*.[36] The embedded paradigmatic messages define, in their totality, the aesthetic for any individual.

The conclusions reached in the previous paragraph need little modification to apply, specifically, to music and dance. In every case it is important to notice that aesthetic satisfaction depends at least as much on the performers as on the composers: I have already noted that the distinction between the two is often blurred in traditional cultures. If, adapting Apel's (1970:14) definition, aesthetics is the study of the relationship of music to the human senses and intellect, then it must be recognised that this relationship is culturally defined. In the Western world, until very recently, the basis of the musical aesthetic was largely mathematical, with parallels being drawn with arithmetic and astronomy – a tradition as old as Pythagoras. This may still be true of many traditional cultures. On the other hand, if music, and indeed dance, are to be judged as heteronomous arts (ibid.: 15), expressing extraneous themes, in a sort of psychological drama, reflecting human temperaments, passions and moods, then it is a question of '*Affektenlehre*'. This is certainly the case in any social context where 'a transformation takes place within the person...which takes him out of the ordinary world and places him in a world of heightened sensitivity' (Spencer 1985:2). Whether this transformation has some sort of a deep structure, with a numerical base, remains an open question: chapter 2 suggests some directions in which one may look for an answer.

10

Games and chance

The definition and classification of games

Games, as a category of human activity, are easier to recognise than define. Taking two such different games, as hide-and-seek, as played by children, and the Mayan ballgame, where to lose was sometimes to be sentenced to death,[1] it is difficult to see what they have in common. Three properties, which, if not sufficient to define the category unambiguously, are in practice common to almost all games.

First, games are fictive, in that their essential form is divorced from the reality of everyday life. In a sense a game is a performance, comparable to drama, but to be distinguished from it by the essential role of the numerical element. Any game contains an element of fantasy. A game may be a contest, but it is not a war between the contestants. A sport, such as boxing, has an equivocal status: much depends upon the context, so that prizefighting is hardly a game at all. Put another way, games are *anti-economic*, in the sense that any relation they may have to an *economy* is always extrinsic.[2] On the other hand, in the realm of number, competitive sports must be taken into account, in part because of the economic and social consequences which turn on the numerical outcome.

Second, games have a clearly defined context – generally both in time and space. It is not only Eton which has playing-fields. The context is defined not so much by the rules of the game, but by the culture in which it is played, in which the game itself will have any number of well-recognised connotations. Bowls, as played in England, and boules, as placed in France, have an almost identical mathematical basis (as would be reflected in any computer representation), but one does not have to be an anthropologist to realise that the games play a quite different role in the local culture. Third, games are an institution defined by fixed rules. If the rules are not obeyed, the game is not being played (Ahern 1981:59). In this sense the rules are *constitutive*, not *regulative*, but there is, once again, an uncertain area in which the definition becomes blurred. There is no doubt about the status of chess – a *constituted* game par excellence – but what about boxing? Is this a *regulated* fistfight, or a sport *constituted* by the Queensberry rules? It is largely a matter of perspective, but the perspective of the anthropologist, at least in the context of numeracy, must be one from which games are seen as *constituted*: this is also essential for any formal numerical analysis.

Now according to the threefold definition given in the preceding paragraphs, games are pre-eminently an instance of what Moravetz (1973:860) has called a 'closed practice'. In the context of numeracy, it is significant that the same is true of anything in pure mathematics. This does not mean, of course, that there is somehow a one-to-one correspondence between instances of games and instances of pure mathematics. It does make it reasonable, however, to investigate the relationship between the two, as will be done in the following section. But first one must continue with the classification of games.

In a study of numeracy it is appropriate to rank games according to the degree to which they are defined, and their strategy determined, by their numerical – or logical – basis. (This is inherent in the *constituent* rules, as I defined above: this need not necessarily involve any such strategy, as appears to be the case among the populations of Papua New Guinea studied by Lancy (1983:117).) In any case, the first thing to look at is the instrumentality of any particular game, that is, the equipment needed for play. A football and an open field have a relationship to the rules of Association Football quite different to that of a chessboard, with the chessmen in the opening position, to the rules of chess. A distinction, such as that between *playing with a football* and *playing football*, can hardly be made in regard to chess. Some types of equipment, such as dice or a pack of cards, have an unequivocal numerical character, without being specific to any one game, but – leaving aside such marginal activities as building card-houses – they can still only be used for games constituted on a logical basis. In practice the distinction between games, such as chess, to which the rules are *intrinsic*, and those such as football, to which they are *extrinsic*, may be most significant in relation to the populations, or culture groups, which choose to play one rather than the other. In any case an *extrinsic* game may be given an *intrinsic* character by imposing upon it a system of scoring, together with any extra equipment as this may require – such as goal-posts in football. At a higher, social level of organisation, the same structure, in such forms as 'league' or 'knock-out' competitions, may be imposed on two quite unrelated games, such as football and chess. The point to be noted here, and to be considered further in the following section, is that the generality of these structures is defined by their common mathematical basis.

Games may also be classified according to a scale whose end-points Caillois (1955:78f.) has defined as 'agon' and 'alea'. *Agon* – a Greek word meaning 'fight' or 'conflict' – is characteristic of an *open* game in which the players are perfectly informed of the state of play, at any time, so that extraneous chance can play no part in determining strategy. It is a common characteristic of boardgames, such as chess and the Japanese *go*, and field-games, such as football, or Tikopia darts. The only uncertainty is then about the other players' future strategy. *Alea* – the Latin word for 'dice' – is characteristic of games of pure chance, in which strategy can play no part at all. There are remarkably few games which satisfy this criterion, and, judged intellectually they are almost bound to be trivial.[3] By extension alea represents the element commonly called 'luck' in any game, so that intuitively games like backgammon or poker – which depend upon the throw of dice or the draw of a card – are seen as combining elements of both *agon* and *alea*.

From the perspective of the individual player, another distinction, between '*paidia*' and '*ludus*' (Caillois 1955:81), provides a basis for classification. *Paidia*, which Caillois derives from the Greek word for 'child', describes a game which is pure diversion. The examples given do not fall within the categories of *agon* and *alea*, and are more akin to play without any discernible regulative basis. *Paidia* is characteristic of the very young child who mimics the playing of a game without having realised that the object is to *win*. It is an element also in such diversions as amusement arcades provide for adults, where the significance of winning is trivial in comparison to the input demanded of the player. *Ludus*, the opposite of *paidia*, characterises those games where the player is wholly intent on a successful outcome. Such solitary pastimes, as solving chess problems or crossword puzzles, or playing any form of patience, fall pre-eminently within this category. Comparing the two categories, *paidia* relates to the theatrical,[4] and *ludus* to the strategical aspects of the game.

The categories introduced above are designed to provide the terms of reference to be used in the rest of this chapter, rather than the basis of a taxonomy of games such as is suggested by Caillois (1955:83f.). The analysis will proceed in two different directions. Games will be looked at, first, intensively, according to their numerical basis, and second, extensively, according to their role in culture and society.

The logical structure of games

Games foreshadow the acquisition of elementary mathematical skills in the intellectual development of the child. More generally, play – which, in the absence of rules fixed by outside convention, may be seen as the precursor of games – is the main source of the symbols used by the child to create its own cognitive universe. At an early stage the child can then accept rules, which define a true game, even though their formal mathematical character is beyond its understanding.

The game which the Japanese know as *janken* illustrates this point. This is the familiar, 'scissors, stone and paper' game, which appears in different symbolic forms in any number of cultures.[5] The two players, after reciting together the incantation '*jan-ken-po*', each indicate one of these three objects by means of a conventional sign made with the right hand. The winner is decided on the principle that scissors cut paper, paper wraps up a stone, while a stone blunts scissors. The game is a tie where both players make the same sign. What could be simpler? Little Japanese children can be seen endlessly playing this game in the school playground. But the mathematical theory is both profound and difficult,[6] and becomes even more so when the game is extended to cover several players, and used to determine which of them should be detailed for some communal chore.[7]

Patol, a game played by Indians of the American south-west, resembles Ludo, in that it is a race around a circular track, with each player having his own starting point, and being subject to the risk of capture. A player moves in turn over a number of separately defined posts – corresponding to the squares in Ludo – according to the points scored by the throw of three flat sticks, marked differently on each side as shown in figure 13. This, the essential numerical basis of the game, is no more than an alternative to throwing a die. Now in a version of Ludo known in France as 'Maisonette', the faces of the die are marked not in spots, but with one of six signs, representing a house, a tree, a tulip, an apple, a bird and a pair of cherries. The squares on the board are marked successively with the same signs, which are repeated some eight times to complete the entire circuit. A player, throwing the die, simply moves to the next square bearing the symbol coming up on top. Now a moment's thought is sufficient to know that the three games – *patol*, ludo and *maisonette* – are simply structural trans-formations of each other. Essentially they are identical, but each has its own cognitive basis, appropriate to the social category of the players: where *patol* is a game for adults, *maisonette* is for children who have not yet learnt to count.

The intellectual basis of games is universal and logical, rather than particularistic and linguistic. In practical terms, any observer of a strange culture will learn to understand its games before any other part of it. Some of the games played may already be part of his own culture, or at least have a common underlying structure. A French visitor to Tikopia would soon note the similarity between the rules of the dart-game (described on page 122) and those of his own *jeu de boules*. The instrumentality of games may vary – as already illustrated by the variants of ludo described above – while the basic rules remain the same. The role of language is essentially subordinate. Even if the use of the Japanese language is essential for teaching a Japanese child *janken*, the child, once it has learnt the game, will have little difficulty in playing it with another who knows not a word of Japanese. The linguistic demands of almost any game[8] are restricted and undemanding,[9] so that, in

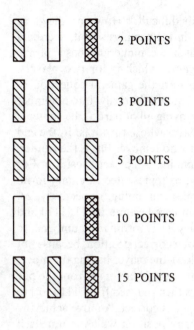

2 POINTS

3 POINTS

5 POINTS

10 POINTS

15 POINTS

ALL MARKED ON ONE SIDE

ONE MARKED ON OTHER SIDE

TWO LEFT ON OTHER SIDE

Fig. 13. The throwing-sticks for the game of Patol.

actual play, an extremely involved game such as contract bridge can get by with a basic vocabulary of less than thirty words, of which about a half will be numerical.[10] It does not matter that a textbook on bridge strategy demands both a much larger vocabulary and some understanding of the syntax of the language in which it is written.

The numerical principles governing strategy are hidden at such a deep level that for many familiar games, such as chess or backgammon, they have only been fully explored in our own generation, and then with the help of electronic computers. In this, games are but an instance of a phenomenon common enough in the realm of mathematics, that the proof of an elementary proposition can be extraordinarily difficult.[11] However, the game of *nim*, to which Hardy and Wright (1945), in their analysis of it, ascribe a Chinese origin (ibid.: 116f.), is one in which the numerical basis of the winning strategy is relatively simple. The game, which is for two players, moving alternately, is purely numerical. To start the game, a collection of identical small objects, or counters, is divided quite arbitrarily, into a number of separate piles. A move then consists of removing all or part of the contents of any one pile, to be freely chosen by the player whose turn it is. In the end there will only be one pile left, and the player who removes this is the winner.

The mathematical analysis depends on defining a 'correct' position. For this the number of counters in each pile must be represented in binary form. Suppose, for example, that there are three piles containing, respectively, 23, 14 and 17 counters. In binary form these numbers become 10111, 1110 and 10001. These are then added up, as if they were ordinary numbers, to produce, in the present case, 21222. This is not a correct position, because not all the digits in this number are even. This allows the player having the move, to convert it to a correct position – in this case by subtracting 8 from the pile containing 14 counters. The binary number is then reduced from 1110 to 110 (= 6), and the total from 21222 to 20222, which is correct. A move achieving this result can be proved to be possible in any position which is not itself 'correct'. A player confronted with a correct position, can only create an incorrect position, since whatever move he makes, by the logic of binary arithmetic, will either add or subtract 1 from one of the even numbers comprising the total, so that in the result, one at least of these numbers will be odd. It follows that the first player making a move which establishes a correct position must win the game, provided he continues to follow the strategy given above with every successive move. If the opening position is correct (which is mathematically improbable, though always possible), then the first player to move will lose if his opponent always moves so as to re-establish a correct position.

The fact that the numerical strategy of *nim* can be explained in a single paragraph means that the game is essentially trivial. True, a certain level of arithmetical sophistication may be necessary to count in binary numbers, but for the Chinese at least, with their familiarity with the *I Ching* and the *mandala*, this was no great problem. In a sense nim is a sort of non-game: its main interest is to be found in the simple arithmetical base of the winning strategy.

The distinction made in the preceding section, between games with an intrinsic, and those with an extrinsic logical structure, takes an extreme form in its application to strategy. In the intrinsic case the logical demands of strategy, for any serious game, such as chess or *go*, transcend the skills of even the best players. A chess player, however good, always plays below par. (It is the absence of such demands which makes *nim* so trivial.) In the extrinsic case the logical demands of strategy are below the level of *nim*: a child of five knows that to win at football you have to score more goals than the other side, and there is really nothing more to be said. Quite simply, the demands of strategy are not in the realm of logic or number.[12] Oddly enough, there is no middle ground, occupied by games with an elementary, though non-trivial, logical basis of strategy, complemented by the sort of non-intellectual skills demanded by, say, football.

The point is extremely interesting, and reflects surprisingly deep philosophical issues. The distinction made in this chapter between *intrinsic* and *extrinsic* corresponds to that between the *transcendental* and the *immanent*. The instrumentality of a game like chess, as represented by the board and the chessmen, is no more than one possible reification of something essentially abstract going on in the minds of the players. This representation can undergo any number of transformations without losing its essential structure: this is what makes it possible to play chess by correspondence. Chess has its own inherent cosmic order. Association Football is order which the rules impose upon the chaos of kicking a ball around an open space, but then the skill shown by sports commentators in evoking the play of a league match is not even a first step on the way to playing football by correspondence. Indeed, in the extrinsic case, the immediate protagonists may be beyond the reach of any sort of rules. As a game between cocks, the Balinese cockfight, as described by Geertz (1973:412–54), cannot be subjected to any logical order, but this does not prevent its being embedded in the numerical culture of Bali. As the following section will show, this approach misses the point entirely, 'for it is only apparently that cocks are fighting. Actually it is men' (ibid.: 417).

Two quite unrelated games, *oware*, a board game to be found not only throughout Africa, but also in other parts of the world,[13] and darts, as played in Tikopia, can be used to exemplify the two categories, of intrinsic and extrinsic games. I chose these two instances to show that both categories can occur in traditional societies, quite independently of any contact with an advanced mathematical culture. There are a number of different versions of *oware*, but in every case it is a game between two players, each commanding a row of six holes in a wooden board, every one of which contains, in the opening position, four seeds or counters, as illustrated in figure 14. In the simplest case, to be found in West Africa (Zaslavsky 1979:118), the board contains no more than the two rows of six holes, so that to begin with each player has 24 counters, equally divided between the holes on his side of the board.

A move consists of taking all the counters out of one of one's own holes, and distributing them, one by one, in an anti-clockwise direction, in successive holes. For this purpose the board is treated as one whole, with the result that the counters can be left, also, in holes belonging to the opponent.

PLAYER TWO

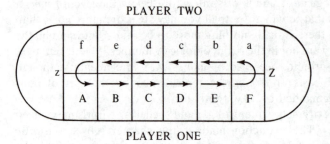

PLAYER ONE

Fig. 14. The layout of the *oware* board.

This is essential for the strategy of the game, since the object is to capture one's opponent's counters. This occurs whenever one can leave one of own's own counters in a hole containing either one or two, but no other number, of the opponent's counters. (It is easy to see that this makes captures impossible in the opening moves of the game.) A player wins by being the first to capture a majority – that is more than 24 – of the counters.

The game seems quite elementary: a player never has more than six possible moves to choose from, and there is no element of chance beyond the uncertainty – common to any such open game – about the future strategy of one's opponent. The game, however, requires great skill, and is a serious pastime in any number of different cultures. Its basis is purely numerical, and it hardly requires counting beyond what can be seen at a glance, by the process known as subitising.

The Tikopian darts game is an example of a wide range of 'field-sports' in which the highest score, in any round, is obtained simply by throwing an object so that it lands closer to a fixed point than similar objects thrown by opponents. As already noted, its formal structure is more or less identical to that of bowls in England, or *boules* in France, and like these games it has its own site or 'arena' – known in Tikopia as the '*marae*' (Firth 1930:65), and comprising an area some 130 yards long, and 6 or 7 yards wide. Successful strategy depends almost entirely on physical skill in throwing the darts – which indeed have more the dimensions of a javelin.

The distinctive feature of the Tikopian darts game is the highly complicated method of scoring, which makes it difficult for either side to obtain a complete victory (Firth 1930:71), simply because a single winning round by one side can wipe out the entire score accumulated by the other (ibid.: 69). (A 'back to square one' rule of this kind is surprisingly common in traditional games.) As in any extrinsic game, the numerical basis is confined to the method of scoring, which is essential to endow the game with any sort of 'winning strategy'.

The classification of games on the basis of the distinction between *agon* and *alea* leaves surprisingly little room for any middle ground, even though any number of games combine both 'skill' and 'chance'. Quite simply, where, in any game, a player has a choice in his reaction to a chance outcome, logic or, indeed, common sense – depending upon the nature of the game – insists that one choice is better than another. Chance determines the cards dealt to a poker-player, but skill determines how he calls them. It may be proved, mathematically, that in the long run skill always wins over chance, although only professional players may realise this.[14] It is absolutely true that only a bad player blames his cards. The point will come up again in the following section, because in the context of almost any culture, intuition always wins over logic – at least when it comes to games.

Hierarchy, opposition and reversal: games in culture and society

Judged in terms of culture, games have something of the character of a *rite de passage*. They represent a temporary shift from a normal to an abnormal order of social relations (Leach 1966:134). As noted on page 115 they take place in a clearly defined context, and are governed by constitutive rules, which outside that context can have no more than metaphorical significance.[15] Furthermore, as Firth (1930:72) has noted of *Tika*, the Tikopia version of darts, a game may have 'a jargon of its own, words which in addition to their normal general meaning have acquired a special meaning in this context, and which are therefore difficult to translate except in descriptive terms of the game itself'. The question which the anthropologist must then ask is what are the social relations which games themselves establish and maintain. The answer to this question is directly related to the cultural significance of games: indeed it is the participants' own understanding of the games which largely determines their social role. The following analysis will focus on games which, according to Geertz's definition cited on page 125, are deep in the sense that society is seriously involved in their outcome. This is an aspect of the distinction made on page 117 between *paidia* and *ludus*: games of pure diversion, falling under the head of *paidia*, even if reflecting significant aspects of the local culture, are much more marginal to society. This remains true even where they are the only games played.[16] The class of participants may extend far beyond the actual players. It may include not only spectators, but any number of people, who, if absent from the actual spectacle, are still involved in the outcome of the game, even sometimes against their own will.[17] In the Tikopia darts game, the choice of the sides 'resolves itself largely along the lines of the traditional opposition of the two districts of the island, Faea and Ravenga' (Firth 1930:68), and anyone who takes part always plays for the same side, with membership being determined by the kinship group in which he is born. The side 'is the basic feature of the match; it persists generation after generation while the individual members drop out and are replaced. The score, the focus of interest, is kept for the side alone, and no total is made of the winning throws of any single player' (ibid.:95).

The whole island community is involved in the darts game, and it is not surprising that it takes place only very occasionally. The fact that the score, at any given time, registers a hierarchical ordering between the two districts of the island is a 'constant factor of discordance' (ibid.: 95), but any meeting between the two is 'apt to be characterized by mutual suspicion and distrust' (Firth 1963:72). On the other hand, both the method of scoring – as described on p. 122 – and the ritual by which the winners, at any stage, console the losers (Firth 1930:70), are designed to maintain equilibrium. The result is that the game reinforces the balanced opposition between the two districts, which is established in Tikopia tradition.

The Balinese cockfight, is an *ad hoc* gathering, brought into focus by a discrete activity – 'a particular process that reoccurs rather than a continuous one which endures' (Geertz 1973:424): this is a characteristic of any game, but in this case gambling is 'the aspect of cockfighting around which all others pivot' (ibid.: 425). This incorporates cockfighting in the money circuit, which is the numerical institution par excellence.

Money, brought into the context of a game, by the institution of gambling, may be seen as a sort of reification of the chances of every player, or collectivity of players. A bet defines the chances of the outcome of the game, as seen by the players at the time it is made. In an intrinsic game – as defined in the preceding section – the exact chances may be determinable by statistical methods, so that strategy consists of foisting on one's opponents odds loaded in one's own favour in terms of the statistical outcome. In the end all one needs to win at a game like poker is to be exceptionally skilled in a rather specialist branch of mathematics.[18] But betting is possible on any uncertain outcome, whether it be the winner of a game, or tomorrow's weather. Gambling, may be defined as betting confined to outcomes which occur in the context of a game.[19] The game may be intrinsic or extrinsic, with this difference, that in the latter case, success depends on what punters call 'studying form', that is, being ahead of one's opponents in one's knowledge of factors, which cannot be measured statistically, such as the present condition of the horses – or the cocks.

In such a situation, the gamblers can form opposing coalitions on the basis of their presumed knowledge, but in a case such as that of the Balinese cockfight, this is conditioned by social factors. Indeed, in this case there are two sorts of bets. The first, for large sums of money and at even odds, is between coalitions clustering around the owners of the cocks. The second is for small sums staked by individuals, at uneven odds, according to the paradigm, 10–9, 9–8 and so on down to 2–1. The first sort of bet is made, almost furtively, at the centre of the ring, with the umpire mediating between the two coalitions, each being led by the owner of the cock. Only when the size of the bet, which may be very large, is announced, do the individual spectators start their round of betting. The bets are small, and, if at first, long odds tend to be offered, they tend to shorten towards the top end of the scale when the centre bet is large, for this reflects the conviction, on the part of those who should know best, that the cocks are evenly matched. In this case also the largest number of separate bets may be expected. The analytical problem is to reconcile the formal asymmetry between the balanced centre bets and the unbalanced side bets (Geertz 1973: 429).

In practice, however, 'the two betting systems, though formally incongruent, are not really contradictory[...]but are part of a single larger system in which the center bet is[...]the "center of gravity", drawing, the larger it is the more so, the outside bets toward the short-odds end of the scale. The center bet thus "makes the game", or[...]signals what[...]I am going to call its "depth" (Geertz 1973:431).

At this point it is worth noting that the operation is conceived of in almost purely mathematical terms. As the centre bet gets larger, the odds on the side bets tend to one, and the game gets deeper[20] – although one should note that 'deep' in this context is a metaphor. The numerical character of a deep game is defined by the fact that the money at stake is more than the protagonists can reasonably afford to lose, so that the whole operation cannot be judged according to the purely economic criteria or utility and disutility. What is at stake – esteem, honour, dignity, respect – is far more than material gain, and it is precisely because money matters so much in Bali, that this is so (Geertz 1973:433–4). On the basis of Geertz's sample, there was a direct correlation between the even matching of the fighting cocks, and the size of the centre bets, so that those who confined their gambling to the largest fights were the most likely to come out even in the long run. The chronic losers were the compulsive gamblers who made too many bets at long odds in 'shallow' fights. Whatever the mathematical logic, the system, as so described, favours those already at the top of the hierarchy in a very status conscious society, so that 'what makes Balinese cockfighting deep is thus not money in itself, but what, the more of it that is involved the more so, money causes to happen: the migration of the Balinese status hierarchy into the body of the cockfight' (ibid.:436). And to adapt an old adage, it is all done with numbers. Finally, to return to a point made at the beginning of this chapter, the cockfight is fictive – a theatrical performance in a society directed 'toward spectacle, toward ceremony, toward the public dramatization of the ruling obsessions of Balinese culture: social inequality and status pride' (Geertz 1980:13).

The theme of reversal is not difficult to establish in relation to the games played in any traditional society. In principle, if games represent an abnormal order of existence, as suggested on p. 115, then, except in games of pure chance where *agon* – as defined on p. 116 plays no part – a hierarchy of players alternative to that of the normal order will emerge. It can hardly be otherwise, unless the necessary skills are in some way inborn in the established hierarchy.[21] The lesson from anthropology is that the alternative hierarchy is recognised for what it is, that is, as belonging to a sort of shadow theatre: it is the outcome of the game which counts in the long run, not the status of the individual players. In human terms, after all, the cocks who fight to the death in Bali can have no status, and if these cocks can be surrogates for men, so also can the best dart-throwers in Tikopia, who are in a way no more than puppets playing according to the text inherent in the constitutive rules of the game. One sees this equally in the modern world, where, in any number of popular sports – of which football is but one example – players are 'bought' and 'sold'. The successful star still lives in a fools' paradise. In short even if the game itself reverses the established hierarchy, as soon as it becomes part of the deep structure of society, the reversal will be undone. The alternative, after all, would be intolerable.[22]

The discussion of games in such general terms is in part justified by the fact that they are seldom specific to any one culture. The deeper the formal structure of a game, the more likely it is to cross cultural frontiers by a process of diffusion, as the case of *oware*, examined in the preceding section, illustrates. Not only this, but as noted on p. 118 in the case of the game known variously as ludo, *maisonette* or *patol*, elementary games, with an identical formal structure, can emerge in quite unrelated cultures. Furthermore, as soon as a game becomes organised within society, a new formal structure emerges, defined purely in terms of which side wins, at any stage, without any regard to which game it is that is being played. The social structure of the Balinese cockfight could equally be based on boxing or chess, although neither of these could be embedded in Balinese culture in quite the same way. In the result games are the element of any culture most accessible to an outsider, however marginal they may be within the culture itself. The fact is that almost any game generates its own elementary formal, or mathematical structure, and that at several different levels. The levels are moreover discrete. Strategy (in the case of any intrinsic game), the constitutive rules, and the incorporation of the game as a competition into an established social matrix, may have separate formal structures, but in the last analysis they all operate in numerical terms.[23] Moreover, between successive levels, according to the above analysis, there is a sort of quantum leap in generality and accessibility to the outside observer. A visitor to Japan, for example, who observed the game of *go* in its social context, would have little difficulty in deducing the formal basis of the competition ladder[24] – which could apply to any other competitive sport – and after some time would even begin to deduce the constitutive rules of the game. To master strategy, however, would require a long apprenticeship, and even then the top rungs of the competition ladder would be beyond his reach. At no stage, however, need *go* be culturally specific: nothing distinctive in Japanese culture is essential to it, however fundamental and distinctive its connotations may be in that culture. Essentially, any game is culturally neutral, or put another way, there is no possible cultural ecology of games. Like money, which is itself instrumental in many games,[25] a true game may cross any cultural boundary.

11

Art and architecture

The role of number in visual representation

From the perspective of the culture of numbers the visual arts dispose of a *tabula rasa*, a blank space which can be filled with any sort of representation suitable to the medium used, with the implicit understanding that it will be intelligible to those who are likely to look at it. What may be represented must fit into the cognitive framework of the local culture, and may be further subject to political or religious restrictions. The representation will be a part of a symbolic universe in which numbers have their own part to play. There is no need for a literate culture, in the strict sense, and even where numbers can be represented in writing, their symbolic representation in the field of art is by no means limited to the standard written forms. From the time of the Ming dynasty (1368–1644) different flowers were used to symbolise the twelve months – which in Chinese are simply named after the numerals from one to twelve – so that the *magnolia*, for instance, connotes the number, two, or the *chrysanthemum*, the number, ten (Medley 1982:412). This does not mean that every representation of a chrysanthemum connotes 'ten': this depends upon the context. In an appropriate case the standard written form for *ten* could conceivably connote a 'chrysanthemum'.[1]

Where art presents its subject in recognisable form, the representation of number is dependant upon the choice of subject, so that the role of art itself is, in a sense, subordinate. To take a theme from the Christian tradition, it is almost inconceivable that the apostles, in any portrayal of the last supper, will be anything but twelve in number. But although the number twelve does have a part in Christian numerology (Horn 1975:357), a picture of the Last Supper is a somewhat oblique way of representing any connotation it may have. The problem of representation in the visual arts is that it leaves too little to the imagination, so that a message which is acceptable in an oral or written tradition somehow loses its impact. Language – and this includes numerical symbols – is a sort of veil, and its effect is to allow any number of choices in interpretation (Sperber and Wilson 1986:9f.). So long as one's knowledge of the Last Supper is confined to the versions of the passion

128

narrative to be found in the Bible, one is left free to conceive of it in one's own way,[2] but once it is portrayed that freedom is limited by the interpretation of the artist.[3] The point can be made clearer by taking as one's example, not some narrative from the four gospels made familiar to us by any number of portrayals in the visual arts, but the complex, esoteric symbolism of the Book of Revelation. Consider the following passage (xii:1–6):

And a great portent appeared in heaven, a woman clothed with the sun, with the moon under her feet, and on her head a crown of twelve stars; she was with child, and she cried out in her pangs of birth, in anguish for delivery. And another portent appeared in heaven; behold, a great red dragon, with seven heads and ten horns, and seven diadems upon his head. His tail swept down a third of the stars of heaven, and cast them to the earth. And the dragon stood before the woman who was about to bear a child, that he might devour her child when she brought it forth; she brought forth a male child, one who is to rule all the nations with a rod of iron, but her child was caught up to God and to his throne, and the woman fled into the wilderness, where she has a place prepared by God, in which to be nourished for one thousand two hundred and sixty days.

What happens when this is represented in pictorial form? If the mind boggles at the idea, it must still take note of the fact that the whole of the Book of Revelation is so represented on a fourteenth-century tapestry, now to be found in the castle at Angers in the west of France. The question is, what is the effect on the impact of the message of changing the form of representation? The answer is quite simple. The pictorial representation highlights the numerical elements, so as to bring to mind all the numerological connotations of the numbers mentioned in the text – in addition to the explanation given in a later chapter of the Book of Revelation (xvii:8–12). This is exactly what the population of fourteenth-century France would themselves have looked for, in complete disregard of the sort of theological interpretation suitable for a sermon.[4] The only problem is the period of time of 1,260 days, which, if impossible to present in pictorial form, was undoubtedly significant in terms of the prevailing number mysticism.[5]

If, in the visual arts, the representation of numbers is no more than incidental, there are still special cases where the form adopted has a numerical basis. A tryptich has, by definition, three components, so that in any specifically religious context, such as the retable of an altar, it can represent many different connotations of the number 'three'.[6] More generally a folding screen lends itself to a pattern repeated according to a numerical formula, so that on each of the six panels of the Japanese Torige Tensho Byōbu there are four pairs of Chinese characters in the *tensho*, interlined with four pairs in the *reisho* script (Nakana 1973:30–1), making two sets of forty-eight characters, with each representing a different version of the same text. This is but one example of such screens to be found in China and Japan, some of which are based upon a much more complicated numerical formula.

Fig. 15. Tiles from the Alhambra recorded by M. C. Escher (© 1989 M. C. Escher Heirs/Cordon Art-Baarn-Holland).

Even more generally, certain media lend themselves to numerical representation, restricting, at the same time, the free hand of the artist. This is particularly true of woven material,[7] such as occurs in tapestries and carpets, so it is perhaps not to be wondered at that some of the finest examples come from Persia, where Islam greatly restricted naturalism in art. In practice work in ivory and precious metals, such as is characteristic of reliquaries or the covers of manuscript books, is often governed by similar principles of design, and the same is true – if in lesser degree – of china and earthenware. In the present age, in which sculpture and the graphic arts dominate,[8] it is easy to forget earlier periods in which they were subordinate to other media.[9]

The lesson here is that the most apt numerical basis in the visual arts is one which corresponds to a pattern, whose geometry is such that it can go on multiplying itself for ever; the border then introduces an arbitrary break in a potentially infinite extension (Ettinghausen 1976:72). In the Japanese example given above, the underlying pattern of the folding screens had this property: the bounded system was determined, in this case, by the length of the 48-character message conveyed by the Chinese characters. In Arabic art, which particularly favours geometric representations, a tiled floor provides an ideal context for such indefinite extension.[10]

The question then is, what indeed is the numerical content of such artistic representation? What numbers can a tiled floor represent, if its extent is indefinite? This is not the right question to ask. Instead, one can make two significant points. The first is that the pattern is inherently capable of being programmed numerically, and this being so, it follows that the programme can then be extended so as to incorporate the instruction to repeat itself indefinitely.[11] Now if this proposition was only proved by Turing some fifty years ago, we look at the matter in this way only because 'the computer is[...]the principal technological metaphor of our time' (Bolter 1986:40). We are concerned only with a change of metaphor. The underlying principle is no more than a restatement of the fundamental character of cardinal numbers, as introduced in Chapter 1. Because in any practical application the number of repetitions of the pattern must be finite, the way is always open to give every instance of it its own label or name, as happens with the Chinese and Japanese screens described in the last paragraph but one. The second point is that pattern, in the present sense, is but an example of the more general case of 'an aesthetic based on modular concepts' (Horn 1975:351). A *module* is then the basic unit to be used in the plan of any structure. This provides the link with architecture, although modular structures are fundamental in other art forms such as music. All that is necessary is that the form of the modular units should be such as to allow the whole structure to be composed of them. How the arithmetical conditions imposed by this rule restrict the numbers which can be represented is the theme of the following section.

The place of numbers in architecture

In medieval Europe, the 'seven sciences', with grammar, rhetoric and dialectic on the one hand, and music, astronomy, geometry and arithmetic on the other, were united by their common attribute of *modulatio*, which was the sensible form of the abstract *numeratio* (Jones 1975:311). In the context of architecture this attribute only requires an established form of construction based upon standard units: this means in practice that the ground-plan must be based on adjacent rectangular units. Figure 16 illustrates a simple case, the Rin'ami house from fourteenth-century Japan, which is based upon a six-by-four grid, with six of the squares being divided into two equal rectangles. While such a simple structure may seem to have only a limited potential to make any significant *numerical* statement, it still shows how the modular units must be capable of fitting together.[12] The reasons for this are both architectural and arithmetical.[13]

As for architecture, principles of engineering impose well-recognised limitations on the design of a viable building, if only because of the need to provide adequate support for the roof. If other mathematical considerations demand a non-viable ground-plan – such as at Stonehenge – this cannot be realised as a building in any architectural sense. This limitation suggests that the use of modulation, in the context of architecture, as a means of symbolic expression, is most likely to occur where local building materials are, by their nature, best suited for modular construction. According to this standard wood is far better than stone. A particular case is given by Horn (1975:379), when he points out that 'modular design has been from the remotest periods an intrinsic feature of northern wood construction. The stability of the timbered Germanic house, whose roof was sustained by two rows of posts dividing the interior into a nave and two aisles, required that its roof-supporting posts be joined together at the top: lengthwise by means of plates, and crosswise by means of beams. These timbers divided the space of the house lengthwise into a modular sequence of timber-framed bays.' Leaving aside the north-European case, it is not surprising that Japan, another country with abundant wood, has perhaps gone furthest in applying the principle of modulation, as is illustrated by figure 17 (Itoh 1972:111).

The arithmetical limitations on modular construction are based upon complex theory in pure mathematics, which is extremely difficult to summarise. Intuitively at least, it is not difficult to see that a large rectangular space, divided up into a grid based on a standard minimum unit, cannot simply be filed by just any collection of rectangles, whose sides are measured in the same unit – even if their total area is the same as that of the whole

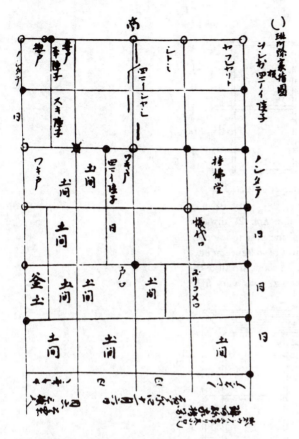

Fig. 16. Plan of the Rin'ami house.

space. Any number of mathematical conundrums depend upon this principle. The problem is largely avoided where the number of units measuring the side of any but the smallest unit, but including the whole structure, is an exact multiple of the corresponding number for all smaller units. Thus if M_1, M_2, M_3... are the lengths of the corresponding sides of the different component units, in ascending order of magnitude, the principle stated requires that M_1 is a divisor of M_2, M_2, a divisor of M_3, and so on. Some flexibility is possible by working with a different series on each axis of the ground plan, but this possibility is likely to be restricted by purely architectural factors. The important point, in any case, is that those who were concerned to use architectural forms for the purposes of number symbolism, were conscious of the arithmetical limitations, in particular because they discouraged the representation of prime numbers. This is one of the points to be illustrated by considering the plan of the early medieval monastic settlement of Saint

133

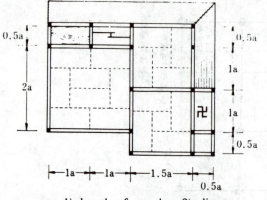

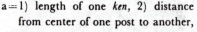

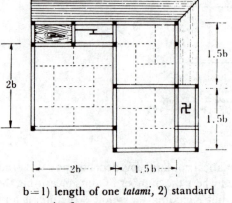

a = 1) length of one *ken*, 2) distance from center of one post to another, 3) standard unit of measurement.
Tatami for any given room are all of the same size, but the size may vary from room to room.

b = 1) length of one *tatami*, 2) standard unit of measurement.
Size of tatami is uniform throughout the plan.
卍 = Buddhist altar

Fig. 17. Japanese modular floor plans.

Gall as explained by Horn (1975), which shows how the modular principles of North-Germanic timber architecture were adapted to the construction of buildings in stone. But by way of contrast it is illuminating to consider first a case from Japan, in which purely numerical principles were allowed to dominate the whole construction.

134

The name of the well-known Buddhist temple of Sanjūsangendō, in Kyoto, means simply the row of 'thirty-three bays', open on one side, which comprise the temple. Architecturally this is the simplest possible case, since the *modules*, identical in size, are laid out along only one dimension. The wooden structure of the building is simply that of a very long barn. This left a free hand to fill it with an immense amount of numerical symbolism, derived from the religious tradition of the Kannon Buddha. The contents consist mainly of 1000 identical statues of the Kannon Buddha, each with 42 hands and 11 small heads surrounding the main head, in 10 rows of 100, to establish a 10×100 modular grid. One much larger statue, of a seated Buddha, but otherwise in the same form, is placed in the centre of the building, to bring the total number up to 1001. Thus four numbers, 11, 33, 42 and 1001 are made explicit by the design of the building and the nature of its contents.

The Kannon Buddha, otherwise known as the 'Regarder of the Cries of the World', is a perfected Bodhisattva characterised by boundless compassion and mercy. In the *Lotus Sutra*, chapter 25 first describes a number of catastrophes in which the Kannon Buddha will come to the rescue, and then goes on to list 33 bodies in which the living will be saved. The number is ultimately derived from the 33 heavens situated on top of the mystical Mount Sumeru, which is ruled by Indra, whose own heaven is located on the central peak, with the 32 other heavens being divided equally between the four cardinal points after the pattern of the Mandala (*The Threefold Lotus Sutra* 1975:147). It is not surprising, therefore, that the number 33 connotes 'boundaries'. It is also a *nombre marginal*, relating directly to the 32 signs distinguishing the body of the Buddha (ibid.:7f.), for by adding to the number 32, with its earthly connotations, the number 1, one enters into the realm of heaven, or unbounded perfection.[14] The number 33 is also to be found in the 33 different figures into which the Kannon Buddha can be transformed, so that the 1001 separate statues in fact represent 33033 separate manifestations of the Kannon Buddha.

The 1,001 statues of the Kannon Buddha also represent a *nobre marginal*. (Compare 1001 with 10001, the binary representation of 33). The 1000 smaller statues represent the product, 25×40, with the number 25 representing the 25 sorts of the life and death of man. The derivation of the number 40 is more involved. Each statue should in principle have 1000 hands, but in fact each hand is taken to represent 25 hands, even though each statue has 42 hands. This number is however reduced to 40, since one pair of hands is clasped together in prayer, while another pair holds a small bowl.[15] As for the 11 smaller heads surrounding the head of the Buddha, the number is made up of three looking forward, symbolising compassion, three looking to the left, symbolising anger, three looking to the right symbolising understanding, one at the back of the head symbolising laughter, and one on top of the head, looking upwards and symbolising perfect harmony. It is important that the heads face in all directions, to show that the Buddha is responsive to all the cries of the world, as well as embracing all possible moral attributes.

In this plan it does not matter that the four key numbers, 11, 33, 42 and 1001 are, arithmetically, not perfectly congruent, since at a certain cost in symmetry the necessary adjustments were made. In particular the absence of fit between the number 1000 (100 × 10), representing the identical statues of the Kannon Buddha, and, 33 (33 × 1), causes no problem, because the first number governs the external dimensions of the building, whereas the second governs the arrangement of its contents. It is still worth noting how the factors, 3, 7 and 11 recur in the four key numbers. Where, however, the principle of *modulatio* is more strictly adhered to, the questions of congruence may well restrict the symbolic representation of certain numbers. For an instance of this case one can return home from Japan, to look at the medieval monastery of Saint Gall, a *locus classicus* of this problem.

The plan of the monastery, shown in figure 18 was designed to incorporate the sacred numbers 3, 4, 7, 10, 12 and 40. In the Christian tradition, three has any number of meanings. Besides the Holy Trinity, there are the three temptations of Christ, and the three days he spent in the tomb. Four is the number of the gospels, and in seven days God created the world. Ten are the ten commandments, and twelve are the twelve apostles.[16] Forty is the number of days Christ remained on earth after his resurrection. The designers were conscious of plenty of other connotations of these numbers (Horn 1975:353–9), but the question is how they were realised in the plan.

To start with, the church is constructed according to a system of squares (figure 19), whose basic unit is the area of the intersection of nave and transept. This forms a forty-foot square *module*, which controls the layout not only of all the remaining units of the church, but also of the entire aggregate of buildings forming the cloister (Horn 1975:358). The entire site is a 16 × 12 rectangle composed of such *modules*. What is more, buildings, or for that matter their contents, too small to be measured in multiples of 40 feet, are measurable as integral multiples of a standard unit of $2\frac{1}{2}$ feet, obtained by halving 40 four times in succession (ibid.: 359). On the basis of square *mini-modules* derived in this way, even the monks' beds can be measured as three adjacent units, so that non-congruent numbers, such as 3, 7 and 12 could still be represented at such microscopic level.

At macroscopic level, as determined by the whole ground-plan, 3, 7 and 12 could not easily be represented, although the whole precinct could be seen as consisting of a 3 × 4 layout of 12 large 160-foot-square *modules* (Horn 1975:355). The numbers could also be represented by buildings of certain restricted categories, such as the three buildings of the northern precinct, or the seven buildings comprised in the core-complex dominated by the church.

136

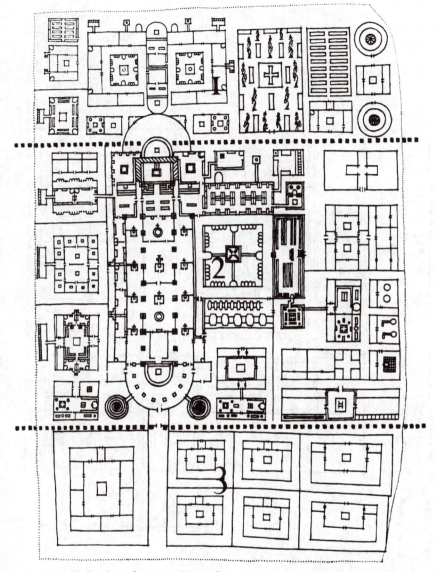

Fig. 18. St Gall, plan of monastery precinct.

The significant distinction between Sanjūsangendō and Saint Gall is that whereas in the former case the numerical demands of Kannon Buddhism were allowed to determine the whole design of the building, as well as the nature and layout of its contents, in the latter case there is not a single instance of 'a sacred number [being] forced upon any part of the Plan, in

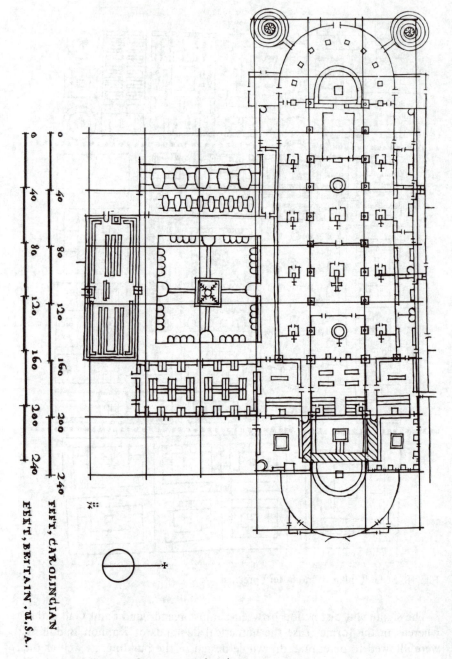

Fig. 19. St Gall, plan of monastery church.

violation of any practical function, or to the detriment of the system of mensuration used in defining these functions' (Horn 1975:384). At the same time, despite the oddness of Sanjūsangendō, it was no more than an instance of well-established principles, ultimately derived from China, where the modular principle had ruled for centuries and architecture made no distinction between sacred and secular buildings (Glahn 1982:442). Saint Gall, in contrast, was highly innovative, and the principles upon which the Plan had been based were only recently established by the construction of the Emperor's palace at Aachen at the beginning of the ninth century. If, at this early stage, there was no question of sacred numbers having binding aesthetic implications (Horn 1975:383), in modular aesthetics the content is still shaped to fit the numerical symbolism chosen (Jones 1975:314). The origins of the modular system, in the context of north European architecture, were – as already noted – to be found in small, purely secular buildings, built in wood. Alternatively, in the context of the graphic arts, the principle was already exemplified in illuminated manuscripts, such as the Lindisfarne Gospels, which were created in Ireland some hundred years before Charlemagne built his palace in Aachen.

The new architecture was the forerunner of all that we think of as Gothic, which extended the modular principle into the third dimension. The principle dominated the design of sacred buildings for seven hundred years, from its first application in Aachen, at the beginning of the ninth century, to such late examples as the Chapel of King's College, Cambridge, which was only completed in 1515. In this latter case the ground plan comprises twelve Pythagorean triangles of $5:12:13$ four-foot *modules*, and the number 26 is dominant. This is a key number in the *kabbala*, a form of Jewish mysticism, already considered in chapter 4, which first appeared in the thirteenth century (Ginsburg 1955:189).

The underlying principle is divine order, which, at least from the time of Augustine of Hippo (354–430), was seen to achieve its most perfect representation in terms of numbers. The scriptural basis is provided by the Wisdom of Solomon (xi:20): 'Thou hast ordered all things in measure, number and weight', so that *modulatio* can be seen as 'the sensible form of the abstract *numeratio*' (Jones 1975:311). Once the principle is established, it generates its own aesthetic, for, following Augustine (De Musica 6.14), 'the inherent beauty results from measure and number, which are successive repetitions of unity'. The same idea is to be found in Hinduism and Buddhism, which require the design of a building to satisfy both physical and metaphysical criteria (Snodgrass 1985:1). *Modulatio* and *numeratio* are the essential principles for the existence of anything, since they are the basis of measurement. The principle that something which cannot be measured, cannot exist, may be strange to us, but the capacity of the principal unity to be infinitely subdivided, is seen as the essential first step in creating cosmos out of chaos (ibid.: 29, 104).

Geomancy and the observation of the heavens

The first two sections of this chapter paid no attention to the location and orientation of the different instances of art and architecture presented. In fact the north–south axis of Sanjūsangendō, or the east–west axis of the abbey church of Saint Gall, are significant, but not in explicitly numerical terms. There are, however, two cases in which location and orientation are at least as important as design and content. Indeed, in cases such as that of Stonehenge, or of any other system of megaliths, the last two factors are of so little importance that a chapter on art and architecture is not the right place to consider them. The same is largely true of the art of geomancy the first case mentioned above, but for a different reason. None the less, because of the critical relationship between geomancy and order, the subject has a place in the present chapter.

Geomancy is a sort of earthly parallel to astrology, with the difference that its foundations could be determined by human designers (Ronan and Needham 1978:198). Put another way, geomancy bears the same sort of relationship to geography as astrology to astronomy. The underlying principle is that in any geographical context there is an ideal arrangement of the topographical features. Any man-made alteration to the landscape, whether relating to the communications infrastructure, or to the design and location of buildings, had to satisfy the requirements of order, as defined in the local culture. In China, geomancy, known as '*fēng-shuǐ*', literally 'wind-water', clearly related the ideal model of order on the face of the earth to that established by the heavenly bodies. The diviner's board, or *shì*, consisted of two layers, an upper disc corresponding to Heaven and a lower square corresponding to Earth (ibid.: 200). In its relation to mathematics, geomancy, not unexpectedly, is closer to geometry than arithmetic: the relation of one to the other is a refraction of that between landscaping and architecture. The idea that there is no essential difference between geometry and arithmetic was really only developed by Descartes at the dawn of the modern age of science (Williams 1978:260), although certain arithmetical equations, such as that relating to a right-angled triangle with all three sides of integral length, had long foreshadowed it. This is no more than an arithmetical instance of Pythagoras' theorem. The point is that once Descartes had established the generality of such equivalences, geomancy was no longer an important factor in design. In any tradition in which it has a prominent place, its close relation to geometry ensured its divorce from the realm of numbers.

The position is significantly changed where astronomical factors determine the location and orientation of buildings and other structures. In this, the second case mentioned above, the observed order of the heavens, as much as any ideal ordering of the earth, is decisive. Two supreme, and indeed related examples are the eighth-century Buddhist temple of Borobudur in Java, and the twelfth-century Hindu temple of Angkor Wat in Cambodia. (Stierlin 1970:134) Both are aligned with other features, both natural and man-made, of the surrounding countryside, according to critical positions of the sun and moon, and similar alignments are incorporated into the layout of internal features. At the same time the modular basis of the architecture is at least as complicated as that of Sanjusangendo[17] or Saint Gall.[18]

Borobudur is essentially a hill covered with stone ornamentation.[19] In spite of periodic restorations[20] the original form of the building is unknown. There is, however, no doubt that it consisted of three square terraces, of diminishing size, connected, on all four sides, by regularly spaced flights of stairs.[21] The uppermost terrace formed the basis for a structure in much the same form, but on a circular ground-plan. This was surmounted by a 'stupa', which was also the form of the whole structure. The *stupa* is a type of Buddhist monument, originating in India, but widespread throughout much of the Buddhist world. Its form is simply that of the monument which the Buddha himself asked to be erected over his ashes after his death. The square base represents the Buddha's folded clothes, the up-turned hemisphere resting upon it, his begging bowl, and the pinnacle, his staff. It relates also to the 'egg of Brahma' in traditional Hinduism. This consisted of a light top half, and a dark lower half, the two being separated from each other by a flat plane representing the earth, the whole structure being held together by a spindle along the vertical axis. The visible, top half, came to be replaced by the world mountain Meru,[22] which was divided into the three worlds of sense, form and shapelessness (Spiro 1971:203). Above this came the four heavens, with the underworld, represented by the bottom half of the egg, being but the mirror image of the whole.[23]

Now every *stupa* embodies a *mandala* (Snodgrass 1985:131), so that the symbolism of the *mandala* is incorporated, at least implicitly. This symbolism is quite explicit in Borobudur, which was designed to be no more than a gigantic *stupa*. What is more, the horizontal surfaces of the monument are covered by a regular succession of smaller and subsidiary *stupas*, laid out according to a perfectly symmetrical ground-plan. The basis of the whole complex, beginning with the one central *stupa* at the highest point of the monument, and then descending through successive levels, is expressed by the numerical series 1, 16, 24, 32, 1472 which in the end leads to an almost uncountable number of *stupas*. This is in fact a deliberate representation of the Buddhist ideal of infinity. This is the basic form of a number of similar, but much smaller monuments, in Java, and elsewhere, where the numbers $1+4$, $1+8$, $1+16$, $1+32$ – which are those of the *mandala* – constantly recur. This representation is also to be found in a number of small stone boxes, divided into 9 or 17 compartments, and dating from an even earlier period, which have been found in Bali and Ceylon, as well as in Java. The *mandala* is indeed the model of Mount Meru, in all its representations.

In Borobudur, as in other similar monuments in Java, everything is focused on the highest point. The fact that the successive layers of squares and circles are connected by any number of flights of stairs makes it clear that Borobudur also represents any number of different ways, each leading ever higher. There is no one correct route to the summit, but an infinity of different possible routes. Whichever is chosen, the pilgrim is confronted also with countless bas-reliefs, covering all vertical surfaces, and representing different events in the history of his faith, and the basic plan remains a rhythmical repetition of the same elements.[24] At the same time, the fact that Borobudur was a replica of the cosmos made its actual position, in relation both to the four cardinal points (which are the basis of *mandala*) and to surrounding natural features, at least as important as the numerical factors incorporated into the design of the building. The architectural and topographical features were but two sides of the same coin.

What did it all mean? In purely political terms the whole complex can be seen as a prestige project of the local prince.[25] The construction of Borobudur and Angkor Wat both placed an almost intolerable demand on the local population, representing therefore not only their most considerable achievement, but also the beginning of the decline of the civilisations which they represented (Bernet Kempers 1960:45). But both constructions were more than just an expression of *folie de grandeur*, for 'it is a recognised phenomenon in the Orient, and elsewhere, that an event only realises its full significance when it is in some way "confirmed" by being linked to some more concrete reality than that in which it actually occurred. This is commonly realised by the building of a monument[26] [...] where the underlying doctrine is represented by texts, pictures and symbols' (ibid.: 126), which, without any doubt, must include also all the numerical factors incorporated into the construction. If only because Buddhism might otherwise be too esoteric to be within the grasp of the common man, the reification of the abstract is almost an obsession, as the example of Sanjūsangendō, considered in the previous section, well illustrates. Numbers are the bridge between the abstract and the concrete. Their purely arithmetical properties can always be represented in wood and stone, for 'architectural work embodies in a tangible form [...] what is intangible' (Snodgrass 1985:4).

While the Hindu temple complex of Angkor Wat is a monumental affair, combining geomantic siting and symbolic architecture, in a parallel tradition to that of Borobudur, the two cases are not entirely comparable. Borobudur is essentially an isolated monument, with no other function than the symbolic representation of Buddhist doctrine. In this sense it is pure display. The medium is the message. Angkor Wat, on the other hand, is a group of buildings, some, such as the two libraries, having a quite practical function. Although it could hardly be called cosy, one could wander – in contrast to Borobudur – around the galleries and temples, in some sort of systematic order, with a roof over one's head. At the same time the group forms a part of a much larger complex – related to the Khmer capital established by King Jayavarman II at the beginning of the ninth century (Stierlin 1970:45). The other groups of buildings are in much the same style, and are clearly related to Angkor Wat by numerical principles.[27] In particular the role of the *stupa* in Borobudur is taken over by the 'prasad', a sanctuary built on a square ground-plan, with one side – generally the east – open, so as to allow access to the interior, and the other three closed. The interior contained no more than a statue of a Hindu god, or a *linga* representing Shiva. Subject to this plan, the external decoration is the same on all four sides, so that the three closed sides contain *false* doors of the same design as that of the open door on the fourth side. The roof is in the form of a step pyramid – generally with four levels – with every succeeding level repeating, on an appropriately reduced scale, the design of the ground floor. The result once again is a representation of Mount Meru.

In the Khmer kingdom the *mandala* was also the basis of any ground-plan, whether that of an entire city, or a single building. The modular elements were known as '*pada*s', and according to the design chosen, a *mandala* would comprise either eight or nine *pada*s (Stierlin 1970:83). In a temple complex, the location of the *prasads* would be determined according to the layout of the *pada*s, as is clearly to be seen at Angkor Wat.[28] The main object was simply the symbolic representation of Hindu doctrine, in which the numerical elements played a dominant role.[29]

The great temple complexes built in different parts of Mexico in pre-colonial times show that many of the principles governing the layout of Borobudur and Angkor Wat were also applied in the new world. Since the conquistadores destroyed almost all the documentary records of the ancient civilisations – which were in any case written in a form which has been but partly deciphered – little is known about the purely arithmetical principles governing the designs adopted. No Mexican layout has been analysed so far in terms of the modular principles which govern the layout of Angkor Wat or Saint Gall, for modern scholars have been almost wholly concerned with the astronomical principles applied. On the other hand the modular layout of the pages of the Maya Dresden Codex (figure 20) – which the Spaniards luckily failed to destroy – suggests that a similar layout could in some way have influenced architectural design.

As for the role of astronomy, a great deal of work has been done to establish theories which explain the alignment of different architectural features comprised in a single complex of buildings. In Teotihuacan, the largest and most influential of all cities in ancient Mexico, the alignment of

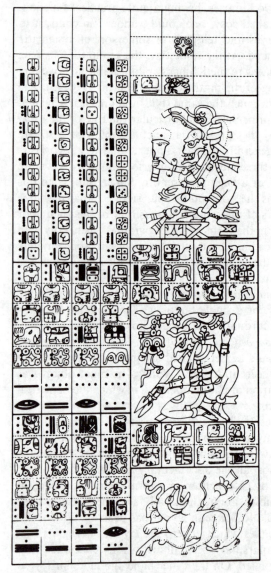

Fig. 20. The Maya Dresden Codex.

two crosses of similar size, made by hammering holes into stone, and separated by a distance of some three kilometres, points in the precise direction of the heliacal rising of the Pleiades, which occurs on the same day as the first of the two annual passages of the sun across its zenith (Aveni 1984:166). The direction of this line – some 17 degrees south of east –

determines the orientation not only of all the main structures of Teotihuacan, but also that of any number of other groups of buildings, of a much later date, in a wide area of Mexico, even though these cases could not have had the same astronomical basis. The explanation given by Aveni (ibid.: 169) is probably correct: 'The priest rulers of these new centres probably looked upon Teotihuacan as a holy city in ruins. Out of reverence for the past, they may have planned their centres with the same directional axes. The sacred alignment could have been transferred astronomically simply by sighting a star which had replaced the Pleiades.' In any case, the purpose was to note the passage of time, which was an obsession with all the ancient cultures of Meso-America. Numerical features quite unrelated to astronomy were also incorporated into all these structures, although their significance remains problematic.

The final point is essentially simple. Sacred art and architecture can turn in either of two directions. Themes can be expressed realistically: the gods can walk on earth in human form, so that the commonplace is somehow sanctified. Alternatively, the sacred can be identified with all that is beyond the reach of man, that is not so much with the invisible, as with the intangible. Realisation in material form must be divorced from any possible practical use. Any idea of using Borobudur or Teotihuacan, except perhaps as a piece in some political chess-game, is inherently far-fetched. To adapt a well-known passage from Lévi-Strauss (1969:162), buildings in this form 'are chosen not because they are good to "use" but because they are good to "think"'. The essence of the thought which they inspire, and which inspired their design in the first place, is to be found in the world of numbers. If we adhere to a culture which, by reason of their association with time and money, sees numbers as profane, we must realise that this is only one possible view.[30] Our problem is that our own tradition, derived from western Christianity, inescapably faces, in two directions,[31] which are difficult to reconcile. Just as the Aztecs resolved the conflicting claims to ascendancy of Quetzalcoatl and Tezcatlipoca by allowing them to govern for alternating periods of fifty-two years, so also, one can see the history of Western art and architecture alternating between periods of idealism and realism. The exaltation of numbers belongs then to idealism, as much as their debasement belongs to realism.

12

The ecology of number

The practical conclusion from the preceding chapters is that the series of natural numbers, together with the basic arithmetical operations of addition and subtraction, multiplication and division, are a resource open to use in almost any culture. On the other hand, the extent of utilization, varies very greatly. The same is true not only of the different types of use, but also of the different ways in which numbers are understood. In sub-Saharan Africa, for instance, numeracy is certainly implicit in a sophisticated game like *oware*, or in any number of intricate musical rhythms, but there is little explicit numerology, or lore of numbers, of the kind which one may take for granted in India, south-east Asia, China and Japan.

What then are the factors which determine the character of a particular numerical tradition? Is there a cultural ecology of numbers? If so, how important is the distinction between traditional and modern? Looking at such questions, one finds that this last distinction is significant, and that in a number of ways. In the first place, the traditional use of numbers, in the sense of numerical institutions which are generally accepted as an integral, stable and long-standing part of any given culture, is seldom *practical* according to the standards of any modern society. Accounting, surveying and engineering, however important they may be to a traditional society, are not often the focus of any general interest in numbers: in the case of Japan, for instance, the necessary 'mathematics was developed and taught in the framework of a number of "schools" – *ryū* – each with its own methods, terminology and notation and its own "mysteries" which were not printed in their books but reserved for oral communication to advanced pupils. In this it resembled the teaching of the military arts, of dancing, acting,[1] sword-making and most other practical techniques' (Dore 1984:147).

But then, is the position so very different in a *modern* society? Accounting, surveying and engineering are recognised *professional* skills. At popular level, skill in the use of numbers is more likely to be applied to working out winning strategies for betting on dogs or horses, often in a setting no less frenzied than that of the Balinese cockfight. At the same time, much of professional mathematics, as taught in universities, is quite beyond any popular reach.

146

The significant difference here is that the professional mathematicians have extended the frontiers of their discipline to the infinite bounds of space, so that they can provide insights into the operation of numbers in daily life. A computer which could play *oware* would not change the rules of the game, indeed, it might not even be able to win against an expert player. On the other hand the process of designing it, and the mathematical principles involved in this process, are far outside the cognitive domain of the traditional African cultures in which *oware* is played. What is more the principles applied would be completely general, so that the same systems designer who concocted the *oware* programme could equally well have turned his skills to chess or *go*. The technology-based institutions of the modern world depend on this sort of *creative* use and understanding of numbers, even though such use may be no more than implicit in the finished product. An African expert would, no doubt, not have any difficulty in playing against an *oware* computer programme while flying in a jet aircraft, but in doing so he would be very conscious that he was caught in a sort of cross-fire between two quite different cognitive domains. He would also be confronted with the realisation that a numerical institution, such as *oware*, is essentially self-contained and context-free.

If there is one lesson to be learnt from the present study of traditional numeracy, it is that diffusion is the most common explanation of the emergence of numerical institutions in any local culture. There are a number of reasons for this. First, and foremost, is the abstract basis of such institutions, which results in their introduction in any given society making few specific cultural demands. These demands are in most cases linguistic, so that it is natural enough that the diffusion of numerical institutions often has a linguistic dimension (Crump 1978). Once such an institution is understood in terms of the local culture, expressed in the local language, it frees itself, almost immediately, from these cultural ties. Somewhat paradoxically, language is no more than a cultural catalyst, necessary for individual conceptualisation, but otherwise not an integral part of the essential cognitive base. Taking once again the case of *oware*, there is no need to presuppose that the two players in any way think differently about it, even if they have no common language, and the game itself is the only element common to their two cultures. In practice, if the game were at all important anywhere it was played, it would no doubt attract cultural accretions, but the point, once again, is that these will not change its rules.[2]

An alternative, but not dissimilar reason for diffusion, is that particular ways of using numbers, even where they do not relate to formal institutions, such as games, do relate to natural phenomena that know no cultural boundaries. In particular the measurement of time by the phases of the sun and moon, and the movement of the stars, explains the historical diffusion of the same units of time across the ancient world.

Even more significant is the fact that there is a sort of 'survival of the fittest' among numerical institutions. The expression of numbers, beyond a certain low threshold, in terms of a polynomial with a single base (generally 10) is absolutely better than any alternative – which, incidentally, explains the dominant position of Chinese mathematics over so long a period of time. So also, when it comes to written numbers, the place value notation, characteristic of Arabic numerals, is absolutely the best possible solution to the problem of written representation (Menninger 1977:399),[3] just as the abacus is the best possible elementary calculator (Crump 1987:19). This sort of pre-eminence of particular numerical institutions extends much further than these basic instances: consider for example the familiar pack of 52 playing-cards, which has long been standard for card games throughout the world. Even more significant is the *mandala*, which provides a numerically based model of wide general application.

The historical origin of a traditional numerical institution is often quite specific. In England, for instance, is there anything more *traditional* than the way in which changes are rung on church bells? Yet what would change-ringing have amounted to without the work of Stedman (see chapter 9, n. 18) in the seventeenth century?

The question still remains as to what it is that makes a specific culture receptive to a given numerical institution made available to it by the process of diffusion. The answer is that such an institution of its nature makes few demands of any local culture. Even where the linguistic resources are insufficient, such an institution may itself provide the means and the opportunity for the necessary enrichment of the local language (consider for example the basic terminology of the game of chess). That this is not always possible is illustrated by the Japanese name science, or *seimeigaku* – discussed in chapter 4 – which presupposes the distinctive form of Japanese names, in the written as well as in the spoken languages,[4] but this case is really quite exceptional. In the general case, even a culture which has no means of conceiving of numbers, for want of words for numerals in the local language, has no difficulty in incorporating them, when circumstance makes this possible. The position has been stated, perhaps too simply, by Dixon (1980:108): 'no special significance attaches to the absence of numeral systems in the Australian languages; it is simply a reflection of the absence of any need for them in traditional culture. Aboriginal Australians have no difficulties in learning to use English numerals[...]'. Once again numbers succeed because they need no culture-specific support: no culture has an inbuilt defence against numeracy. Numeracy is a sort of Trojan horse (Crump 1978), for, once it is admitted, the institutions it supports tend to become dominant in every domain, whether it be the local economy, leisure and play, religion or whatever.

The economic dimension is probably the most important when it comes to the transformation of the way of life. The detailed, number-based calendric rituals, characteristic of wet-rice cultivation in Bali and Japan, presuppose an appropriate local ecology – which is to be found throughout much of the orient.[5] The use of such rituals is none the less a consequence of the diffusion of Hinduism and Buddhism, but this was a part of a historical process which may also have brought with it specific techniques of rice-cultivation. Put otherwise, the calendric rituals and the cycle of cultivation they govern may have been part of the same historical package in Bali and Japan. Yet this does not require any essential link between the two: the religious origins are also to be found in a part of India where wheat rather than rice is the staple crop. Even if it is true that for numerical institutions to be adopted from outside they must in some sense be functional, the function need not have any ecological rationale. In fact it may be characteristic of numerical institutions that such a rationale is the exception rather than the rule. It may be that a culture such as that of the Bemba of Zambia, whose numerical institutions are extremely rudimentary, is of itself less receptive to a religion such as Buddhism than were the indigenous cultures of Bali and Japan, but the question is purely academic: the Bemba were never confronted with Buddhism,[6] and their recent experience of Christianity was in a form bereft of many traditional numerical elements.[7]

The historical importance of diffusion, and to a lesser extent innovation, would seem to require that the meaning of tradition in relation to the use of numbers be reconsidered. Too often, the idea of tradition has been associated with that of an enclosed society, which can be looked at in isolation from the rest of the world. The correct reaction to this point was suggested by Leach (1970:7) more than thirty years ago, when he noted 'the social anthropologist normally studies the population of a particular place at a particular point in time and does not concern himself greatly with whether or not the same locality is likely to be studied again by other anthropologists at a later date', a process leading to an almost inescapable 'confusion between the concepts of equilibrium and of stability'. This approach may explain, at least in part, why so few anthropologists have been interested in numerical institutions, which of all cultural phenomena are the least apt to be tied either to a particular place, or a particular point in time. But this does not prevent such institutions being traditional, or stable, or in equilibrium. One can go even further than this. A numerical institution, such as place-value notation, which has achieved a form of absolute perfection in the sense given earlier in this chapter, is assured of almost unimpeachable stability, so that it is equally certain to be well entrenched in any cultural tradition to which it belongs.[8] This is true as much of the societies which we call 'modern' as of those we call 'traditional'. On the other hand, for reasons I have already suggested, it is difficult for any society, however traditional, to defend itself against numerical institutions superior to those it already possesses,[9] once these are knocking at the door.

Finally, it is worth noting that many of the most remarkable achievements of modern mathematics can be related to traditional numerical praxis. Turing's demonstration that 'to "process information" by computer is nothing more than to replace discrete symbols one at a time according to finite set of rules' is another way of saying that any numerical process which reaches a result has the structure of a game defined by constitutive rules. It is significant how important are the concepts of von Neumann's games theory in modern mathematical thinking. There is at the same time a pragmatic approach to mathematics that is little concerned with the search for secure foundations (Davis and Hersh 1983:351).[10] This sees the use of numbers in terms of winning strategies, which is, essentially, not only the approach of the modern computer programmer, but also that of the expert user of the abacus.[11] If we were really fair in our judgment, we might just have to accept not only that the world of traditional numeracy has achieved more than we would give it credit for, but also that, in the achievements of modern mathematics, with all their lack of transparency, there is less than meets the eye.[12]

Notes

Chapter 1

1 A possible solution to the problem of infinity is suggested by Hodes (1984:149): 'The answer to our difficulty is as old as Aristotle: the notion of infinity required by mathematics is merely that of a potential infinity. Even if at every possible world only finitely many objects exist, still any world has access to a richer world with more objects.' More generally, the present book very seldom goes beyond the bounds of the natural numbers, so that negative numbers, fractions, irrational and imaginary numbers are hardly mentioned. For the extension to the class of natural numbers which these require see Russell (1920), which is a basic text for the present chapter.

2 Compare Lévi-Strauss' appreciation of the arithmetical consciousness of primitive societies, cited below on p. 2. It is still a characteristic of modern societies to use numbers, in a social context, to name the parts of a whole, so that in the British Army, the 'sixtieth' is known to refer to the 'sixtieth regiment of foot'; none the less there is still a bias towards the use of natural symbolism, as in the 'Fifty-first *Highland* Division'.

3 'Isomorphism applies when two complex structures can be mapped on to each other, in such a way that to each part of one structure there is a corresponding part of another structure, where "corresponding" means that the two parts play similar roles in their respective structures' (Hofstadter 1980:49).

4 See for instance chapter 5, nn. 27, 28 and 29.

5 See for instance the science of Japanese names, described in chapter 4.

6 Many traditional cultures distrust instruments whose manner of operation is concealed from the user: the continued popularity of the abacus in Japan (Crump 1987:18) in a time when pocket electronic calculators are available at half the price comes largely from the fact that the latter are regarded as a 'black box' whose workings are not visible to the operator. It is significant that the National Abacus Education Institute, which is supported by the Japanese government, is continually researching new and more complex algorithms to deal with the arithmetical demands of a modern industrial society.

7 Consider here the way in which Hindu mathematics uniquely emphasised large numbers, particularly in relation to time, which included the cycle of the *kalma*, or 4,320,000,000 years. This, as Restivo (1983:218) notes, is "mathematics for transcending experience, but not in the direction of rationalist abstraction. Numbers are used to mystify and impress; they are symbols of a mathematical rhetoric designed to stimulate religious awe.' This is hardly within the reach of

151

Brouwer's approach. For the redevelopment of the axiomatic foundations characteristic of Greek mathematics see Lloyd (1979:112f.).

8 This is not necessarily true of periods of time of measurable duration. What, for instance, is the ordered relationship between Lent and the month of March, which always includes some, though never all the days of Lent?

9 See the discussion of Maya chronology in chapter 7.

10 The key to this sentence is a *demonstrative*, in the philosophical meaning of this term. The class comprises, essentially, four instances, 'this', 'I', 'here' and 'now' (Ayer 1963:148), which are in ordinary usage assumed to have a denotation on each occasion of their use. In particular, in the case of the demonstrative 'I', the fact that someone uses it correctly entails that its reference succeeds (ibid.: 149).

11 'One, as the antithesis of Many, had already taken a special position as far back as the Table of Ordinal Concepts established by the Pythagoreans. Plato constantly emphasized this: Like the Now in time and the Point in space, the One among numbers cannot be further subdivided. Hence it conceals within itself no plurality which it collects together into unity, and since it is in this that the essence of number lies, One is not a number. Since, according to Euclid, "a number is an aggregate composed of units", One is itself not a number, though it is the source and the origin[...]of all numbers. Throughout the Middle Ages no one thought differently' (Menninger 1977:19).

12 An obvious case is provided by the letters of the alphabet, but then the Japanese *kana* syllabaries, each with some fifty characters, have two alternative orders, one phonetic, and the other based on a poem known as the *i-ro-ha*, comprising all the sounds, but with a definite meaning.

13 The Ponam do, however, have a 'well-developed system of ordinals for naming successively born children in a family'. Compare the Balinese case examined in chapter 5. Note also how this conflicts with the heuristic assumption made by Hurford (1987:67) that '*both* a command of order and a command of one-to-one mapping of collections are taken to pre-exist the human command of number and *jointly* to create the conditions in which number and numerals can arise'.

14 Since Russell (1920) was published, Gödel's theorem, proved in 1931, 'showed that no fixed system, no matter how complicated could represent the complexity of the whole numbers, 0, 1, 2, 3,...': Hofstadter (1980:19).

15 Today the Japanese makes a clear distinction between *shuzan*, that is, calculating with the abacus, and *hissan*, calculating with Arabic numerals, which have only been in common use in the last hundred years. The first part '*shu*' of *shuzan*, refers to the beads of the abacus, whereas '*hitsu*', the first part of *hissan*, refers to the brush traditionally used for writing Japanese. *San* simply adds the meaning of 'calculation': in the general case this is *keisan*, and it is significant that Arabic numerals, which are essential to *hissan*, are also known as *keisan sūji*, that is 'calculation numerals'. See also n. 6 above.

16 In traditional societies ordinal numbers are characteristically small numbers, particularly in any preliterate culture. Large ordinal numbers, which order whole populations for the purposes of allocating telephones, passports, car licences etc., are a distinctive and novel feature of modern society. Even then it is to be noted how alternative orders govern the same large class of individuals: just consider how useless a telephone directory would be, which listed subscribers in the order of telephone numbers.

17 The trouble with any theory which allows for the existence of an independent mathematical reality 'does not lie in the puzzling nature of its ontology but in the

circular character of its epistemology. It presupposes precisely what it sets out to explain' (Bloor 1973:182).

Chapter 2

1 To give one example, almost all the studies made of the cognitive basis of written Japanese, are based on these exceptional cases (Paradis, Hagiwara and Hildebrandt 1985). For mathematics note the case studies contained in Deloshe and Seron (eds.) 1988.

2 Normal distribution has here its meaning in mathematical statistics, as explained in Moroney (1951: ch. 9), and illustrated by the distribution of IQ's (ibid.: 64). The idea of IQ, which begs all kinds of cultural questions, is but one instance of the sort of problem encountered in any anthropological study of cognition. But then 'anthropological critiques of psychological experimentation have never carried much weight with psychologists, nor have anthropologists been very impressed with conclusions from psychological tests[...]their mutual indifference stems in part from a difference of opinion about the inferences that are warranted from testing and experimentation, and in part because the anthropologist relies mainly on data that the psychologist completely fails to consider: the mundane social life of the people he studies' (Cole and Bruner 1971:868).

3 This sentence is not necessarily incompatible with Lave's (1988:20) conclusion that 'arithmetic relations are underdetermined, enacted, embodied, and generated in dialectical relations with the settings in which they occur'. Although Piaget's theory about the development psychology of the child may have to be modified to deal with this sort of point relating to adult cognition, there is little doubt that he '[...]remains by far the most influential figure in developmental psychology in his generation' (Bryant 1983:597).

4 Piaget (1972:62) is content to note that 'The demonstration of the connection between neural co-ordinations and organic regulations at all levels is of course the task of biology.' The problem, in the context of development psychology, is that much the best results are obtained with elementary organisms, such as crickets (Huber and Thorson 1985), and even at this level there are many unsolved problems. Quite simply, 'we all know how difficult it is to understand undocumented software written by someone else' (ibid.: 54). For a recent discussion see Churchland (1986, Chapter 8) "Are mental states irreducible to neurobiological states?". See also n.15 below.

5 The same sort of process has been recognised not only in the history of science (Kuhn 1962:52), but is seen by theologians as fundamental to the revelation of religious truth: 'one thing I know, that though I was blind, now I see' (John ix:25). This is closely related to what Karl Buhler called the 'Aha-experience', which 'is accompanied, and in fact caused, by a characteristic change in the cognitive structures at issue. In terms of Gestalt psychology, unsolved problems have the character of "defective structures": they are structures with apparently missing parts that contradict each other. Generally speaking, problems are structures in disequilibrium: during the process of productive thinking, we observe sudden spurts of equilibration. It is these sudden gains of equilibrium and harmony that are emotionally reflected by the "aha-experience"' (Piatelli-Palmarini 1980:236–7). In this context it is not necessary to postulate, as Chomsky does, 'in each new-born child a disposition to extrapolate in the same way from his first linguistic experiences' (Hurford 1987:38).

6 The spots on dice, or the layout of the symbols for the different suits on playing cards, both depend, implicitly, on 'subitizing'.

7 At this level numerical skills may well be regarded as esoteric, as they were in Japan in the pre-modern era (Dore 1984:147), so that teachers would only communicate them, orally, to certain selected pupils.

8 The problem for the development psychologist is to discover the connections between the procedures of formalisation, which are essential to any 'advanced' mathematics, and those of natural thought. Piaget (1972:63) accepted that 'the procedures of formalisation run counter to the spontaneous tendencies of natural thought[...]if we accept a definition of natural thought in terms of the content of the subject's consciousness: ordinary thought tends to be forward-looking, whereas formalisation is retrospective – it aims at determining the necessary and sufficient conditions of all assertions and making explicit all intermediate steps and consequences[...]formalisation[...]exhibits a freedom and richness of combinatorial possibilities which largely transcend the bounds of natural thought'. Here it is interesting to consider two sorts of arithmetical strategies noted by Reed and Lave (1979:572): (i) those that deal with quantities (e.g. abacus, pebbles, pencil marks) and (ii) those that deal with number names and a ritual litany of symbols divorced from reality. If at first sight formalisation may appear to go further with (ii), it is important to note how very far it can go with (i) in certain special cases such as the use of the Japanese abacus.

9 The designation 'pre-literate' is somewhat unfortunate in the case of the Vai of Liberia, among whom much important research into numeracy has been carried out, simply because the Vai, uniquely for West Africa, developed their own form of writing. The cognitive consequences, described in Scribner and Cole (1981), make an interesting comparison with Vai numeracy, as described by Reed and Lave (1979).

10 Note here Cole and Bruner (1971:872, 874), that only 'Quite recently, psychologists have started to face up to the difficulties of assuming "all things are equal" for different groups of people.[...]The problem is to identify the range of capacities readily manifested in different groups and then to inquire whether the range is adequate to the individual's needs in various cultural settings. From this point of view cultural deprivation represents a special case of cultural difference that arises when an individual is faced with demands to perform in a manner inconsistent with his past [cultural] experience.'

11 The occurrence of such contradictions and the consequent adjustment of established paradigms to take them into account, is a major factor in scientific advance (Kuhn 1962:52f.) in modern societies. This is a sort of parallel to the individual process of passing through successive stages of cognitive clarity, described in the previous section.

12 At the present time even the traditional shopkeepers will be able to write out prices in Arabic numerals, and add them up with the help of a pocket calculator, which just proves the point. For a comparative study of the mathematical abilities of children in Japan, Taiwan and the United States, see Stigler et al. (1982).

13 Lave (1988) now goes a long way towards making good this omission

14 Miller (1982, ch. 4) is a devastating critique of Tsunoda's thesis, to the point indeed of overkill. The detailed arguments considered in Paredes and Hepburn (1976–7), in which both anthropologists and psychologists took part in the discussion, are not mentioned by Miller. To be fair to Tsunoda, he draws no 'numerical' conclusions from his research, although its numerical implications

may well provide an additional reason for rejecting the premises upon which it is based.

15 Harnad and Steklis (1976:321), commenting upon Paredes and Hepburn (1976), assert that there is nothing in 'current neuropsychological research' which justifies localisation of such functions in any part of the brain. The most interesting and intensive work in this field relates to the processing of written Japanese, which is unique in making use of two different forms, one, *kanji* – directly derived from Chinese – operating on the principle of every word having its own separate character, and the other, *kana*, providing a set of some fifty characters to represent, phonetically, every syllable occurring in spoken Japanese. The clear differentiation between the two forms, which are combined in any normal narrative text, has made possible a vast amount of experimental work, largely carried out with subjects suffering from different types of brain lesions. This research is summarised in Paradis, Hagiwara and Hildebrandt (1985), whose conclusions are somewhat contradictory, as indeed are the results of the experiments upon which they are based. On the one hand 'there is at present no clear model of cerebral asymmetry of function' (ibid.: 58), while on the other, 'oral reading, and kana processing in particular, depend upon a preserved left temporal area, whereas reading comprehension and kanji processing depend on a preserved left parieto-occipital area' (ibid.: 195).

16 Compare also Roll's (1970) test of the conservation of number among different social classes in the city of Medellin, Colombia.

17 The Kpelle adjective for 'clever' cannot be applied to technical skills, but is restricted to the social sphere. A father can be clever in the way he brings up his children, but not in the way he builds a house (Cole, Gay, Glick and Sharp 1971:220).

18 Chomsky's (1980:109) conclusion on this question is not generally disputed: 'in particular cognitive domains, for example in the domain of language, but not only there, the individual goes through a series of states and reaches what in effect is a steady state, which is a state that doesn't change very much except in marginal respects. In the case of language, it seems that the steady state is invariably attained about puberty.'

19 The general references to Piatelli-Palmarini (1980) refer also to the contributions of other scholars to the symposium on which the book is based: these include both Piaget and Chomsky. The text of this chapter should make it clear whose views are being considered at any given stage of the argument.

20 This is generally the conclusion of Hurford (1987), following Chomsky, and discussed in Chapter 3. Lancy (1983:183) seems to support it, but Vygotsky (1978:55), contends that 'the first use of signs demonstrates that there cannot be a single organically predetermined internal system of activity that exists for each psychological function'.

21 Cognitively, of course, this statement still takes much for granted, but logically such a search for the foundations of arithmetic could only lead back to one set of premises.

22 Piaget himself (Piatelli-Palmarini 1980:34) is weak on the question of exceptional intellectual gifts: 'As for what the scientist keeps from his younger years, it is not a collection of innate ideas, since there are tentative procedures in both cases, but a constructive ability: and one of us went so far as to say that a physicist of genius is a man who retained the creativity inherent to childhood instead of losing it in school.' In contrast to this, Posner (1973:113) considers the processes of 'so-

called lightning calculators[...]who can perform complex numerical manipula-
tions[...]in their heads. They are often gifted at using special short-cuts they have
learned. However, by making up special problems, experimenters can reduce the
use of such short-cuts. When this is done, it is found that the time these people
require to produce the answers indicates that the rates at which information is
handled is well within the limits obtained for normal subjects. They differ
primarily in their ability to hold in store the subproducts of operations so that
they can complete and report the results.' In this case the so-called *idiots savants*,
examined in detail in Treffert 1989, are a special case.

23 The Classification System published by the American Mathematical Association
in 1980 lists 3,400 sub-categories in mathematics, most of which are known to no
more than a handful of specialists, who communicate with each other but with no
one else. In the light of this information it is difficult to see what Bruner (cited
Lancy 1983:175) had in mind with his 'multiembodiment' principle which 'holds
that any mathematical concept, no matter how abstruse, can be "embodied" in
a form comprehensible to even very young children'.

24 In some cases, such as the use of the letters of the Hebrew alphabet to enumerate
the stanzas of the Psalm 119, these mnemonics pre-suppose a literate culture.

25 The Dutch grand master, Jan Timman, carries in his head some 2,000 games
played by those whom he is likely to compete against in international
competitions.

26 It is interesting to see how Goody (1977:87) sees written lists as a means of
organisation of information which has no parallel in the spoken language.
Indeed, in relation to the actual case examined he admits, 'I do not know how this
type of information is stored in the long-term memory and then retrieved
according to some specified criteria. But the general outline of the kind of sorting
that occurs through writing is clear enough, and is illustrated by the list of
"rituals and sacrifices to various gods according to the days of a certain month".'
Although Goody leaves the question open, it must be that memory, to be efficient,
must be controlled in some way – particularly in pre-literate cultures. The
question is examined in some detail by Vansina (1965:40f.), who gives some
remarkable instances of texts and information remembered over a period of
several centuries.

27 Here change-ringing (ch. 9) provides an almost perfect example: thousands of
successive permutations can be achieved, with no repetition, simply by
remembering a short programme of the different possible transformations of one
peal into its successor. The 'recursive' principle used in this case is one of great
efficiency in relation to the required memory input.

Chapter 3

1 An elaborate ritual of this kind, to be found in Zinacantan in southern Mexico,
is based on counting the value of a sacred hoard of coins against a fixed number
of maize kernels kept in a sack (Vogt 1976:128 and Crump 1981:288).

2 Quite apart from the *null* cases from Australia cited by Dixon, these needs can be
very limited, as among the Bemba of Zambia, who in contrast to the cattle-
owning Bantu tribes, have little interest in large numbers (Richards 1939:204). A
comparative perspective, within a comparatively small area of Papua New
Guinea, is to be found in Philp & Kelly (1977:262).

3 These new needs are frequently the result of culture contact, so that the problem
then arising may be solved by resorting to the numerical system of the dominant

culture. For an example from Nigeria see Welmers (1973:304) and for one from Mexico, Crump (1978).

4 In the modern world the Pythagorean view of number is probably strongest in Japan (Crump 1986).

5 In Renaissance Italy 'abaco' was the normal term for written arithmetic (Murray 1978:170). Ronan and Needham (1981:35) suggests that the word may well derive from the Semitic 'abq' (dust).

6 'Algorithm' derives from 'Al-Khwarismi', 'the name of the great emporium on the Caspian where the Arabs had learned the Indian art of arithmetic' (Murray 1978:191).

7 In fourteenth century Italy the distinction between *abaco* and *algorismo* corresponded remarkably closely to the modern distinction between hard- and soft-ware.

8 Note Turing's proof of the theorem cited in ch. 12 that '"to process" information by computer is nothing more than to replace discrete symbols one at a time according to a finite set of rules' (Bolter 1986:47). This process will prove to be remarkably similar to that adopted in many traditional numerical institutions.

9 An exception is the autochthonous Japanese 'futatsu' for '2' derived from 'hitotsu', '1'.

10 As ch. 7 shows many systems of measuring time make it extremely difficult to calculate the age of an individual at any particular time.

11 A language may maintain separate 'evocative' sets of numerals for use in special cases. The Bingo numbers are a modern example.

12 Lancy (1983:102f.), on the basis of some 225 languages spoken in Papua New Guinea, identified four types of counting system:

> *Type I*. Body-parts tally system: parts of the body above the waist are enumerated, beginning with the fingers on one hand and going up one side of the body and down the other.
>
> *Type II*. Tally systems based on objects, like sticks. The basis number words are primary lexemes and do not name parts of the body.
>
> *Type III*. Mixed-based systems based on 5 and 20, the former often represented by the word for 'hand', and the latter by 'one man'.
>
> *Type IV*. Base 10 systems in which no body parts are indicated.

13 It is still astonishing to note how often a standard text, such as Stevenson (1972) completely disregards the acquisition of numerical skills.

14 Such exotica as 'quintillion' do not count in this analysis.

15 Salzmann (1950) lists sixteen similar cases from Indian tribes in South America, but indicates that the number is much greater.

16 If 'derived' morphemes are left out, the number is reduced to fourteen.

17 These are defined by Schubert (1887:13) as *Stufenzahlen*, lit. 'step-numbers'.

18 The logical impossibility of determining the end of such a list is not important in the present cognitive analysis.

19 The implied limitation here is a property of the spoken language, which written numerals can often transcend.

20 Salzmann's system is also applied by Lévi-Strauss (1978:337) to the analysis of the numbers occurring in North-American Indian myths. An algebraic analysis is given in Crump (1978:504).

21 Compare the French '*deux-mille-huit-cent-quatre*'.

22 One special case of this is examined in detail in Dixon & Kroeber (1907).

23 For numbers from 40 to 100 Danish counts in 20s as French does from 60 to 100, but so that the numbers 50, 70 and 90, are expressed in the form '*halv-*

tre(3)/fir(4)/fem(5)-sinds-tyve(20)'. To add to the confusion, 'tyve', in 20, 30 and 40 is an old plural form of 'ten', but then, in ordinary speech 'sinds-tyve' is reduced just to 's' in the expression of numbers above 50, so that 57, for example, becomes '*syv-og-halv-tres*'. This process, which occurs in only a very small number of languages, is called 'overcounting': it is discussed in detail in Hurford (1975:235–9).

24 The question of difficulty is partly subjective, but a Yoruba cited by Welmers (1973:304) said, 'Any Yoruba who knows some English tries very hard to avoid the Yoruba numeral system.'

25 Japanese rules of assonance equate 'f' with 'h'.

26 This is explained in detail in Shiratori 1937.

27 There are also survivals for numbers above 10, so that 'ya-o-ya', lit. 'eight-hundred-shop' is the normal word for a 'grocery'. The normal word for 'eight-hundred' is the Chinese derived 'happyaku', and an expression such as 'ya-o-en' for ¥ 800 would simply not be understood.

28 For other cases of such 'stray' number systems see Lounsbury (1946).

29 For an Indonesian analysis see Barnes (1982:2f.).

30 There are also languages whose grammars contain dual, and even 'trial' (Milner 1972:17) numbers, in addition to singular and plural.

31 There appears to be no complete list of the *josūshi* in any English study of Japanese, but readers of Japanese are referred to *Nihon o shiru jiten* (1971:426–7).

32 The particle *no* is required by the rules of syntax. *Wa* connotes simply wing, as can be seen from the Chinese character used in the written form: this counter, curiously, is also correctly used for *usagi*, meaning 'rabbit', in place of the normal animal classifier.

33 But such connotations can occur in proper names, such as that of the Kyoto temple of San-jū-san-gen-dō, where *san-ju-san* is simply the Japanese for 'thirty-three'. See ch. 11.

34 The point is that although the existence of order may be implicit in the succession of number words committed to memory, the reification of such order by means of special lexical forms does not necessarily follow. That is, numerical *order* can be part of the cognitive domain, where *ordinals* have yet to appear in it.

35 This may not be apparent in English, but in the Slavonic languages, for example, the grammatical form of numerals, and of the nouns they govern, varies according to extremely complex rules: these are examined in detail in Hurford (1987:187f.).

36 In this context it is interesting to note, also, the necessity for specially designed computer languages, which then gain international currency far transcending their original linguistic base. In Japan, for instance, BASIC, FORTRAN, PASCAL, and so on, may be the only 'English' in which computer users are really at home.

37 This explains why the English 'second' or the Polish 'drugi' need not be cognate with the word for the cardinal number, '2'.

38 The effect of deceased children is left out of account in this analysis, but on this point see Geertz (1973:370f.) on Balinese birth-order names.

39 One sees this in the transition to seven-figure telephone numbers in a city such as London, so that the old exchange-names fell out of use. Anyone familiar with London before about 1970 knows that GROsvenor has a snob-ranking higher than WHItechapel; but is this ranking preserved in 460 and 866?

40 For the consequences for the measurement of time see ch. 7, p. 84.

41 The cardinal points are a more involved case, since they can be endlessly subdivided on a binary scale. See particularly the discussion of the mandala in ch. 5.

42 This is of course another instance of the *Pythagorean* use of numbers.

43 Computer storage is perhaps more refined, but it is hardly accessible in popular terms.

44 Four different cases are given by Ifrah (1987:36f.).

45 Of course if feet are included as well as hands, twenty becomes the base, as one sees in the Maya languages which express the numeral '20' as 'one man'. Limiting the representation to one hand explains the quinary systems, which indeed often combine with vigesimal systems: see for example Dixon & Kroeber (1907).

46 It is significant that the Babylonian system based on '60' – the only important system not immediately related to the human anatomy – is known exclusively through the written record.

47 Adapting a passage from Goody (1977:104), 'Writing draws out, crystallises and extends the discontinuity of numbers by insisting upon a visual, spatial location which then becomes subject to possible rearrangement.'

48 A skilled operator can largely overcome this restriction. The Japanese abacus champions, who use their fingers to operate on an imaginary abacus, can calculate the cube root of a twelve figure number in four seconds.

49 Note the etymology of 'manipulate' as well as that of 'calculate'.

50 This is the number used in the illustration of written Chinese on p. 36.

51 An alternative model of the abacus is based on stones which are moved over a flat board.

52 In practice a quinary system is incorporated into the abacus, so that a bead above the bar represents 5, while those below the bar each represent a single unit.

53 The different theories are discussed by Ronan and Needham (1981:32f.).

54 In practice the abacus always seems to have been used in contexts where a written language was available, but there is no essential objection to its use outside such contexts. Indeed shopkeepers in China and Japan constantly use the abacus, for adding up customers' bills or working out the correct change, without making any written record.

55 At a much more elementary level, the hoes used by the Plateau Tonga for the payment of bridewealth also transcend the limitations of the spoken language.

56 The form of the earliest Chinese numerals is to be found in Ronan and Needham (1981:1f.). The eventual adoption of a logographic form, which consistently represented the spoken form of all numerals, may be seen as a major factor in ensuring the survival to the present day of the logographic (as opposed to the orthographic) form of the whole written language.

57 'The decline of Greece and the rise of Roman imperialism stifled mathematical work' (Restivo 1983:253). Although this author consistently prefers a political to a cultural view of the history of science, in terms of chronology the statement cited is substantially true. Restivo finds the first signs of revival as late as the sixteenth century.

58 Both the Kabbala and the Book of Changes are considered further in ch. 4.

59 Medieval Europe referred, correctly, to Indian Numerals (Murray 1978:167).

60 There is no evidence of diffusion from China to India: if anything the process went the other way, as witness the spread of Buddhism.

61 The word 'cipher' comes from the Arabic *al-cifr* 'the vacant one', which referred to the zero-coefficient in an 'Arabic' numeral.

62 The numerals now used in modern Arabic texts are different from the so-called 'Arabic numerals' used in the west, but the underlying place-value system remains identical.

63 Compare the special abacus schools in Japan, which are still in business.

64 This followed from the demands of the calendar: see ch. 7, p. 85.

65 Jedediah Buxton, a calculating prodigy in the time of George II (1727–60), was illiterate (*Scientific American*, May 1984:23f.).

Chapter 4

1 Gellner (1972:173) seems to imply that every society can choose between these alternatives. But then (ibid.: 174) 'it is of the essence of the savage mind, that there is a lower degree of functional specificity. The tacit but persistent propaganda by modern philosophy, in quite a broad sense, on behalf of functional specificity, introduced "innocently", as a neutral analytic device, in fact favours the mechanistic, disenchanted vision of the world as against magical enchantment[...]A sense of the separability and fundamental distinctness of the various functions is the surest way to the disenchantment of the world.'

2 This is the view of scientists rather than musicians: J. S. Bach and Alban Berg, to name but two composers, would have found it quite unacceptable.

3 Ethnoscience is a term which became popular in the 1960s: it may be taken to refer to the 'system of knowledge and cognition typical of a given culture'. Where ethnoscience refers to the 'reduction of chaos' achieved by a particular culture, cosmology may be taken to be 'the highest possible and conscious degree to which such chaos may be reduced'. (Sturtevant 1972:130). Ethnoscience is relative, where cosmology is absolute, but the difference between the two is essentially one of perspective.

4 cf. Jeans (1930:5): 'The universe shows evidence of a designing or controlling power that has[...]the tendency to think in the way which, for want of a better word, we describe as mathematical.'

5 The truth is otherwise, needless to say: on this point see particularly Restivo (1982). For the essential characteristics of a modern scientific community see Kuhn (1962:167), but note also Gellner's (1972:165) criticism: 'In Kuhn's[...]scheme[...]there is no room for any such direct intercourse with Objective Reality: the scientist is only capable of checking little theories against the socially imposed Paradigm, and there seems to be no way of checking these paradigms themselves against reality, for science cannot do without some paradigm.' However just this criticism is of the modern scientific world (which is, after all, Kuhn's subject matter), it is not a bad summary of the world of traditional cosmologies.

6 For a description of this world see Davis and Hersh (1983:17–20).

7 For a modern review of Galileo's trial before the Inquisition, and its historical and scientific background, see Lerner & Gosselin (1986).

8 Although worship of the Kannon Buddha (to whom Sanjūsangendō is dedicated) still continues in modern Japan, the temple is now mainly a tourist attraction.

9 Note Sahlins (1976:54): 'The real issue for Marxism and anthropology comes down to the relation between praxis and the symbolic order.'

10 The duration of pregnancy is commonly measured from the end of the last menstruation, so that there are ten months of pregnancy: for a modern instance, from Japan, see Ohnuki-Tierney (1984:183), but compare Wisdom of Solomon vii: 2.

160

11 The dog is one of the twelve animals of the lunar calendar, corresponding to the zodiac. It is also one of the twelve kan used in chapter 3, figure 3.

12 Any number of passages in the New Testament support this distinction, but note the well-known words of St Paul (1 Cor. xii:9): 'For our knowledge is imperfect and our prophesy is imperfect; but when the perfect comes the imperfect will pass away', or simply, as Jesus said (Joh. xviii:36), 'My kingdom is not of this world.'

13 Precision is not rated so highly in western popular culture. Fieldwork carried out in Japan disclosed a quite different case, so that virtues such as punctuality, whose underlying basis is precision, are particularly esteemed.

14 The classification is all-pervasive: to give but one example, the twelve intervals of Chinese music to be found on p. 106 are alternately classified as Yin and Yang.

15 In the simplified characters now used in China, 阴 for Yin, incorporates 月 the character for moon (or month), while 阳 for Yang incorporates 日 the character for sun (or day). The original characters, 陰 and 陽, had quite other connotations (for which see, inter alia, Ronan and Needham 1981:164), and are still used in Japan, where their normal pronunciation is 'on' and 'yō'.

16 The same is true of French, and in the same order, except that French inevitably lacks the relationship to the five elements. (In the traditional European scheme of four elements – earth, fire, air and water – the fifth, or quintessential element, formed an ideal basis of the other four.)

17 Note the parallel with English change-ringing, as this is described in ch. 9.

18 The kana syllabaries in their present form comprise only 47 characters.

19 For the same reason it would be confusing to represent the elements of the game of Jan-ken, discussed in ch. 10, as ternary numbers.

20 The importance of recruitment to the Japanese household is made clear by Bachnik (1983), so the decision about names is no trivial matter.

21 The ekisha's traditional task was to interpret the 'ekikyo', the Japanese version of the I Ching.

22 There has been no detailed study of this process in Japan (save possibly in Japanese), but for Korea see Janelli (1977).

23 This is surprisingly similar to the purported origins of the Book of Mormon, which the angel Moroni 'communicated' to Joseph Smith in 1832.

24 Such as the appearance of Halley's comet during a period of seventy days in the year 1264.

25 The 231 possible combinations of two letters are particularly significant, for 231 is the triangular number, $1+2+3+ ... +21$. Such numbers are also significant in the New Testament (Crump 1982:281).

26 An elementary example of this two-way process is provided by the Pythagorean right-angled triangle with its sides, 3, 4 and 5 units in length. 3, then, as all odd numbers, connotes the male, 4, as all even numbers, the female, and 5 – by virtue of the fact that $3^2+4^2 = 5^2$ – connotes marriage (Burkert 1972:429).

27 See *City of God*, Book XI, ch. 30 and 31. Book XV, ch. 20, Book XVII, ch. 4, Book XX, chh. 5 and 7. More generally there is a considerable volume of literature on the significance of different numbers, particularly in the west. For '2', see Halle (1957), for '3' Usener (1903) and Lease (1919), for '4' Buckland (1896), for '7' Andrian (1901) and Roscher (1901). (The concentration of interest in this theme at the turn of the twentieth century is quite remarkable (Crump 1985:169). For Japan, Mori (1980) is an encyclopedia of numbers, giving the significance of many of the numbers occurring in Japanese history and culture.)

28 The position is apparently obscured by the medieval obsession with astrology, which involved 'the most complex arithmetic its epoch knew' (Murray 1978:201).

It must not be thought, however, that the Church rejected astrology as such; it was far too deeply embedded in popular culture. As Aquinas (*Summa* Ia, CXV, Art. 4) makes clear, the Church rejected determinism according to the movements of the stars, as contrary to free will, but this did not deny the theory that 'the planets had an effect on events and on psychology, and, much more, on plants and minerals' (Lewis 1964:103).

Chapter 5

1 The classic example here is André Weil's essentially numerical analysis of the prescribed-marriage system of the Murngin of Australia, contained in Lévi-Strauss (1971:275–65).

2 Such at least is the implicit view of Gudeman (1986:44, 106).

3 This result was actually achieved by the repeal of the Corn Laws in 1845. The link between policy and economic theory has become steadily closer since Ricardo's day, as witness the enormous influence of J. M. Keynes. For a comparatively recent perspective see Johnson (1965).

4 In practice many of the models constructed by economic theorists are quite incapable of being brought down to earth: indeed this was never the intention of the model-builders.

5 This approach is carried to its extreme in Geertz's (1980) study of nineteenth-century Bali, in which Leach's 'frills' become the substance of daily life, so that Bali 'was a theatre state. [...] The stupendous cremations, tooth filings, temple dedications, pilgrimages, and blood sacrifices, mobilizing hundred and even thousands of people and great quantities of wealth, were not means to political ends: they were the ends themselves, they were what the state was for' (ibid.: 13).

6 Here Leach is adopting Wittgenstein (1922) 6.421.

7 In technical economic terms, money has perfect inelasticity of substitution (Keynes 1936:231).

8 Such division is the essence of share-cropping, in which those who own and work land divide its annual produce: for a comprehensive analysis see Robertson (1980:411–29).

9 In modern corporate practice this distinction corresponds to that between the variable dividends on common or ordinary stock, and the fixed dividends on preference stock.

10 Thus at bridge the cards can be allocated to the four players simply be applying the process of dealing until the pack is exhausted: this is sufficient to ensure, even without counting, that each player gets a hand of thirteen cards. In poker, it is necessary to count to five rounds, simply because the rules of the game require the dealer to retain the residue of the pack. It is worth noting that 'delen', the Dutch cognate of the English 'deal', is also the ordinary word for 'share'.

11 The model discussed is basically static, but in practice the patterns of stratification in the Indian village are subject to continuous change under modern conditions: for a recent discussion see Beteille (1965).

12 Etymologically, the *jajman* is the master of the house who employs a Brahman priest to carry out a sacrifice on his behalf (Dumont 1966:129).

13 Parry, in his Appendix on reckoning *pari* (*Man* 1980:106f.), notes that 'there is a good deal of vagueness about how the original shareholders were related to each other, and even more about how they relate to present-day kinship groups. The majority are quite indifferent on these matters, but generally suppose that all the original descent lines are now extinct. But despite this apparent lack of concern

to fit the present with the past, the five ancestor model is in fact crucial to the operation of the system in that it acts as a mnemonic device for cross-checking the day on which your *pari* should occur. Each *pari* belongs to the *kunt*, or "stake" of one of the five named ancestors[...]and these stakes follow each other in regular sequence.'

14 For a discussion of the merits of the term 'bridewealth' as opposed to the older 'brideprice', see Gray (1968:259f.).

15 An example is given, for payments made in goats, among the Sonjo of Northern Tanzania, in Gray (1968:263).

16 Evans-Pritchard (1940:69) records that when rinderpest threatened the system of prescribed payments stability was restored by lowering the number of cattle to be paid for bridewealth, though not, apparently for homicide.

17 This question is central to the theme of Gudeman (1986), but the spirit of this book, in its relation to traditional cultures, is decidedly anti-numerical. This may be justified by the actual cultures investigated, but any consideration of cultures related to Hinduism or Buddhism would lead to a quite different conclusion, as any number of examples given throughout the present book demonstrate.

18 An analysis of the Nuer case, in the spirit of Gudeman (1986), is given by Evans-Pritchard (1956:163f.):

> If a man has a right to cattle in the division of a girl's bridewealth he does not lose that right at death. Indeed, if he is dead he not only retains the right but his claims are given precedence, as being "the right of a ghost" over those of the living. These cattle are ghok jookni, "cattle of the ghosts", and they must be handed over to his sons.[...]The rights of the dead in bridewealth cattle derive not only from the fact that it is their kinswoman who is being married but also from the feeling Nuer have that a line of descent is attached to its herd. Whatever individual may have control over the herd it is thought of as being in a vague general sense owned by the ghosts who once tended it, for though the animals change the herd is felt to have a sort of continuity. This is partly why ghosts are addressed at invocations at weddings. It must be explained to those on the bride-groom's side that the cattle are leaving the herd so that a girl of another lineage may come into the family to bear sons who will continue their own lineage; and it must be explained to those on the bride's side that she is being married with cattle which will enable her family to acquire a wife who will bear sons to continue their lineage.

By way of comparison it is interesting to note Goody's (1962: ch. VIII) discussion of the fixed payments made on deaths occurring among the LoDagaa of Northern Ghana, where again there is no suggestion of given numbers having any particular mystical significance. This question is also mentioned briefly in the preface to this book.

19 The allocation of proportionately equal amounts of water, needed for wet rice cultivation, from the village tank of Pul Eliya in Ceylon, as described by Leach (1961:160f.) shows the application of principles homologous to those applied by the Mahabrahman in Benares. In the Ceylonese case, however, the allocation has no basis in *jajmani*, in spite of the presence of castes.

20 The Japanese commonly make this distinction between cardinal and ordinal numbers explicit by using Arabic numerals for the former and Chinese characters for the latter, so that March, April and May are written as 三月, 四月 and 五月, where 三, 四 and 五 are simply 3, 4 and 5, and 月, 'month'.

21 $(k(a^2-b^2))^2 + (2kab)^2 = (k(a^2+b^2))^2.$

22 Its importance in relation to time is a major theme of chapter 7.

23 Age-sets are to some extent a case apart, particularly since alternate generations are often equated with each other, as among the Jie of Uganda (Gulliver 1955:250), or in any case in which names tend to be repeated, establishing a

recurrent cycle over the generations, as among the Rendille of Kenya (Spencer 1973:33).

24 The most exhaustive treatment is to be found in Yano (1973), though the subject is of course dealt with in any number of standard texts. Failure to understand the Japanese obsession with rank, and its consequences, made President Reagan look absurd in the eyes of the Japanese, when he addressed the prime-minister, Nakasone, by his given name, Yasuhiro. Indeed, according to the rules set out by Yano (1973), there is almost certainly no one in Japan, except possibly an older brother of Nakasone, who can address him in this way. Significantly, boys' names such as Ichiro, Jiro, Sanro, incorporating the series of natural numbers, are very common – whatever the requirements of *seimeigaku*, as given in ch. 4.

25 One wonders how much the enormous popularity of golf in modern Japan is related to the fact that the system of handicaps not only ranks the players in order of proficiency, but the 18 holes of the course in order of difficulty. The Japanese, also, are obsessed with the numerical aspects of baseball (Whiting 1977:6f.).

26 *Dan* has many different meanings, both concrete and abstract, but implicit in all of them is the idea of an ordered series, such as of a flight of steps, or of the terraces used in wet-rice cultivation. Such phenomena are typical of Japan, to the point even that the way to the top of the highest mountain, Fuji, largely consists of flights of steps, with numbered 'stations' occurring at regular intervals. On this point see also Snodgrass (1985:282f.) 'The symbolism of the stairways'.

27 Note how Shorto (1963:581) refers to the 'series, subsumable under the formula $2^n + 1$, which recurs time and again in political contexts in South East Asia'.

28 These were the 32 townships in the traditional division of the Mon Kingdom of lower Burma. Shorto (1963) is without doubt an analogue of Tambiah's (1976:101f.) *mandala* model.

29 The 37 *nats* are according to tradition the individual members of the Burmese pantheon. Shorto (1967) derives the number, on the implicit basis of the *mandala*, from the sum $1 + 4 + 32$.

30 The *mandala*-based topography of the old Japanese capital of Kyoto, as well as that of the old imperial palace at the centre, is still maintained, and this is reflected in the names of the nine original wards, which in English are, simply, *centre*, *upper*, *lower*, *left*, *right*, *north*, *east*, *south* and *west*. The principle is not affected by the addition of Fushimi and Yamashina, which increase the number to eleven.

31 Some idea of the different forms of symbolic representation to be found in the *mandala* is given by Snodgrass (1985:111f.).

32 Tambiah (1976: ch. 7) is a much more thorough treatment, which is essential to any complete understanding of the *mandala*.

Chapter 6

1 'It is more important to investigate the circumstances under which primitive people perform the operation of genuine measurement and the extent to which they use it, than it is to determine the fact that they employ this or that customary unit of measurement' (Hallowell 1942:63).

2 Harris (1979) is a work which takes a position directly opposed to that of Sahlins, although no mention is made of Malinowski. The debate is critical for the determining factors of any culture, and the particular part played by numerical phenomena has been largely ignored – notwithstanding the contribution of authors such as Hallpike (1979, ch. 6). In the context of this debate numbers are a case of their own, but the question may be shortly stated in the following form.

Do numerical systems develop in response to the demands of some sort of 'utility', or is such 'utility' no more than a cultural construct which will only emerge where an already pre-existent numerical system can provide it with the operational means for satisfying its demands? In spite of the stand taken by Harris, the secular trend of modern anthropology is more in the direction of the second alternative.

3 'There is no means of bringing linear concepts of all kinds into a single unified category of spatial attributes because the units of measure expressing the distance travelled on a journey, for example, are categorically distinct from those applied to the length of a piece of string' (Hallowell 1942:65). Even in the modern world there is not much cognitive identification between an inch and a mile, save possibly in regard to the scale of large-scale maps.

4 In Africa, also, there is a proliferation of local measures (Zaslavsky 1973:86).

5 This does not mean that the farmer has necessarily 'measured' the area under cultivation. As a practical point, measurement is easier for 'manipulable' than for 'non-manipulable' areas (Hallpike 1979:254): the former term refers to objects which can be handled, such as grain, where the latter would refer, in this case, to the ground from which the grain was harvested.

6 The Chamula farmers know perfectly well whether it is more advantageous to sell corn in small lots, measured in *cuartillos*, in the local market, or in bulk, measured in *toneladas*, to the Mexican government warehouses.

7 The problems arising by trying to combine time with money are a special case, which is dealt with in ch. 8.

8 As stated in ch. 8: 'The strength of money as a cultural institution, is derived from its capacity to represent quantity in the most abstract and general terms.'

9 This is essentially the case of the Indian populations in the highlands of Chiapas, discussed in the previous section. Here the preliterate local cultures have absorbed many elements of the literate Spanish culture of the Mexican state. This process is described, in its relation to money and number, in Crump (1978).

10 In Japanese, the character 分 has much the same range of meanings, but as a verb it has an autochthonous reading 'wakeru', while as a noun it is generally 'bun', which is derived from Chinese.

11 The Chinese approach to time is described in ch. 7.

12 The twentieth century has witnessed a further step in the process of mensuration, with new definitions derived from fundamental wave theory. The metre is thus defined in terms of a multiple of the wavelength of radiation emitted by the atom of Krypton 86.

Chapter 7

1 Macey (1980) is an excellent study of the profound cultural changes brought about by the invention of the clock: the modern position is given by Bolter (1986).

2 Whitrow (1961:292, 313) considers, in some detail, whether it is necessary to assume time in order to explain time, allowing that if this is so, time must be regarded as 'ultimate'. He refuses, however, to regard time as no more than a 'mysterious illusion of the intellect', but sees it rather as an essential feature of the universe. This is essentially how physicists view time, but further discussion is beyond the scope of the present book.

3 For classical Greece, this point is considered in some detail by Leach (1966:127).

4 Dempsey (1971) is a short survey of work in this field done by experimental psychologists.

165

5 The use of the word 'co-ordinate' refers to the mathematical idea of an axis with a fixed point from which numerical co-ordinates are measured according to a given scale. In the western calendar the origin is then the point separating the years B.C. and A.D.

6 Geertz (1973:365f.) is an interesting discussion of the question of simultaneity in relation to the Balinese conceptualisation of time.

7 Evans-Pritchard (1940, ch. VI) is the classic description of such a system.

8 The cognitive problems involved by terms such as 'yesterday' and 'tomorrow' are discussed by Hallowell (1937:651f.).

9 Time is of course related to distance in traditional society, as is to be seen from such expressions as 'three days' journey', but then it becomes a substitute for the measure of distance by some other standard. Numerical concepts, such as speed or wages, combining two separate dimensions, are largely absent in traditional cultures (Hallowell 1937:649), as also are equivalences between different units of time. It is remarkable how a cognitive system can work with durations as different as a century and a second, although the two can hardly occur together in any one context. The idea of defining equivalences, so that there are sixty minutes in an hour, or twenty-four hours in a day, first occurred in Babylon and Egypt long before the beginning of the Christian era. In the history of the Church the doctrine of purgatory, which first emerged in the twelfth century (Le Goff 1981:183), projected an essentially worldly time structure on to the life hereafter, with far reaching consequences for popular belief and devotion. In the scheme of Dante's Divine Comedy, Purgatory, in contrast to both Heaven and Hell, was a kingdom in time (ibid.: 475), where, eventually, the time spent could be shortened by the intervention of those of the faithful still living in the world, first by means of suitable devotions, and finally by gifts, in money, to the Church. In the context of numeracy this last development, in its implicit equation of time with money, represents a fascinating synthesis of the traditional and modern. Its implications for modern European history, starting with Luther's attack on the whole system and the protestant reformation, have been far-reaching.

10 It is significant that the Anglican prayer-book (with its very limited number of holy-days), and whose introduction more or less coincided with that of the clockwork timepiece, is much less 'Pythagorean' than any of its Roman Catholic predecessors. The nineteenth Sunday after Trinity requires only the measurement of the lapse of nineteen weeks, and connotes little more than the collect, epistle and gospel for that day.

11 Cultures, such as that of the Kapauku Papuans, which the local ecology has left quite unconscious of the natural succession of years, play no part in the present analysis, simply because there is no need to measure time. The Kapauku have, however, a highly developed decimal counting system, which is essential for the monetary transactions which are a constant feature of their daily lives (Pospisil 1963:94). As a numerical phenomenon money is essentially arithmetical and based on cardinal numbers. It has no place in any Pythagorean system. In its relation to time, see below, n.28.

12 The days of the week are in fact alternative forms of the ordinal numbers from 1 to 7, for use only in this single case: see p. 38 above.

13 See ch. 3, fig. 3. On this basis any one hour in a sixty-year cycle is uniquely identified by a combination consisting of four pairs of characters. This provides the common basis for Chinese horoscopes (Palmer 1986:37).

14 Thompson (1970:281) identifies the successive days with the thirteen gods who

rule over the numbers one to thirteen, noting that 'they, being attached to the day-names, are also repeated through all eternity'.

15 Only in 1539 did the Mayapan calendar reform represent the conversion of the Maya to lineal time (Edmonson 1976:716).

16 The Mayan archeological sites are covered with hieroglyphic texts, many of which record the dates of past events, often in terms of the highly complex Initial Series system, in which the common starting point for all component cycles has been reckoned to correspond to the year 3113 B.C. in our calendar (Thompson 1972:23). This is almost a thousand years earlier than the traditional first date for the publication of the Chinese Almanac.

17 It is as if one had to calculate the number of days separating Thursday, the 4th and Saturday, the 22nd, in any year of our calendar.

18 The phases of the moon are however important for fishing at sea, which may be a reason why the lunar calendar remains so popular in Japan. Among the major religions, the lunar calendar still governs Islam, so that Ramadan, the ninth month of the lunar year, during which the faithful must fast during the daylight hours – in recognition of the original revelation of the Quran – may occur at any season.

19 Is this also the case in the West? In Hardy's (1940:78) view, 'the mathematics[...]which can be used by economists or sociologists hardly rises to "scholarship standard"', whereas stellar astronomy stands at the highest level in popular estimation (ibid.: 4).

20 The astronomical explanation is simple. Five Venus 'years' are almost exactly equal to eight normal years.

21 This led Japanese court astronomers to over-predict, so as to be on the safe side when the catastrophes associated with eclipses occurred (Nakayama 1969:52).

22 After all it was only in the eighteenth century that Halley was able to demonstrate the periodicity of the comet now named after him, and which history now shows to have appeared at critical moments in the more distant past.

23 In the last six hundred years only the K'ang Hsi emperor (1662–1723) has reigned so long. In the whole of Japanese history, where the same system of dating is used, the Showa Emperor, who died in 1989, was the first ever to enter the sixty-first year of his reign. The Japanese emperors have, however, never had the same power over the calendar as the Chinese emperors. The fact that in the *Shōwa* era the year known as *kinoe no ne* – the year (1986, according to the sixty-year cycle, has the same name as that of the year 1926) creates few serious problems in the present bureaucratic culture, which is content simply to refer to this year as Showa 61. This is a case of *kanreki* (see p. 91 below), but the numerological implications for an emperor's life on the throne had to be worked out for the first time in 1986.

24 Not only Chinese emperors had the prerogative to rule time: the Book of Daniel (vii: 25) reproaches the Emperor Antiochus Epiphanes that he 'shall think to change the times and the law'.

25 The invention of increasingly accurate clocks and chronometers, from the end of the seventeenth century, turned this process on its head, so that by knowing the exact time, it was possible then to determine one's exact location, an important matter for navigation at sea (on which question see also the discussion of Caroline-islands navigation in ch. 4). The necessary calculations also required the development of more advanced mathematics, enabling the publication of

almanacs accurately predicting the movements of the heavenly bodies to be sighted.

26 The whole somewhat involved process is well explained in Krupp (1984:192).

27   [...]the higher Nilus swells
        The more it promises: as it ebbs, the seedsman
        Upon the slime and ooze scatters his grain,
        And shortly comes the harvest.
                Shakespeare, Antony and Cleopatra, Act II, Scene VII.

Note also the Andamanese 'who have adopted an original method of marking the different periods of the year by means of the odoriferous flowers that are in bloom at different times. Their calendar is a calendar of scents' (Radcliffe-Brown 1922:311f.).

28 'The extraordinary fascination exercised by money is better understood if one realises how it provides for the measurement of time and of the events which define a man's life until his complete disappearance beyond the land of the dead.' (de Coppet 1970:37). Note, however, that the 'Are 'Are recognise no smaller divisions of the day or night (ibid.: 18).

29 The correct transliteration 'Motecuçuma', means Courageous Lord (Collis 1954:50). Collis' fascinating book tells the numerological story in great detail, and provides the basis for the present text.

30   Men at some time are masters of their fates;
        The fault, dear Brutus, is not in our stars,
        But in ourselves[...].

These words of Cassius in Shakespeare's Julius Caesar (I.ii.134) find hardly an echo in the cultures now being considered, to which our whole concept of fault (which is Shakespeare's also) is quite alien. Indeed, to us, time like money (Crump 1981:284f.) is profane, and the best things in life have nothing to do with either. In the present context, a poem such as John Donne's *The Sun Rising* must be seen as the rankest heresy:

        Busy old fool, unruly Sun,
        Why dost thou thus,
        Through windows, and through curtains call on us?
        Must to thy motions lovers' seasons run?
        [...]
        Love all alike, no seasons knows, nor clime,
        Nor hours, days, months, which are the rags of time.

31 Over the long term species do of course become extinct, and modern computer science has even shown that this is part of a mathematical process (Dewdney 1986).

32 There are special points of interaction between cosmos and nature, such as the tides which depend upon the phases of the moon. King Canute, when, in the presence of his courtiers, the rising tide would not turn at his command, showed that even a King was powerless to challenge the cosmos in its control of nature.

33 In the Japanese context one should compare the three natural disasters (known as 'sansai'), fire, flood and storm, which represented nature in a form which man could not control.

34 Since the twelve months of the lunar calendar are less than a year, a thirteenth, intercalary month, is included about every third year. This simply repeats one of the twelve named months, but the appropriate festivals are not celebrated a second time. It follows also that important dates, such as that of the winter solstice or the spring equinox, do not in successive years occur on the same date in the lunar calendar.

35 According to Tsuboi (1970:28⁹), the Japanese word *manebi* for 'copy' is cognate with *manabu*, 'to learn'.
36 See the traditional use of the *obi* described in chapter 4, p. 49. The tradition may date back to the Heian period (794–1185) (Ohnuki-Tierney 1984:182).
37 These ceremonies are simply referred to as *shichi-go-san*, lit. 'seven-five-three'.
38 Death, like birth, is the occasion for bestowing a new name, which will be chosen by the temple priests, then to be inscribed on the tombstone. For this a very large fee is charged – although this does pay for all rites carried out in later years.
39 This is true even if the marriage is childless, because the problem of succession can always be solved by adoption (Smith 1983:89–90).
40 The scheme set out in the present text is based on two popular works, Miyako (1980) and Tsuboi (1970) but it must be appreciated that there is no rigorous separation of the domains of Buddhism and Shinto, whose definition can vary from one community to another. Following Embree (1939:221) in his chapter on traditional religion, 'The only religious system[...]is the festival calendar, marking as it does the phases of the moon and the seasons of the year.'

Chapter 8

1 Holtz (1984) is the most recent general study of the origins of money.
2 The Kula ring, first made known to anthropology by Malinowski (1922), has its cognitive base in a similar concept, which also provides a bridge between otherwise quite unrelated local cultures.
3 A well-known present day exponent of this approach, which finds a classic demonstration in Clower (1969:297).
4 Whose views are no more than standard for most western monetary theorists.
5 Marxist theoreticians, in particular, are inclined to argue the contrary, but in doing so they ignore the cognitive base of the local culture, and impose instead their own theoretical position. For a specific example see Godelier 1974.
6 *Kula* in fact means 'ring'.
7 The economy of the Kapauku of western New Guinea, as described by Pospisil (1963), provides one clear exception to this statement.
8 Atiyah (1979) expounds, in detail, the legal-historical background.
9 For all the meanings of this symbol, see Nelson (1974:183).
10 This point is analysed in detail in Crump (1981:4).
11 This explains also the popular designations of coins, such as *nickel*, *stuiver*, *tanner*, *sou* etc.
12 The mathematical analysis to be found in such texts almost invariably uses a purely algebraic notation, without ever making explicit any recognised monetary denomination.
13 For the fallacies which may then arise, see Crump (1981:268f.).
14 The most common case of the self-liquidating transaction is represented by a sale of goods according to the provisions of s.28 of the (British) Sale of Goods Act 1893, whereby 'the delivery of the goods, and the payment of the price, are concurrent conditions'. This is no more than a standard provision of commercial law in any modern jurisdiction.
15 This ideal is to be found in many quite unrelated cultures. In the Judeo-Christian tradition it is the theme of Isaiah xl:4, in the Old Testament, which is constantly taken up again in the New Testament (e.g. Matthew vi:12).
16 This is a generic term used by de Coppet for want of a better translation. In fact the 'Are'Are dead are not generally buried, so the term is hardly apt. It must be

taken to refer to the role of those who prepare the resting place of the deceased, whatever form this may take. On the point see the photographic illustrations in de Coppet & Zemp (1978).

17 The status and functions of the big men are described in de Coppet (1968:50f.).

18 The supply of 'Are 'Are money is maintained by trade, on a very restricted scale, with the outside world. It is a point worth noting that what to the 'Are 'Are will be money need not be so to the outside suppliers. The classic instance of this happening is provided by the Maria Theresa thaler, which originated in Austria in the eighteenth century but whose circulation, in the twentieth century, has been confined to Ethiopia (Pankhurst 1965:373f.).

19 Note how the title to de Coppet 1970 distinguishes between the two monetary cycles applying respectively to homicide and natural death.

20 'The money game' is the theme (and title) of ch. 2 of Crump (1981), which looks at 'Are 'Are money from this perspective, and in some detail.

21 Compare chapters 5 and 7, for the way in which the ranking of individuals may be determined by considerations of time.

22 The original '*le regime du produit rarefié*' is much clearer.

23 In this case any definition of money in terms of exchange is bound to be tautologous.

24 Boas (1898:54–5), notes, in relation to the North-West Coast Indians of British Columbia, that the capital represented by outstanding debts far exceeds the quantity of valuables available for discharging them, and points out how this position is comparable to that of any modern monetary system.

25 Compare the Uruk bookkeeping system described by Schmandt-Besserat (1979:40). In ancient Egypt all taxes paid in kind were invoiced as 'labour', which was in practice a measure based on time. In this way, as Goody (1977:88) notes correctly, accounting systems can be used to develop a generalised system of equivalences even in the absence of a generalised medium of exchange. The question is whether the unit used in such a system is ever a unit of time.

26 According to the medieval Church, money was also a fungible, because when money was lent, what was returned was a generally equivalent amount of money, but not the identical coins which had been lent. It is this complete absence of separate identity which establishes money as a phenomenon of *cardinal numbers*.

27 Three possible interpretations are given in Peake (1962:790). Note also the way in which the living could buy indulgences to lessen the time the departed spent in purgatory: ch. 7, n.9.

28 For the tensions which arise in such cases see Ortiz (1973:154f.) (Colombia) and Watson (1958:106f.) (Zambia).

29 The concept of 'stickyness' comes from Keynes (1936:304) who maintained that it was essential for maintaining the 'stability of values in a monetary system'. The title of his book *The General Theory of Employment, Interest and Money* embraces precisely those two qualities which are related to money by means of time.

30 That this is not always the case is shown by Birch (1971), which describes the Pardhi, a tribe of central India, whose monetary operations consist exclusively of lending at interest to outsiders. It is the three ethical religions of the western world, Judaism, Christianity and Islam, which have the strictest rules relating to usury (Crump 1981:74), but it should still be noted that the arithmetical and bookkeeping demands of lending at interest may be beyond the intellectual resources of many traditional societies. This factor is undoubtedly related to the uses and development of literacy (Goody 1977:88f.), which is in no way essential to the emergence of money.

Chapter 9

1 This is what makes car-horns, tuned to recognised musical intervals, so irritating to anyone who cares for music, for they represent an anomalous and deliberate confusion in function between music and noise.

2 To demonstrate the existence of harmonics, a piano can be used in the following way. Press any key, slowly, so that the note is not actually sounded, and hold it down. Strike hard the key for an octave higher, and immediately release it. The note will then continue to resonate, quite audibly, on the undamped strings of the lower octave. The experiment can be carried out not only with the first harmonic, the octave, but with every succeeding harmonic, but the volume of resonance will continually decline (Apel 1970:10). This phenomenon was observed in China by Tung Chung-Shu in the second century B.C. (Ronan and Needham 1981:364).

3 Expressed mathematically, if a_0 is the amplitude of the note itself, and a_1, a_2, a_3, ... those of the successive harmonics, so that the series a_n converges uniformly (and generally quite rapidly) to zero, then the timbre is defined by the successive ratios $a_0:a_1$, $a_1:a_2$ and so on. It is particularly to be noted that since the octaves are defined in terms of successive powers of two, the harmonics will become much 'denser' in the higher octaves, where their amplitudes will generally be very small. Since the ear is insensitive to high frequencies, some harmonics may be inaudible, so that the note actually heard will differ, very marginally, from that played. This phenomenon can be demonstrated by listening to music being played over the telephone, which is even less sensitive to high frequencies than the human ear. It should also be noted that the most recent computer-based research has demonstrated that the above explanation is somewhat oversimplified. For the latest, but more complex analysis, presented in popular form, see Mathews and Pierce (1987:93).

4 Of the 176 scores of primitive music given by Schneider (1957:61f.) not one is so elementary.

5 Rhythm, according to the above analysis, is strictly 'isometric' (Apel 1970:729), but there are other so-called 'multimetric' rhythms, such as that of Gregorian chant. The isometric rhythm remains fundamental, none the less.

6 This is a somewhat simplified conception of 'melody'. According to Apel's (1970:517) analysis, 'each musical sound has two fundamental qualities, pitch and duration, and both these enter into the successions of pitch-plus-duration values known as melodies. To consider melody and rhythm separate or ever mutually exclusive phenomena[...]is misleading. If a distinction between the pitch quality ("high-low") and the time quality ("long-short") is needed, the proper terms are motion and rhythm. Melody may thus be said to consist of motion plus rhythm, and every melody can be separated into a motion skeleton and a rhythm skeleton[...]'

7 Compare the Emperor's power over the calendar, discussed in ch. 7 (p. 86).

8 Needham (1969:313f.), in his discussion of the Chinese word *lu*, which refers both to 'statutes' and 'regulations' and to the series of standard bamboo pitch-pipes, suggests that the Chinese never considered that the latter were governed by 'any kind of law in the non-human phenomenal world'.

9 'certain common features in the Chinese and Pythagorean methods of drawing up scales make a common origin seem likely; the Babylonians, with their highly developed string instruments, may well have been this source' (Ronan and Needham 1981:374). No one has yet been able to discover what Babylonian music actually sounded like (Farmer 1957:233, 239).

10 The mathematical theory is discussed in Hardy & Wright (1945: chapter XI), 'Approximation of Rationals by Irrationals'.

11 Schönberg, and other modern composers, have indeed worked with twelve-tone systems, but this is but one instance of the so-called serial music in which 'the traditional rules and conventions governing all aspects of music – tonality, melody, harmony, rhythm, etc. – are discarded[...]' (Apel 1970:766).

12 'Scale', derived from the Latin 'scala', originally meant no more than 'ladder'.

13 The black keys on a piano correspond to a pentatonic scale, and the white keys to a diatonic scale.

14 The major and minor keys correspond to two modes.

15 One should note here the great number of instruments, including the human voice, which can only produce one note at a time.

16 'According to the Pythagorean theory, the smaller the numbers that express the ratio of the frequencies of intervals (or the lengths of the corresponding strings), the more consonant the intervals' (Apel 1970:201).

17 Scottish highland dancing would seem to provide a good instance of this, but the tradition dates only from the nineteenth century.

18 Although change-ringing is truly traditional, Stedman's 'Tintinnalogia' (1668) and 'Campanologia' (1677) entirely transformed the art (Morris 1974:34).

19 The purists would call this a 'touch', for nothing less than 5,000 changes is deemed a 'peal' (Morris 1951:103).

20 Note the criticism of Dr Burney (quoted in Morris 1974:37): 'melody has not been consulted in the choice of changes: there seems a mechanical order and succession in them all, without the least idea of selecting such as are most melodious and agreeable'.

21 It has also a curious affinity to the *I Ching*, or Chinese Book of Changes, discussed in ch. 4. In particular the 'changes' which transform one hexagram into another can be equated to the dodge in change-ringing.

22 The treatment of oral poetry in the present section is based largely on Finnegan 1977.

23 Alliteration, rather than metre, is the governing principle of Somali poetry, whose cultural role is described in Andrzejewski and Lewis (1964).

24 Finnegan (1977:79f.) stresses that in 'oral' cultures, poetry is 'performed' although in some cases, such as that of worksongs, the performers and the audience will be one and the same.

25 Wodehouse (1953) is a humorous novel, revolving around a Canadian poet, whose main contribution to the narrative is the single line, 'Across the pale parabola of joy'. One recognises the poem, not by the language – which is nearly meaningless – but by the metre, which is numerically defined: this line is a perfect iambic pentameter.

26 It is interesting to note that with the protestant reformation, when the scriptures were presented for the first time in the vernacular, the Reformed Churches considered it important to adopt metrical versions of the psalms, as a more biblical form of musical worship. The usage continues to this day, particularly in Scotland.

27 There are also ancilliary languages, admittedly of limited scope, based on whistling.

28 Finnegan (1977:57) notes 'an instructive contrast between different kinds of work songs among Texas prisoners. Thus songs which accompany critically-timed tasks, such as a team of men cutting down a tree, give little scope for change or development in the singing.[...]But songs for less rigorously timed group-work

like cotton picking or sugarcane cutting give more opportunities for solo songs and for lyrical and ornamental development by the leader.'

29 The musical accompaniment for dancing can be sung as well as instrumental. An example is provided by the Faroese *grindadansur* (Wylie and Margolin 1981:114f.), a dance which represents the ordering of the local island society in relation to the mass slaughter of a school of pilot whales.

30 As Spencer (1985:1) makes clear, dancing can merge into many other kinds of physical activity, in one and the same event. The Tonga Islanders use the word '*heliaki*' to imply an additional, deeper meaning, in any action or utterance, so that, it represents, also, the imponderable element, which transforms movement into dance (Kaeppler 1985:96f.). The principle of *heliaki* has, however, no numerical connotations.

31 Difficult but not impossible: considering what he achieved with the Musical Offering (Hofstadter 1980:9f.), the task would hardly have been beyond J. S. Bach, whose obsession with numbers – in the field of musical composition – is equal to Dante's in the field of poetry.

32 There may be cases – such as that of tap-dancing – where the audible marking of the rhythm is part of the action, but this is not music: so, also, a dancer who sings, or plays an instrument, while the dance is in progress, provides no more than incidental music, not inherent in the action of the dance. This latter instance is, however, rare.

In contrast to this, the Tonga have a ritual – not, apparently, recognised as a dance – by which foodstuffs presented on certain ceremonial occasions are counted. It is no doubt the absence of any appropriate *heliaki* (see above, n.30) which prevents the actions performed from constituting a dance.

Compare also the Lugbara, who have no dances without song, and use the same word, *ongo*, for both song and dance (Middleton 1985:168).

33 A twentieth-century example would be Planck's constant, which measures the smallest quantum of energy.

34 The formula for the Divine Comedy is based on three-line stanzas, with the first and third lines rhyming, and the second line providing the rhyme for the following stanza: this is the terza (that is 'third') *rima*. This formula, although used successfully in a number of modern translations, such as that by Dorothy Sayers of necessity fails to make the same impact on contemporary English readers as it did on the inhabitants of thirteenth-century Italy.

35 Milner (1971:253) notes that humour is often based upon accidental similarity and resulting ambiguity in 'surface structure' corresponding to dissimilarity in 'deep structure'. This is why Wodehouse's line, cited in note 25, is so successful.

36 Mori (1980) does not suggest any such connotations under the entries for 17 and 33.

Chapter 10

1 The only evidence for the death sentence is to be found in the bas reliefs decorating the ball-court at Chichen Itza (Blanchard and Cheska 1985:105). These provoked one visitor to comment, 'It would have been no good to say, "as number two we have to try harder".'

2 It may still be important. The importance of gambling on cockfights for the local economy of Bali is noted by Geertz (1973:432, n.18). For a modern economy compare Rothschild (1976:11f.).

3 Roulette, however seriously it may be taken by addicts, is pure *alea*, as is 'beggar-

my-neighbour'. It is interesting how many games of pure chance, such as for instance, roulette or craps, give unequal chances to the players. This indeed provides yet another way of classifying games, that is, according as to whether all players have the same status. In some cases, such as cricket or baseball, balance may be achieved by reversing the status of the competing sides in the course of the game, but still, in this case, 'winning the toss', which may be absolutely decisive, is pure alea. It is however no accident that casino's prefer to offer games loaded in favour of the bank, which then never passes out of their hands.

4 Compare Huizinga's (1950:173) theories of ontogenesis: 'civilization is in its earliest phases, played[...]it arises in and as play and never leaves it'.

5 An American Indian version, known as 'Tillikum', is described in Macfarlan (1985:168f.).

6 The most elementary representation is known as a 'digraph', that is a directed graph, but Hage and Harary's standard work (1983) does not deal with this, or any other game in this context.

7 Suppose n children out of N – with n < N – must be chosen to fetch firewood. All N children then play *janken* until a round with only two out of the three possible signs occurs. The losers, if exactly n in number, will constitute the whole detail. If there are less than n losers, these are chosen in any case, and the game continues so as to make up the detail out of the remaining children. In the same way, the losers on a given round, if more than n, must go on playing until the number is brought down to n. Japanese children, playing the game with great speed, reach this result surprisingly quickly. The mathematics belongs to the theory of Markov chains, for which see, generally, Hage and Harary (1983:145f.).

8 The existence of specifically linguistic games, such as scrabble, does not affect the point being made. The structure is still logical rather than linguistic. After all to play scrabble, in say Albanian, one would have to learn Albanian, not scrabble. I have myself successfully introduced boggle – another word game – into a Japanese family with children at primary school, notwithstanding my relatively poor command of Japanese. Indeed once the object of the game was understood, it more or less explained itself.

9 The use of language in games is seldom syntactic, as in a normal text, but deictic, in that it refers, directly, to a position in the game. The use of the word 'check' in chess is a prime example. Many games, indeed, can be played without using language at all. For another case of deictic usage, see Crump (1988:138).

10 In numerical terms *knave* is but another word for 'eleven', *queen* for 'twelve', and *king* for 'thirteen'. At the same time the four suits are also ranked in terms of the first four ordinal numbers, but in this case it is more than convenient that each has its distinctive name, since the order is changed when one suit becomes 'trumps'.

11 A well known example is the four-colour theorem, of which the statement is elementary, but the proof so difficult that it required hundreds of hours of mainframe computer time (Appel & Haken 1978).

12 Significantly, the strategy required by computer football, where the field is represented on a television screen, is still that of actual football, even though the physical skills needed are much more restricted, while the underlying mathematical base, inherent in the computer programme, adds an entirely new element. Bar football falls somewhere between these two extremes.

13 The diffusion of *oware* is related in Zaslavsky (1973: chapter 11), which is also the main source for the discussion in the present chapter.

14 Statistically, in any chance event, such as the throw of a die, deviation from the

mean outcome, becomes progressively smaller as the number of such events increases. Thus, where, with six throws of a dice, the chance of each face coming up once is small, in a run of 6000 throws, each face will come up 1000 times to a degree of approximation smaller than the margin of skill possessed by a player who must choose a strategy depending on the outcome of every throw, and if this is not true for 6000 throws, it will be for 60,000, or some larger number. The margin of skill between any two players may be taken to be a mathematical constant, which, however small, must in the end always exceed the deviation from the mean outcome, as it steadily decreases to a zero limit.

15 One could make a whole study of the use of metaphors borrowed from games: 'stalemate', borrowed from chess, is, for instance, a common metaphor in political reporting. It would be interesting to know of any such metaphorical uses to be found in traditional societies.

16 Mead (1970:334) contrasts the rich symbolism of Bali with that of the Lepchas of Sikkim, 'who have virtually no symbolic life at all[...][and whose] children play hardly any games'.

17 It is easy enough to cite examples from the modern world, if only by taking the case of all those involved in football hooliganism. In an extreme case, in 1969 war broke out between Honduras and El Salvador, following the outcome of a qualifying match for the World Cup played in Mexico City.

18 The point is well made by David Slansky, the son of a professor of mathematics, quoted in Alvarez (1984:135):

'In poker, if you're better than anyone else you make immediate money. If there's something that I know about the game that the other person doesn't, and if he's not willing to learn or can't understand, then, I take his money.[...]But in the business world things aren't like that. I was always being told what to do by incompetent people, and I hated it. The world is full of idiots, and I can't handle it. I can't handle the politics involved. But this town [Las Vegas] gives me what I want. I like the freedom of the gambler's life, I like being my own boss, I like the way you are rewarded directly according to your ability, not according to what people think of you.'

There is hardly any element in Slansky's philosophy of life which would be acceptable in a traditional society. The culture of poker, which is examined also in Hayano (1982), belongs to the modern world, but this does not exclude gambling, even on intrinsic games, from traditional societies, as witness the Chinese obsession with Mah Jong, as described by Fleming (1983:178, 193).

19 This provides the basis for the distinction between gambling and insurance, which also involves placing money on an uncertain future event. An 'insurable risk' however is one in which the 'bettor' is involved even where he has placed no bet. A farmer whose crops are destroyed by bad weather makes a real loss, measurable in terms of money, whether or not he has insured against it. To the non-player at least, there is no risk in the outcome of a game, on which no bet has been placed.

20 In mathematical notation, if the amount of the centre bet is C, the odds on the side bets, s, and the depth, D, then as $C \rightarrow \infty, s \rightarrow 1$ and $D \rightarrow \infty$.

21 It is interesting to note here the devotion of the upper classes, in many a western society, to games such as polo, which for economic reasons are beyond the reach of the masses.

22 If war is seen as a game – and the dividing line is not always clear – historical periods in which the war-game was played so as to involve the whole population, as in fifteenth-century England or sixteenth-century Japan, are regarded as chaotic. The Tudors in England, or the Tokugawas in Japan, are esteemed for the restoration of order by putting an end to such nonsense.

23 This is essentially a consequence of Turing's theorem, discussed in ch. 12.
24 The word '*dan*', familiar also to western Judo fans, means no more than the rung of a ladder, although in any sport it means the formal level attained by a player: see ch. 5, n.26.
25 See ch. 2, 'The Money Game', in Crump (1981).

Chapter 11

1 In Japanese (as well as Chinese, where it is pronounced *shi*) the written form for 10 is ┼, pronounced in Japanese *jū*. Because of this the normal word for the Cross (of Christ) is *jūjika*, lit. 'ten-sign-frame'. Other examples of such interpretation of numbers are to be found in Crump (1986a:91).
2 This point is very strongly argued by Street (1984:151), who points out that oral tradition may be fixed, while written texts are malleable and open to a constant process of change.
3 In this context it is interesting to compare the silver-gilt antipendium and the wooden retable of a late fifteenth-century altar now displayed in the Cathedral Treasury at Aachen. The former represents the twelve apostles, in stylised form, in two rows of six panels. The latter represents, the life of the Blessed Virgin in two rows of four panels, but the incidents are portrayed naturalistically. The seventh panel represents the Assumption of the Virgin, in the presence of the apostles, but that they number twelve only becomes apparent by counting them. These two sides of the same altar represent, therefore, a transition in the structure of design, leading in the end to the atrophy of the modular principle in the graphic arts.
4 Peake's (1962:1051) twentieth-century comment on this passage is simply 'we must not press for the Christian meaning of the details'.
5 Taking a 360-day year (such as was the basis of the calendar in the ancient Mediterranean (Usener 1903:349)), 1,260 days is exactly three and a half years, which is the precise duration of the rule of Antichrist as prophesied in the Book of Daniel (xii:7) in the Old Testament.
6 The most obvious is the divine Trinity, but note also the three temptations of Jesus, and the three days spent in the tomb. So also, such devotional formulae of the liturgy as the *Agnus Dei*, the *Mea Culpa* and the *Domine, non sum dignus*, are repeated three times. Usener (1903) is a full treatment of the symbolism of the number three (and other numbers, also), as it has developed in the western world.
7 The Hindu symbolism of weaving is worth noting: 'The loom is the cosmos. The warp [top] beam is the Essential pole of the universe; the bottom beam is its Substantial pole; or transposing the symbolism, the upper beam is Heaven and the lower beam is Earth. The weft threads are the planes of existence or the levels of being; the warp threads are the rays of informing Light or Breath, linking the upper and lower Principles. Joined together by its supporting side beams the loom forms a rectangle framing an interlaced gridwork of threads, which is precisely the form of the mandala' (Snodgrass 1985:116).
8 The graphic arts were, of course, often dominant in prehistoric times, as witness the cave paintings of Lascaux and Altamira.
9 Note, in relation to the Gothic revival of the nineteenth century, the role of William Morris, who wrote that 'we found [...] that all minor arts were in a state of complete degradation [...] and accordingly [...] I set myself to reforming all that: and started a firm for producing decorative articles' (Morris 1984:30).

Morris is perhaps best-known for his wall-papers, tapestries and carpets, all of which were designed on modular principles.

10 The modern Dutch graphic artist, M. C. Escher, derived a major part of his inspiration from the tiles incorporated into Moorish architecture in Spain, particularly in the Alhambra in Granada (Escher 1981:24). (See also figure 15.)

11 The way in which the possibilities for computerised design extend far beyond mere repetition is explained by Dewdney (1986), where the illustrations have a remarkable resemblance to the traditional tile and mosaic patterns of the Islamic world.

12 The Japanese word *kata*, whose general meaning is 'form' or 'shape', also has a specific meaning, 'module', in the sense of the present chapter. The *tatami*, or mats of standard size, which cover the floor of any Japanese house, are an everyday expression of the principle of *kata*.

13 Such architecture may well be subject to essentially negative injunctions. To give one example (Barnes 1982:14), 'Kedang say that odd numbers are the numbers of life, while even numbers are the numbers of death. A house, for example, may not be built with an even number of spars on any side of the roof.'

14 Another example of the connection between the number 33 and the Kannon Buddha is provided by the sanjūsansho (literally, '33 places'), which refers to 33 temples in and around Kyoto. It was believed in medieval Japan that anyone who had visited all of these temples would be preserved from hell.

15 The Buddha with 1,000 hands (depicted in the same way) is to be found also in seventeen of the temples comprising the sanjūsansho (see above, n.14).

16 Note how these numbers occur in the traditional English song 'Green grow the rushes O' (see ch. 9).

17 Since Sanjūsangendō belongs to essentially the same religious tradition, it will certainly reflect the same approach to number mysticism. There is however no space for a detailed comparison.

18 It is significant the chief works supervisor with the building of Borobudur was the *sutradhara*, literally 'the one who holds the measuring rope' (Bernet Kempers 1963:46).

19 The description, and interpretation of Borobudur are based on Bernet Kempers (1960).

20 The most recent is described in Morton (1983) by the architect who actually carried it out.

21 For the enormous variety of symbolic meaning attached to the stairways see Snodgrass (1985:282f.).

22 This is needless to say the same as the Mount Sumeru mentioned on p. 135 in connection with Sanjūsangendō, with the 32 heavens there represented corresponding to the four heavens of the original Hindu cosmology.

23 Compare the relationship betweenhell and purgatory as represented in Dante's Divine Comedy (Anderson 1980:251, 257).

24 The basic message of the bas-reliefs is that the body and mind of man are a constantly changing combination and interchange of elements or *dharmas*. The instantaneous combination of certain *dharmas* is to be explained by *karma*, the law of cause and effect, which reaches beyond the limits of life and death (Bernet Kempers 1960:65).

25 See ch. 5 for a similar relation between Sanjūsangendō and to the Japanese Emperor Goshirakawa.

26 Compare the importance of tombs for the Merina states of Madagascar as described by Bloch (1981:137–47).

177

27 In Hinduism there are four sacred periods of time, known as the *Krita Yuga*, *Treta Yuga*, *Dvapara Yuga* and *Kali Yuga*, which last, respectively, for 1,728,000 years, 1,296,000 years, 864,000 years and 432,000 years, which are in the ratio 4:3:2:1. Distances in the same ratio are incorporated into the design of the temple complex, but with minor discrepancies in length to fit in with the fixed astronomical alignments (Pennick 1979:135). Such compromises are almost inevitable in any structure – not necessarily architectural – overloaded with numerical symbolism.

28 In the whole temple complex there was no building which could be used as a meeting point for prayer or worship. At the centre there would be a *cella*, a small building of the same basic design as the *prasad*, but its sole purpose was to provide a place where the High Priest would commune with the God of the Temple.

29 The elaborate geometrical principles, which also governed the design of the Khmer temples, are explained in Stierlin (1970:130).

30 The struggle between two cults is to be found in a number of instances in the history of the Christian Church. The iconoclastic controversy, which was at its height at the turn of the eighth century, was basically concerned with the permissible forms of artistic expression in the service of the Church. It was essentially the realism of icons which made them so objectionable, because in this way the humanity of Christ was emphasised at the cost of his divinity, destroying the balance between the two 'natures', of man and God. Although this controversy was mainly confined to the Eastern Church, it had some influence also in the domain of Charlemagne. One is led to wonder whether this, in turn, related to the emergence of modular principles in ecclesiastical architecture. It is worth noting also that some 750 years later the Western Church, as a result of the reformation, was subject to a similar controversy.

31 In the history of western art the gradual mastery of perspective, in the course of the fifteenth century (Symonds 1961:168), is one factor leading to the emphasis of geometrical as opposed to numerical factors in the graphic arts. This development may be identified with the triumph of realism over formalism.

Chapter 12

1 Dancing and acting, if hardly 'practical' according to western standards, were none the less highly professional in pre-modern Japan.

2 Geertz's (1973:412–53) explanation of the Balinese cockfight would seem to provide a classic illustration of this point, provided it can be accepted that the cockfight is a game. The Kula ring, in its classic description by Malinowski (1922), may also be seen as a 'game' involving a number of otherwise unrelated cultures, each of which it interprets it in its own way. It is, however, not strictly, a numerical institution.

3 The same is true of music 'since a close relationship exists between notational capabilities and the ability to organize musical materials' (Cohen and Katz 1979:101).

4 On the other hand the Japanese game of '*go*', which is now popular in the west, has almost unlimited potential for diffusion.

5 See also ch. 5, n.19. For further discussion, in an evolutionary perspective, see Tambiah 1976:128–9.

6 It is characteristic of the world's ethical religions, whether Buddhism, Christianity or Islam, that they not only make the adaptations necessary for crossing cultural boundaries, but also mould pre-existent local cultures to adapt them to their own

canons. The point is well-illustrated by the cultural history of Turkey, where until the end of the Byzantine period almost unrestricted representation of the human figure was allowed; this was anathema to the Islamic faith of the Ottomans, whose art was predominantly modular, and therefore numerically based, in the sense discussed in ch. 11(*Treasures from Turkey* 1986:167f.).

7 For the historical importance of such elements see ch. 5, especially nn.27 and 28. It may be that Roman Catholic missionaries brought with them the numerical elements of the doctrine of purgatory discussed in ch. 7, n.9.

8 The computer age is witness to the challenge of binary numbers, which have their own mystique expressed in words such as 'byte', but they hardly threaten the decimal system in the popular domain.

9 Difficult but not absolutely impossible: the English-speaking world has been remarkably obtuse about abandoning non-metric systems of weights and measures.

10 This development has much to do with Gödel's (1931) proof that 'for any formal system that contains arithmetic there must be true statements of the system that cannot be proved within it'.

11 An instance from Japan is instructive: in the Kyoto District Technical High School the same course provides students with instruction in the use of fourth generation main-frame computers and of the latest abacus procedures: the latter part of the course, which is highly competitive, is taught by a former national abacus champion, who solves complex arithmetical problems with breath-taking rapidity.

12 The point is really one of the definition of 'generality': professional mathematicians conceive of generality in terms of theories and constructs which have the potential to apply to a wide range of different conceivable instances, none of which need have any practical application, nor indeed be of any interest to any but a small number of specialists; the anthropologist, in contrast, is concerned with the actual instances in which a given institution occurs. The difference can be illustrated by the application of the theory of Markov chains to the game of *janken* when this is played by more than two players – as quite commonly happens in Japan. For a mathematician such application is specific to this one – for him, quite trivial – case, and for this reason, it is not even worth a footnote. On the other hand, for the anthropologist the other potential applications of the theory are so esoteric as to have little possible relevance to anything he may come across in the course of his research: the game of *janken* may then well be, for the Japan specialist, the only *general* instance of the theory applying. The gap between the two approaches is so wide as to make any communication between mathematicians and anthropologists very difficult.

References

Ahern, E. M. 1981. *Chinese Ritual and Politics*. Cambridge University Press.
Alvarez, A. 1984. *The Biggest Game in Town*. London, Fontana.
Anderson, W. 1980. *Dante, the Maker*. London, Routledge & Kegan Paul.
Andrian, F. von. 1901. Die Siebenzahl im Geistesleben der Volker. *Mittheilungen der anthropologischen Gesellschaft in Wien*.
Andrzejewski, B. W. and Lewis, I. M. 1964. *Somali Poetry*. Oxford University Press.
Apel, W. (ed.) 1970. *Harvard Dictionary of Music*. London, Heinemann.
Appel, K. and Haken, W. 1978. The Four-Color Problem. In L. A. Stern (ed.) *Mathematics Today*. New York, Springer Verlag. pp. 153–90.
Ascher, M. and Ascher, R. 1981. *Code of the Quipu*. Ann Arbor, University of Michigan Press.
Atiyah, P. S. 1979. *The Rise and Fall of the Law of Contract*. Oxford University Press.
Augustine of Hippo. 1972. *City of God*. Pelican Classics.
Aveni, A. F. 1984. Astronomy in ancient Meso-America. In E. C. Krupp (ed.) *In Search of Ancient Astronomies*. London, Penguin.
Ayer, A. J. 1963. *The Concept of a Person and Other Essays*. London, Macmillan.
Bachnik, J. M. 1983. Recruitment Strategies for Household Succession: Rethinking Japanese Household Organization. *Man*, N.S. 18:160–82.
Baddeley, A. D. 1985. *The Psychology of Memory*. London, Harper & Row.
Barnes, R. H. 1974. *Kedang: a Study of Collective Thought of an East Indonesian People*. Oxford, Clarendon Press.
1982. Number and number use in Kedang, Indonesia. *Man*, N.S. 17:1–22.
Barthes, R. 1967. *Elements of Semiology*. London, Jonathan Cape.
Bateson, G. 1958. *Naven*. Stanford University Press.
Beidelman, T. O. 1959. *A Comparative Analysis of the Jajmani System*. Locust Valley, N.Y., J. J. Augustin.
Bennett, W. C. 1878. *Final Settlement Report on District Gonda*. Government of India Printing Office.
1963. Lore and learning: numbers, measures, weights and calendars. *Handbook of South-american Indians*, vol. 5, pp. 601–10.
Bernet Kempers, A. J. 1960. *Borobudur*. Wassenaar, Servire.
Beteille, A. 1965. *Castle, Class and Power*. Berkeley, University of California Press.
Birch, S. 1971. Beggar money-lenders of Central India. In G. Dalton (ed.) *Studies in Economic Anthropology*. Washington D.C., American Anthropological Association.
Blacking, J. 1968. Percussion and transition. *Man*, N.S. 3:313–14.
1985. Movement: Dance, Music and the Venda Girls' Initiation Cycle. In P. Spencer (ed.) *Society and the Dance*. Cambridge University Press. pp. 64–91.

180

Bibliography

Blanchard, K. and Cheska, A. 1985. *The anthropology of Sport*. South Hadley, Mass., Bergin & Harvey, Publishers Inc.

Bloch, M. 1981. Tombs and States. In S. C. Humphreys and H. King (eds.) *Mortality and Immortality: the Archaeology and Anthropology of Death*. London, Academic Press.

Blofeld, J. 1968. *I. Ching. The Chinese Book of Change*. London, Allen & Unwin.

Bloor, D. 1973. Wittgenstein and Mannheim on the sociology of mathematics. *Studies in History and Philosophy of Science* 4: 173–91.

1976. *Knowledge and Social Imagery*. London, Routledge & Kegan Paul.

1983. *Wittgenstein: a Social Theory of Knowledge*. London, Macmillan.

Boas, F. 1898. *12th Report on the North-Western Tribes of Canada*. British Academy for the Advancement of Science.

Bogaert, R. 1966. *Les Origines Antiques de la Banque de Depot*. Leiden, A. W. Seythoff-Leyde.

Bolter, J. D. 1986. *Turing's Man*. London, Penguin.

Bovet, M. C. 1974. Cognitive processes among illiterate children and adults. In J. W. Berry and P. R. Dasen (eds.) *Culture and Cognition*. London, Methuen.

Brainerd, C. J. 1973a. The Origins of Number Concepts. *Scientific American*. March, 101–9.

1973b. Mathematical and behavioral foundations of number. *Journal of General Psychology*. 88:221–81.

Brinson, P. 1985. Epilogue: Anthropology and the Study of Dance. In P. Spencer (ed.) *Society and the Dance*. Cambridge University Press.

Bruner, J. S. 1964. The course of cognitive growth. In *American Psychologist*. 19:1–15.

Bryant, P. E. 1983. Jean Piaget. In A. Bullock and R. B. Woodings (eds.) *The Fontana Companion to Modern Thought*. London, Collins.

Buckland, A. W. 1896. Four as a sacred number. *Journal of the Anthropological Institute*. 25:96–102.

Burkert, W. 1972. *Lore and science in ancient Pythagoreanism*. Cambridge, Mass., Harvard University Press.

Burridge, K. 1969. *New Heaven, New Earth*. Oxford, Blackwell.

Caillois, R. 1955. Structure et classification des jeux. *Diogène*. 12:72–88.

Cancian, F. 1965. *Economics and Prestige in a Maya Community*. Stanford University Press.

Candler, H. 1910. On the symbolic use of number in the 'Divina Commedia' and elsewhere. *Transactions of the Royal Society of Literature*. Series 2:30; 1–29.

Carraher, T. N., Carraher, D. W. and Schliemann, A. D. 1985. Mathematics in the streets and in the schools. In *British Journal of Development Psychology*. 3:21–9.

Chomsky, N. 1980. The Linguistic Approach. In M. Piatelli-Palmarini (ed.) *Language and Learning*. London, Routledge & Kegan Paul.

Churchland, P. S. 1986. *Neurophilosophy*. Cambridge, Mass, The M.I.T. Press.

Clower, R. W. 1969. *Monetary Theory*. London, Penguin.

Cohen, D. and Katz, R. 1979. Notational systems and musical information. *Yearbook of the International Folk Music Council* 100–13.

Cole, M. and Bruner, J. S. 1971. Cultural Differences and Inferences about Psychological Processes. *American Psychologist* 26:866–76.

Cole, M., Gay, J. and Glick, J. 1974. Some experimental studies in Kpelle quantitative behavior. In J. W. Berry and P. R. Dasen (eds.) *Culture and Cognition. Readings in Cross-cultural Psychology*. London, Methuen.

181

Cole, M., Gay, J., Glick, J. and Sharp, D. 1971. *The Cultural Context of Learning and Thinking*. New York, Basic Books.

Collis, M. 1954. *Cortes and Montezuma*. London, Faber and Faber.

Crump, S. T. 1978. Money and Number: the Trojan Horse of Language. *Man* 13:503–18.

　　1981. *The Phenomenon of Money*. London, Routledge & Kegan Paul.

　　1982. The alternative meanings of number and counting. In D. Parkin (ed.) *Semantic Anthropology*. London, Academic Press.

　　1985. Le Problème linguistique du nombre. In J. Thomas (ed.) *Linguistique, ethnologie, ethnolinguistique*. Paris, SELAF.

　　1986a. The Pythagorean View of Time and Space in Japan. In J. Hendry and J. Webber (eds.). *Interpreting Japanese Society*. Oxford, JASO.

　　1986b. Literacy and Hierarchy in Modern Japan. In *Sociolinguistics* XVI:56–71.

　　1987. Gendai no Nihon Soroban Kyoiku [Abacus education in Modern Japan] *Zenchu Renkaikoku* 111:18–20.

　　1988. Alternative meanings of literacy in Japan and the West. *Human Organization* 47:138–45.

Dantzig, T. 1930. *Number: the Language of Science*. London, George Allen & Unwin.

Davis, P. J. and Hersh, R. 1983. *The Mathematical Experience*. London, Pelican.

de Coppet, D. 1968. Pour une étude des échanges cérémoniels en Mélanésie. *L'Homme* 8:45–57.

　　1970. Cycles des meurtres en cycles funéraires: esquisse de deux structures d'échange. In J. Pouillon and P. Miranda (eds.) *Mélanges offerts à Claude Lévi-Strauss à l'occasion de son 60ème anniversaire*. The Hague, Mouton.

de Coppet, D. and Zemp, H. 1978. *'Are 'Are. Un peuple mélanésien et sa musique*. Paris, Seuil.

de Lemos, M. M. 1973. The development of conservation. In G. E. Kearney, P. R. de Lacey and G. R. Davidson (eds.) *The Psychology of Australian Aboriginals*. Sydney, John Wiley and Sons.

Deloshe, G. and Seron, X. (eds.) 1988. *Mathematical Disabilities: a Cognitive Neurophysiological Perspective*. Hillsdale, N.J., Erlbaum.

Dempsey, A. D. 1971. Time Conservation Across Cultures. *International Journal of Psychology*. 6:115–20.

Dewdney, A. K. 1986. Wallpaper for the mind: computer images that are almost, but not quite, repetitive. *Scientific American*. September, pp. 14–23.

Dixon, R. M. W. 1980. *The Languages of Australia*. Cambridge University Press.

Dixon, R. B. and Kroeber, A. L. 1907. Numeral systems of the languages of California. *American Anthropologist* 9:663–73.

Dore, R. 1984. *Education in Tokugawa Japan*. London, Athlone.

Douglas, M. 1966. *Purity and Danger*. London, Routledge & Kegan Paul.

Dumont, L. 1966. *Homo Hierarchichus*. Paris, Gallimard.

Edmonson, M. S. 1976. The Mayan Calendar Reform of 11.16.0.0.0. *Current Anthropology* 17:713–49.

Embree, J. F. 1939. *Sure Mura. A Japanese village*. University of Chicago Press.

Escher, M. C. 1981. (1976) *Leven en Werk*. Amsterdam, Meulenhoff.

Ettinghausen, R. The Man-made Setting: Islamic Art and Architecture. In B. Lewis (ed.) *The World of Islam*. London, Thames and Hudson.

Evans-Pritchard, E. E. 1940. *The Nuer*. Oxford University Press.

　　1951. *Kinship and Marriage among the Nuer*. Oxford University Press.

　　1956. *Nuer Religion*. Oxford University Press.

Faber, E. 1873. The Chinese Theory of Music. *The China Review* I, 324–8, 384–8.

Bibliography

Farmer, H. G. 1957. The Music of Ancient Mesopotamia. In E. Wellesz (ed.) *Ancient and Oriental Music*. Oxford University Press.
Finnegan, R. 1977. *Oral Poetry*. Cambridge University Press.
Firth, J. R. 1930. A Dart Match in Tikopia. *Oceania* 1:64–97.
    1963. *We, the Tikopia*. Boston, Mass., Beacon Press.
Fleming, P. 1983. *One's Company*. London, Penguin.
Freeman, J. D. 1955. *Iban Agriculture*. London, H.M.S.O.
Friberg, J. 1984. Numbers and Measures in the Earliest Written Records. *Scientific American*. 250:2:78–85.
Fry, D. 1979. How did we learn to do it? In V. Lee (ed.) *Language Development*. London, Croom Helm.
Gay, J. and Cole, M. 1967. *The New Mathematics in an Old Culture. A Study of Learning among the Kpelle of Liberia*. New York, Holt, Rinehart and Winston.
Geertz, C. 1973. *The Interpretation of Cultures*. New York, Basic Books.
    1980. *Negara. The Theatre State in Nineteenth-Century Bali*. Princeton University Press.
Gellner, E. 1972. The Savage and the Modern Mind. In R. Horton and R. Finnegan (eds.) *Modes of Thought*. London, Faber and Faber.
Gerschel, L. 1962. La conquête du nombre: des modalités du compte aux structures de la pensée. *Annales E.S.C.* 17:691–714.
Ginsburg, C. D. 1955. *The Essenes and the Kabbalah*. London, Routledge & Kegan Paul.
Ginsburg, H. P. (1977) *Children's Arithmetic: the Learning Process*. New York, D. van Nostrand Co.
Ginsburg, H. P. and Allardice, B. S. 1984. Children's Difficulties with School Mathematics. In B. Rogoff and J. Lave (eds.) *Everyday Cognition*. Cambridge, Mass., Harvard University Press.
Gladwin, T. 1964. Culture and logical process. In W. H. Goodenough (ed.) *Explorations in Cultural Anthropology*. New York, McGraw-Hill.
Glahn, E. 1982. Art and Architecture. In B. Hook (ed.) *The Cambridge Encyclopedia of China*, pp. 439–45. Cambridge University Press.
Godelier, M. 1974. *Un Domaine Contesté: l'anthropologie économique*. Paris, Mouton.
Goody, J. 1962. *Death, Property and the Ancestors*. London, Tavistock.
    1977. *The Domestication of the Savage Mind*. Cambridge University Press.
    (ed.) 1975. *Literacy in Traditional Societies*. Cambridge University Press.
Gray, R. F. 1968. Sonjo bride price and the question of African "Wife Purchase". In E. E. LeClair Jr. and H. K. Schneider (eds.) *Economic Anthropology*. New York, Holt, Rinehart and Winston.
Green, J. 1972. *Suite Anglaise*. Paris, Plon.
Greene, G. 1982. *The Lawless Roads*. London, Penguin.
Greenfield, P. M. 1966. On culture and conservation. In J. S. Bruner, R. R. Oliver and P. M. Greenfield (eds.) *Studies in Cognitive Growth*. New York, Wiley.
Gudeman, S. 1986. *Economics as Culture*. London, Routledge & Kegan Paul.
Gulliver, P. H. 1955. *The Family Herds*. London, Routledge and Kegan Paul.
Hage, P. & Harary, F. 1983. *Structural Models in Anthropology*. Cambridge University Press.
Halle, M. 1957. In defence of the number "two". In E. Pulgram (ed.) *Studies Presented to Joshua Watmough on his Sixtieth Birthday*. The Hague, Mouton.
Hallowell, A. I. 1937. Temporal Orientation in Western Civilization and in a Pre-literate Society. *American Anthropologist*. 39:647–670.

183

Bibliography

1942. Some Psychological Aspects of Measurement among the Saulteaux. *American Anthropologist* 44:62–77.

Hallpike, C. R. 1979. *The Foundations of Primitive Thought*. Oxford, Clarendon Press.

Harding, T. G. 1967. *Voyagers of the Vitiaz Strait*. Seattle, University of Washington Press.

Hardy, G. H. 1940. *A Mathematician's Apology*. Cambridge University Press.

Hardy, G. H. and Wright, E. M. 1945. *The Theory of Numbers*. Oxford University Press.

Harnad, S. R. and Steklis, H. D. 1976. The Split Brain and the Culture and Cognition Paradox. *Current Anthropology* 17:320–2.

Harris, M. 1979. *Cultural Materialism*. New York, Vintage Books.

Hayano, D. M. 1982. *Poker Faces. The Life and Work of Professional Poker Players*. Berkeley, University of California Press.

Hodes, H. 1984. Logicism and the ontological commitments of arithmetic. *Journal of Philosophy* 81:123–49.

Hofstadter, D. R. 1980. *Godel, Escher, Bach: an Eternal Golden Braid*. New York, Vintage Books.

Holtz, J. 1984. *Kritik der Geldentstehungstheorien*. Berlin, Dietrich Reimer Verlag.

Horn, W. 1975. On the selective use of sacred numbers and the creation in Carolingian architecture of a new aesthetic based on modular concepts. *Viator* 6:351–90.

Huber, F. and Thorson, J. 1985. Cricket Auditory Communication. *Scientific American*. December: 46–54.

Huizinga, J. 1950. *Homo Ludens: A Study of the Play Element in Culture*. Boston, Beacon Press.

Hurford, J. R. 1975. *The Linguistic Theory of Numerals*. Cambridge University Press. 1987. *Language and Number*. Oxford, Blackwell.

Ifrah, G. 1987. *From One to Zero*. London, Penguin.

Itoh, T. 1972. *Traditional Domestic Architecture of Japan*. New York, Weatherhill.

Izikowitz, K. G. 1951, *Lamet: Hill Peasants in French Indochina*. Göteborg, Etnologiska Museet.

Janelli, D. Y. 1977. *Logical contradictions in Korean learned fortunetelling*. University of Pennsylvania. Ph.D. Thesis.

Jeans, J. 1930. *The Mysterious Universe*. Cambridge University Press.

Johnson, H. G. 1965. Monetary Theory and Policy. In *Surveys of Economic Theory*. London, Macmillan.

Jones, C. W. 1975. Carolingian Aesthetics: Why Modular Verse. *Viator*. 6:309–341.

Junod, H. A. 1927. *The Life of a South African Tribe*. London.

Kaeppler, A. L. 1985. Structured Movement Systems in Tonga. In P. Spencer (ed.) *Society and the Dance*. Cambridge University Press.

Katz, F. 1956. Die sozialökonomischen Verhaltnissen bei den Azteken im 15. und 16. Jahrhundert. *Ethnographisch-Archäologische Forschungen*. 3:2:10–166.

Keynes, J. M. 1936. *The General Theory of Employment, Interest and Money*. London, Macmillan.

Kobayashi, M. (1951) *Seimei no hikani* [The Light of Full Names]. Tokyo, Seikōkai.

Krupp, E. C. 1984. Astronomers, pyramids and priests. In E. C. Krupp (ed.) *In Search of Ancient Astronomies*. London, Penguin.

Kuhn, T. S. 1962. *The Structure of Scientific Revolutions*. University of Chicago Press.

Lancy, D. F. 1983. *Cross-cultural Studies in Cognition and Mathematics*. New York, Academic Press.

Lancy, D. F. and Strathern, A. F. 1981. "Making twos": Pairing as an alternative to the taxonomic mode of representation. *American Anthropologist*. 83:775–95.

Lave, J. 1988. *Cognition in Practice*. Cambridge University Press.

Lave, J., Murtaugh, M. and de la Roche, O. 1985. The dialectic of arithmetic in grocery shopping. In B. Rogoff and J. Lave (eds.) *Everyday Cognition*. Cambridge, Mass., Harvard University Press.

Leach, E. 1961. *Pul Eliya – a Village in Ceylon*. Cambridge University Press.

1964. Anthropological Aspects of Language: Animal Categories and Verbal Abuse. In E. H. Lenneberg (ed.) *New Directions in the Study of Language*. Cambridge, Mass., M.I.T. Press.

1966. *Rethinking Anthropology*. London, Athlone Press.

1970. *Political Systems of Highland Burma*. London, Athlone Press.

Lease, E. B. 1919. The number three, mysterious, mystic, magic. *Classical Philology*. 14:56–73.

LeGoff, J. 1981. *La Naissance de Purgatoire*. Paris, Gallimard.

Lemoine, J. G. 1932. Les anciens procédés de calcul sur les doigts en orient et en occident. *Revue des Etudes Islamiques*. 6:1–58.

Leontiev, A. N. 1981. *Problems of the Development of the Mind*. Moscow, Progress Publishers.

Lerner, L. S. & Gosselin, E. A. 1986. Galileo and the Specter of Bruno. *Scientific American*, November.

Lévi-Strauss, C. 1969. *Totemism*. London, Pelican.

1971. *Les Structures Elémentaires de la Parenté*. Paris, Mouton.

Lévi-Strauss, C. 1973 *From Honey to Ashes*. New York, Harper & Row.

1975. *The Raw and the Cooked*. New York, Harper and Row.

1978. *The Origin of Table Manners*. New York, Harper & Row.

1985. *La Potière Jalouse*. Paris, Plon.

Lewis, C. S. 1964. *The Discarded Image*. Cambridge University Press.

Lewis, D. 1972. *We, the Navigators*. Canberra, Australian National University Press.

Lloyd, G. E. R. 1979. *Magic, Reason and Experience* Cambridge University Press.

Lounsbury, F. G. 1946. Stray Number Systems among Certain Indian Tribes. *American Anthropologist*. N.S. 48:672–5.

Lu Gwei-Djen and Needham, J. 1980. *Celestial Lancets. A history and rationale of acupuncture and Moxa*. Cambridge University Press.

Macey, S. L. 1980. *Clocks and the Cosmos*. Hamden, Conn., Shoe String Press.

McClain, E. G. 1979. Chinese cyclic tunings in late antiquity. *Ethnomusicology*, 205–23.

Macfarlan, A. and P. 1985. *Handbook of American Indian Games*. New York, Dover Press.

McMullen, D. L. 1982. The examination system. In B. Hook (ed.) *The Cambridge Encyclopedia of China*, pp. 129–31. Cambridge University Press.

McPhee, C. 1979. *A House in Bali*. Oxford University Press.

Malinowski, B. 1922. *Argonauts of the Western Pacific*. London, Routledge & Kegan Paul.

Marshack, A. 1972. *The Roots of Civilization*. New York, McGraw-Hill.

Mathews, M. V. and Pierce, J. R. 1987. The computer as a musical instrument. *Scientific American*. February.

Mauss, M. 1968. Essai sur le Don. In *Sociologie et Anthropologie*. Paris, P.U.F.

Mead, M. 1970. The Arts in Bali. In J. Belo (ed.) *Traditional Balinese Culture*. New York, Columbia University Press.

Medley, M. 1982. Art and Architecture. In B. Hook (ed.) *The Cambridge Encyclopedia of China*, pp. 395ff. Cambridge University Press.

Melitz, J. 1974. *Primitive and Modern Money*. Reading, Mass., Addison-Wesley Publishing Company.

Menninger, K. 1969. *Number Words and Number Symbols*. Cambridge, Mass., M.I.T. Press.

Middleton, J. 1985. The Dance among the Lugbara of Uganda. In *Society and the Dance* (ed. P. Spencer). Cambridge University Press, pp. 165–82.

Miller, G. A. 1956. The magical number seven, plus or minus two: some limits to our capacity for processing information. *Psychological Review*. 63:81–97.

Miller, R. A. 1982. *Japan's Modern Myth; the Language and Beyond*. New York and Tokyo, Weatherhill.

Milner, G. B. 1971. The Quartered Shield: Outline of a Semantic Taxonomy. In E. Ardener (ed.) *Social Anthropology and Language*. London, Tavistock Publications.

1972. *Fijian Grammar*. Suva, Fiji, Government Press.

Miyako, J. 1980. *Seikatsu no naka no shūkyō* [Religion in life.]. Tokyo, NHK books.

Moravetz, T. 1973. Commentary: the Rules of Law and the Point of Law. *University of Pennsylvania Law Review*. 121:859–73.

Mori, M. 1980. *Meisū Sūshi Jiten* [Dictionary of numbers]. Tokyo, Tokyodo.

Moroney, M. J. 1951. *Facts from Figures*. London, Penguin.

Morris, E. 1951. *Bells of all nations*. London, Robert Hale.

1974. *The History and Art of Change Ringing*. Wakefield, E. P. Publishing.

Morris, W. 1984. *News From Nowhere and Selected Writings and Designs*. London, Penguin.

Morton, W. B. 1983. Borobudur. *National Geographic Magazine*, January.

Murra, J. V. 1980. *The Economic Organization of the Inka State*. Greenwich, Conn., JAL Press.

Murray, A. 1978. *Reason and Society in the Middle Ages*. Oxford, Clarendon Press.

Nakane, C. 1973. *Japanese Society*. London, Pelican.

Nakayama, S. 1969. *A History of Japanese Astronomy*. Cambridge, Harvard University Press.

Needham, J. 1956, Vol. 2. *History of Scientific Thought; Science and Civilisation in China*. 1959, Vol. 3. *Mathematics and the Sciences of the Heavens and the Earth*. Cambridge University Press.

1969. *Within the Four Seas*. London, Allen & Unwin.

1980. *Science and Civilisation in China. Vol. 5, Part 4 (Chemistry and Chemical Technology/Spagyrical Discovery and Invention: Apparatus, Theories and Gifts)*. Cambridge University Press.

Needham, R. 1967. Percussion and Transition. *Man* N.S. 2:606–14.

Nelson, A. N. 1974. *The Modern Reader's Japanese–English Character Dictionary*. Rutland, Vermont, Charles E. Tuttle Company.

Nihon o Shiru Jiten (The 'know' Japan Dictionary).

Norbeck, E. 1955. Yakudoshi, a Japanese complex of supernatural beliefs. *Southwestern Journal of Anthropology*. 11:106–20.

Ohnuki-Tierney, E. 1984. *Illness and culture in contemporary Japan*. Cambridge University Press.

Oppenheim, A. L. 1964. *Ancient Mesopotamia*. University of Chicago Press.

Ortiz, S. 1973. *Uncertainties in Peasant Farming*. London, Athlone Press.

Palmer, M. 1986. *T'ung Shu. The Ancient Chinese Almanac*. London, Rider and Company.

Pankhurst, R. 1965. The history of currency and banking in Ethiopia and the Horn of Africa from the middle ages to 1935. *Ethiopia Observer*. 8:358–408.

Bibliography

Paradis, M., Hagiwara, H. and Hildebrandt, N. 1985. *Neurolinguistic Aspects of the Japanese Writing System*. New York, Academic Press.

Paredes, J. A. and Hepburn, M. J. 1976/7. The Split Brain and the Culture and Cognition Paradox. *Current Anthropology* 17:121–7, 318–26, 503–11, 738–42; 18:44–50.

Parry, J. 1980. Ghosts, greed and sin: the occupational identity of the Benares funeral priests. *Man* N.S. 15:88–111.

Peake's *Commentary on the Bible*. 1962. London, Nelson.

Pennick, N. 1979. *The Ancient Science of Geomancy*. London, Thames and Hudson.

Philp, H. and Kelly, M. R. 1977. Cognitive development in Papua New Guinea – some comparative data. *Australian Journal of Education* 3:256–67.

Piaget, J. 1952. *The Child's Conception of Number*. London, Routledge & Kegan Paul. 1972. *The Principles of Genetic Epistemology*. London, Routledge and Kegan Paul.

Piatelli-Palmarini, M. (ed.) 1980. *Language and Learning*. London, Routledge & Kegan Paul.

Picken, L. 1957. The Music of Far Eastern Asia. In E. Wellesz (ed.) *The New Oxford History of Music*. Oxford University Press.

Pieron, H. 1959. Qu'est-ce que l'hominisation. *Cahiers Rationalistes* 10:211.

Posner, M. I. 1973. *Cognition: an Introduction*. Glenview, Ill., Scott, Foresman and Company.

Pospisil, L. 1963. *The Kapauku Papuans of West New Guinea*. New York, Holt, Rinehart and Winston.

Price-Williams, D. R., Gordon, W. and Ramirez, M. 1969. Skill and conservation: a study of pottery-making children. In J. W. Berry and P. R. Dasen (eds.) *Culture and Cognition: Readings in Cross-cultural Psychology*. London, Methuen.

Radcliffe-Brown, A. R. 1922. *The Andaman Islanders*. London.

Reed, H. J. and Lave, J. 1979. Arithmetic as a tool for investigating relations between culture and cognition. *American Ethnologist* 6:868:82.

Reischauer, E. O. 1977. *The Japanese*. Cambridge, Mass., Harvard University Press.

Resnick, L. B. and Ford, W. W. 1981. *The Psychology of Mathematics for Instruction*. Hillsdale, N.J., LEA.

Restivo, S. 1981. Mathematics and the limits of the sociology of knowledge. *Social Science Information*. 10:679–701.
1982. Mathematics and the sociology of knowledge. *Knowledge: creation, diffusion, utilization*. 4:127–44.
1983. *The Social Relations of Physics, Mysticism and Mathematics*. Dordrecht, D. Reidel Publishing Company.

Richards, A. I. 1939. *Land Labour and Diet in Northern Rhodesia*. Oxford, International African Institute.

Robertson, A. F. 1980. On Sharecropping. *Man* N.S. 15:411–29.

Robinson, J. & Eatwell, J. 1973. *An Introduction to Modern Economics*. London, McGraw-Hill.

Roll, S. 1970. Conservation of number: a comparison between cultures and sub-cultures. *Revista Interamericana de Psicologia*. 4:13–18.

Ronan, C. A. and Needham, J. 1978. *The Shorter Science and Civilisation in China* (vol. 1). Cambridge University Press.
1981. *The Shorter Science and Civilisation in China* (vol. 2). Cambridge University Press.

Roscher, W. H. 1901. Zur Bedeutung der Siebenzahl im Kultus und Mythus der Griechen. *Philologus*. 10:360–73.

Rothschild, Lord (Chairman) 1978. *Report of the Royal Commission on Gambling.* London, H.M.S.O.

Russell, B. 1920. *An Introduction to Mathematical Philosophy.* London, Allen & Unwin.

1946. *History of Western Philosophy.* London, Allen & Unwin.

1980. *An Inquiry into Meaning and Truth.* London, Allen & Unwin.

Sahlins, M. 1976. *Culture and Practical Reason.* Chicago University Press.

Salzmann, Z. 1950. A method for analyzing numerical systems. *Word.* 6:1:78–83.

Sayers, D. L. 1959. *The Nine Tailors.* London, New English Library.

Schmandt-Besserat, D. 1979. The Earliest Precursor of Writing. *Scientific American.* June, 38–47.

Schneider, M. 1957. Primitive Music. In E. Wellesz (ed.) *The New Oxford History of Music.* Oxford University Press.

Schubert, H. 1887. *Zahlen und Zahl.* Hamburg.

Scriba, C. J. 1973. Number. *Dictionary of the History of Ideas.* New York, Scribner. Vol. III, 399–407.

Scribner, S. 1984. Studying Working Intelligence. In B. Rogoff and J. Lave (eds.) *Everyday Cognition.* Cambridge, Mass., Harvard University Press.

Scribner, S. and Cole, M. 1981. *The Psychology of Literacy.* Cambridge, Mass., Harvard University Press.

Shiratori, K. 1937. The Japanese Numerals. *Memoirs of the Research Department of the Tōyō Bunkō* 9:1–78.

Shorto, H. L. 1963. The 32 Myos in the Medieval Mon kingdom. *Bulletin of the School of Oriental and African Studies.* XXVI, 572–91.

1967. The Dewatau Sotapan: a Mon prototype of the 37 Nats. *Bulletin of the School of Oriental and African Studies* XXX, 127–41.

Skemp, R. R. 1980. Mathematics as an activity of our intelligence. Paper presented at the *Seventh Annual Conference for Diagnostic and Prescriptive Mathematics,* Vancouver.

Smith, R. J. 1983. *Japanese Society.* Cambridge University Press.

Snodgrass, A. 1985. *The Symbolism of the Stupa.* Ithaca, N.Y., Cornell University Press.

Spencer, P. 1973. *Nomads in Alliance.* Oxford University Press.

1985. Introduction: Interpretations of the Dance in Anthropology. In *Society and the Dance.* Cambridge University Press.

Sperber, D. and Wilson, D. 1986. *Relevance.* Oxford, Blackwell.

Spiro, M. 1971. *Buddhism and Society.* London, George Allen & Unwin.

Stark, W. 1958. *The Sociology of Knowledge.* London, Routledge & Kegan Paul.

Stevens, S. S. 1958. Measurement and Man. *Science.* 121:383–9.

Stevenson, H. W. 1972. *Children's Learning.* New York, Meredith Corporation.

Stierlin, H. 1970. *Angkor.* Fribourg, Office du Livre.

Stigler, J. W., Lee, S-Y., Lucker, G. W. and Stevenson, H. W. 1982. Curriculum and achievement in mathematics: a study of elementary school children in Japan, Taiwan and the United States. *Journal of Educational Psychology* 74:315.

Stoller, P. 1984. Sound in Songhay cultural experience. *American Ethnologist* 11:559–570.

Street, B. V. 1984. *Literacy in theory and practice.* Cambridge University Press.

Sturtevant, W. C. 1972. Studies in Ethnoscience. In J. P. Spradley (ed.) *Culture and Cognition.* San Francisco, Chandler Publishing Company. pp. 129–67.

Symonds, J. A. 1961. *The Fine Arts. The Renaissance in Italy.* New York, Capricorn Books.

Bibliography

Tambiah, S. J. 1976. *World conqueror and world renouncer*. Cambridge University Press.

Thompson, J. E. S. 1970. *Maya History and Religion*. Norman, University of Oklahoma Press.

1972. *Maya Hieroglyphs without Tears*. London, British Museum.

The Threefold Lotus Sutra. 1975. New York, Weatherhill.

Treasures from Turkey. 1986. Rijksmuseum van Oudheden in Leiden.

Treffert, D. A. 1989. *Extraordinary People*. London, Bantam Press.

Tsuboi, H. 1970. Nihonjin no seishikan [The Japanese way of life and death]. In *Minzokugaku kara mita Nihon* [Japan in the light of folklore], pp. 18–34. Tokyo, Kawade Shoboosha.

Tsunoda, T. 1978. *Nihonjin no Nō* [The Brain of the Japanese]. Tokyo, Taishukan Shoten.

Usener, H. 1903. Dreiheit. *Rheinisches Museum n.F.* 58: 1–48, 161–208, 321–62.

Vansina, J. 1965. *Oral Tradition*. London, Routledge & Kegan Paul.

1973. *The Tio Kingdom of the Middle Congo*. Oxford University Press.

Viner, J. 1978. Religious thought and economic society. *History of Political Economy* 10:1.

Vogt, E. Z. 1976. *Tortillas for the Gods*. Cambridge, Mass., Harvard University Press.

Vygotsky, L. S. 1962. *Thought and Language*. Cambridge, Mass., M.I.T. Press.

1978. *Mind in Society*. Cambridge, Mass., Harvard University Press.

Watson, W. 1958. *Tribal Cohesion in a Money Economy*. Manchester University Press.

Weiner, H. 1971. *9:9½ Mystics. The Kabbala Today*. New York, Collier Books.

Welmers, W. E. 1973. *African Language Structures*. University of California Press.

Whitehead, A. N. 1932. *Science and the Modern World*. Cambridge University Press.

Whiting, R. 1977. *The Chrysanthemum and the Bat*. New York, Dodd, Mead & Co.

Whitrow, G. J. 1961. *The Natural Philosophy of Time*. London, Thomas Nelson & Sons Ltd.

Williams, B. 1978. *Descartes: the Project of Pure Enquiry*. London, Pelmon.

Wittgenstein, L. 1922. *Tractatus Logico-Philosophicus*. London, Routledge & Kegan Paul.

1964. *Remarks on the Foundations of Mathematics*. Oxford, Blackwell.

1970. *Lectures and Conversations on Aesthetics, Psychology and Religious Belief*. Oxford, Blackwell.

Wodehouse, P. G. 1953. *Leave it to Psmith*. London, Penguin.

Wylie, J. and Margolin, D. 1981. *The Ring of Dancers. Philadelphia, University of Pennsylvania Press*.

Yano, Y. 1973. *Kazoku no komyunikeeshon seikatsu*. [*Communication Life of the Family*]. In T. Ota, Y. Fujioka, T. Nogawa and T. Inoue (eds.) *Toshi ni okeru Kazoku no Seikatsu* [The life of the family in the year]. Kyoto University Institute for Humanistic Studies.

Zaslavsky, C. 1979. *Africa Counts*. Westport, Lawrence Hill.

Index

Cambridge Studies in Social and Cultural Anthropology

Editors: ERNEST GELLNER, JACK GOODY, STEPHEN GUDEMAN,
MICHAEL HERZFELD, JONATHAN PARRY

*Available in paperback

*Available in paperback